W9-AGM-777

# Bicycling Magazine's

## Complete Guide To

# Bicycle Maintenance And Repair

# Bicycling® Magazine's

## Complete Guide To

# *Bicycle Maintenance And Repair*

## By the editors of **Bicycling**®

 Rodale Press, Emmaus, Pennsylvania

Copyright © 1986 by Rodale Press, Inc.

All rights reserved. No part of this publication may be reproduced or transmitted in any form or by any means, electronic or mechanical, including photocopy, recording, or any information storage or retrieval system, without the written permission of the publisher.

Printed in the United States of America on recycled paper containing a high percentage of de-inked fiber.

Senior Editor: Ray Wolf

Editor: Larry McClung

Technical Editors: Jim Redcay, Hal Jeffrey Davis

Photographers: Robert Walch, Rodale Press Photography Department

Book Design: Sandy Freeman

Illustrator: Sally Onopa

Copy Editor: Cristina Negrón Whyte

Due to the variability of materials, skills, and manufacturing differences, Rodale Press, Inc., and the Authors assume no responsibility for any personal injury, property damage, or other loss of any sort suffered from any actions taken based on or inspired by information or advice presented in this book. Make sure you completely understand any procedure before beginning work. If in doubt, get help from a competent mechanic.

**Library of Congress Cataloging in Publication Data**
Main entry under title:

Bicycling® magazine's complete guide to bicycle
    maintenance and repair.

    Includes index.
    1. Bicycles—Maintenance and repair. I. Bicycling!
II. Complete guide to bicycle maintenance and repair.
TL430.B55    1986        629.28′772        85-23306
ISBN 0-87857-603-7    hardcover
ISBN 0-87857-604-5    paperback

    4    6    8    10    9    7    5            hardcover
                    10    9                    paperback

# CONTENTS

# ACKNOWLEDGMENTS

A book of this type is a team effort, the result of a lot of ideas and effort from many different individuals. But, special thanks goes to the various authors who contributed chapters.

Jim Redcay handled the complicated subjects of frames and gears and provided the information on chains and pedals. Jim spent eight years custom designing and building bicycles under his own name before joining Ross bicycles as frame engineer and designer. Jim was head of Ross's Signature division for two years before joining the staff of *Bicycling* magazine as technical editor. Jim served both as a writer and technical editor for this book.

The most prolific contributor to this book was Hal Jeffrey Davis, who drew on his considerable experience as a bike mechanic to write the chapters on hubs, cranksets, freewheels, gearshift levers, front and rear derailleurs, headsets, saddles and seatposts. Jeff is on the staff of *Bicycling* magazine as associate editor. Previously he worked for the American branch of Campagnolo, the prestigious bicycle component firm. During the four plus years he spent with Campy, Jeff worked in varied technical capacities. After leaving Campagnolo, Jeff served as consultant on their official technical manual and developed a program of technical seminars. In addition to writing, Jeff functioned as technical adviser throughout the preparation of this book.

Eric Hjertberg drew on his considerable expertise and more than 15 years experience as a master wheel builder in preparing the lengthy chapter on wheels. Eric is cofounder of Wheelsmith Fabrications, which produces and markets top-quality wheels and wheel parts. He has served as a wheel builder for U.S. national and Olympic cycling teams off and on since 1968, and has contributed numerous technical articles to *Bicycling* and other cycling journals.

The chapters on handlebars and stems and brakes were prepared by *Bicycling* contributing editor, Richard Jow. Richard has been a regular contributor of technical articles to *Bicycling* since 1969.

Robert Walch and Michael Koenig worked long hours creating the hundreds of photographs used to illustrate the repair and maintenance sections of this book. Mike served as the model mechanic, while Bob expertly wielded the camera. Allen Schaeffer, manager of George's Schwinn Cyclery in Emmaus, Pennsylvania, lent us components used in the photo sessions.

Larry McClung served as general editor for the book. In addition, Larry wrote all of the repair sections, and coordinated their photography. Larry spent two years as a freelance writer and editor before joining the staff of Rodale Press as assistant editor. He is a cycling enthusiast, a member of *Bicycling*'s bike testing crew, and has edited six books on cycling.

# INTRODUCTION

This is a book about caring for your bike. Our hope is that this book will bring you and your bike closer together, and in the process provide you with countless hours of trouble-free cycling.

The bicycle is an amazing piece of technology, when properly maintained. But, the bicycle is not perfect, and from time to time even the trustiest of bikes needs attention. That is where this book comes in.

When we started work on this book we had a lofty goal, we wanted to create the definitive home maintenance and repair guide for cyclists. This is not the kind of book you sit down and read from cover to cover and then put away. This book is designed to be on your workbench. Keep it close to where you work on your bike and refer to it often. Think of this book as another tool for working on your bike.

This is not a shop manual that even experienced technicians have trouble understanding. This book is targeted at everyday cyclists, those with only modest amounts of mechanical ability. We not only tell you what needs to be done, but we tell you exactly how to do it. For those of you blessed with more mechanical ability, the information in this book will enable you to attempt even the most difficult of repair jobs.

Our goal throughout has been to create a book that will enable even the first-time bike mechanic to properly do a job. The key to this approach is the use of repair spreads, photographic step-by-step sessions that walk you through the entire process of fixing a part of your bike. To use the repair spreads, first read the preliminary chapter and then study the individual repair spread that pertains to the task you are working on.

It is important to remember that today's bike uses many ultralightweight materials. Although these materials make riding easier and more enjoyable, they do not stand up well to abuse. If you are having trouble getting a nut or bolt to move, take a minute to reread about the job you are doing, before applying extra force. The fine threads used on bicycle components can easily be permanently damaged.

We hope this book improves the relationship you have with your bike. To fully enjoy the cycling experience, the feeling of being at one with an extremely efficient machine, you have to know your equipment inside and out. Hauling your bike off to the local shop for every little repair is not only costly and deprives you of riding time, it also does nothing to help you understand and get to know your bike. Perhaps the biggest benefit of maintaining and repairing your bike on your own is that you get to intimately know and understand what a marvelous piece of equipment it really is.

Ray Wolf
for the editors of *Bicycling* Magazine

# 1

# HOME BICYCLE REPAIR

Many people feel lucky if they master a single area of knowledge and are content to trust the expertise of others in most aspects of their lives. Thus, it would never occur to them to try to do their own plumbing, carpentry, or appliance maintenance and repair.

Often such an attitude makes sense. Repairing and maintaining houses, refrigerators, and automobiles requires a level of skill that cannot be acquired overnight, plus a sizable investment in tools. Moreover, some of us who have attempted home repair jobs have discovered after considerable time and frustration that we still must call on an expensive expert to come in and show us how to do the job right.

But many people who spend their workdays in an office or a classroom find the home workshop a haven of rest, a place to relax and temporarily forget the tensions and problems they experience at their jobs. Even jobs that might become frustrating or boring if done as a full-time occupation can be immensely enjoyable when pursued as a hobby or occasional pastime. The emotional satisfaction that one gains from such work is as important as the practical result.

## Becoming Your Own Bike Mechanic

Once you give it a try, you may discover that working on your bike is a pleasant diversion from your regular work routine and a good way to satisfy some of your creative impulses. It can also be a way to save some money.

Being your own bike mechanic can save you money because most bike maintenance and repair jobs involve little expenditure for materials and new parts. The most important and most frequent maintenance tasks involve cleaning, lubricating, tightening, and adjusting various parts of the bike. In short, bike maintenance tends to be labor intensive. You must buy the materials involved whether you do the work or have someone else do it. But the labor you can provide yourself. Otherwise, you must pay for it, unless you have a friend who loves bike repair so much he will work on your bike for free.

But there are good reasons why you should become your own bike mechanic other than merely saving money or even fulfilling your creative needs. The bicycle is a marvelous machine, a good source of fun and exercise as well as a highly efficient means of getting around. Unfortunately, it is a machine that works so well that it is often taken for granted. All too many cyclists abuse and neglect their bikes, allowing them to break down and fall apart for lack of proper care. Only when the bikes become nuisances rather than joys to ride do these bike owners give thought to their repair. Unfortunately, at that point many bikes are left to rust away in a damp basement or simply tossed onto a junk pile.

Making the commitment to work on your own bike helps prevent you from taking it for granted. And the more you work on it, the more you learn about it. You soon discover how little effort it really takes to keep the bike running well. The rewards for your efforts are immediately evident and you soon become unwilling to settle for second- or third-rate performance. You learn which problems are easy to solve and which are difficult, and then you begin to take extra pains to avoid allowing the latter to develop. You see the value of preventive maintenance in minimizing the need for expensive repairs.

## You Are in the Saddle

When you work on your own bike, you are the person in the saddle in more ways than one. Whereas before you may have been a passive passenger, constantly at the mercy of your maladjusted bike's special quirks, you now become an active agent who knows how to make it respond to your needs. As mechanic-rider, you gain a control over your bike that you previously never had and see that it is a willing partner, eager to please, if only you give it the special care it needs to live up to its potential.

Not only is caring for your own bike useful to you as its rider, it is also appropriate, since no one is in a better position to give it the attention it needs than you. Precisely because you are the one in the saddle most of the time, you know the bike better than the mechanic in the shop who sees it only on rare and brief occasions. The way the bike shifts or brakes while suspended on a shop repair stand is never quite the same as what you experience when you are out riding on the open road or climbing and descending hills. You know how this bike responds in a wide variety of situations, few of which can be easily duplicated in a bike shop.

Once you begin to work on your bike, you start to know it more intimately than ever. You become more attentive to its operation; you listen, feel and observe any unusual sounds, vibrations, or patterns of behavior in ways you never did before. You come to understand and appreciate your bike's strengths and weaknesses, what it can and cannot do. Your bike, in turn, appreciates the attention you give it and rewards you for your efforts.

Finally, doing your own bicycle repair and maintenance is good discipline. It helps you become more self-sufficient and self-reliant and teaches you to be resourceful. This has a highly practical payoff. The time will come when you are in a situation where you may have to deal with special problems. Your experience with repairing and maintaining your bike will be of particular value then.

This principle was vividly illustrated for us one Thursday evening, when members of our staff were out on their weekly group ride. A few miles out into the country, we were joined by an experienced cyclist whom we had not previously met. About a mile farther down the road one of the skinny tires on the newcomer's expensive racing bike suddenly went flat.

What looked like an aborted ride turned out not to be much of a problem. Without a moment's hesitation this veteran hopped off his bike, released the wheel from the frame, and began tugging at the flat tubular, which was glued to the rim. Soon the tire was off and a spare rolled on in its place. The tire was pumped up, the wheel replaced, and we were on our way again. The whole process lasted maybe three minutes, not enough time to seriously interrupt our 25-mile ride. This man clearly was prepared for such emergencies and knew how to make the needed repair quickly and efficiently.

Of course, good maintenance will minimize chances that emergency situations will arise. Doing your own work will help you evaluate the quality of your bike's components and help you make wise decisions about upgrading them. If you have a component with a particular flaw, you will know what to expect from it and what to look for in a new one. The man in our story knew his tubular was on its last legs and ready to go flat. This did not bother him since he was prepared to deal with the problem when it happened. If it had been a different component not so easily replaced on the road, he would have undoubtedly repaired it before leaving for the ride.

### Knowing When to Consult an Expert

Clearly, no one is in a better position to know when something is out of adjustment or in need of repair on your bike than you, the one in the saddle. However, being able to spot a problem does not always mean you will be able to fix it. While most aspects of bicycle repair are within your grasp, there are some that probably are not. Some repair processes are either so complicated or call for the use of such expensive and specialized tools that it is simply not wise for anyone other than a professional bike mechanic to do them. Several such processes are identified in later chapters of this book.

However, even when a problem arises that you cannot solve, the more experience you have working on your bike the more capable you will be of recognizing the problem for what it is. Like the medical doctor in his clinic, the mechanic at your local bike shop is best able to diagnose and cure problems when the patient has been a careful observer. But, when the patient is vague about what ails him, it is much harder for the doctor to accurately focus in on the problem.

### Setting Aside a Special Work Space

In our part of the country, home workshops are generally located in basements. Elsewhere, they may more likely be found in garages. Pick whatever location suits you, but try to create a specific and permanent workspace. This will give you a place to organize and store all the tools and supplies you will need for working on your bike. If every time you decide to do a simple repair job you have to search all over your house for the needed wrench, it is easy to get discouraged and postpone the work.

One simple method that helps keep track of tools in the *Bicycling* bike shop is to assign each one a specific location when it is not in use. In our shop most of the tools are hung on a sheet of plywood attached to the wall over the workbench. The profile of each tool has been traced around it on the board, so that when we finish using a tool it is easy to quickly return it to its proper place on the board. Having your tools readily at hand when you need them certainly speeds your work and helps you avoid procrastination.

Ideally your work space will be equipped with a bench on which you can set tools and bike parts while you work. It is also important to provide your work space with adequate lighting so you can see what you are doing. It is not easy to properly examine parts for wear or recover an escaped ball bearing in a dimly lit place. Creating a good work space and keeping it well organized will help you develop a good maintenance routine.

*Photo 1-1: Home bicycle maintenance is easier to perform if you have a special place set aside for the work and a method for keeping your tools organized and accessible.*

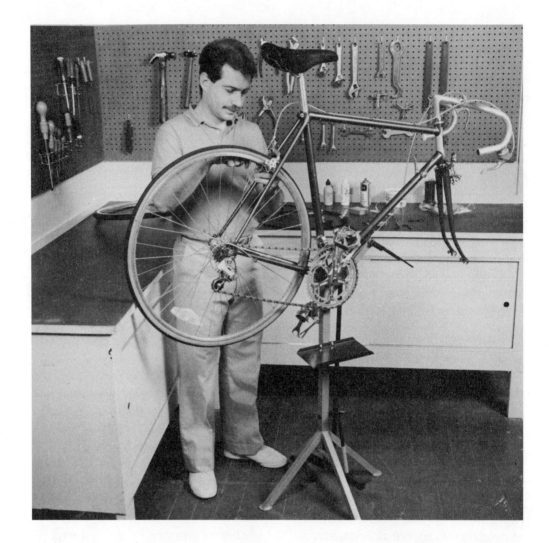

You may also want to prepare a schedule of periodic maintenance tasks and hang it on the wall over your workbench next to a calendar for checking off tasks as you complete them.

## Make or Buy a Repair Stand

When you are working on your bike you need some method of holding it steady, preferably with its wheels suspended a couple of feet above the floor. There are a number of ways in which you can do this. The most convenient way is to use a bike repair stand. The professional bike shop models are heavy-duty items equipped with arms that can be set at different heights, clamps that can be rotated to different angles and adjusted to fit tubes of different diameters, and a tray to hold tools. These stands, of course, cost too much to be practical for the individual bike owner.

Scaled-down versions of the professional repair stand are available, however, and some of them appear to work quite well. You will find several different brands and models advertised in bike component catalogs and in the pages of *Bicycling* magazine. Possibly, you will find one for sale in your well-stocked local bike shop.

Before buying a stand, check to see how it clamps to the bike. Some models clamp to the down tube in a manner that conflicts with exposed gear cables. Make sure the model you choose does not conflict with the routing of gear and brake cables on your bike.

One repair stand owner to whom we spoke complained that his light-weight stand tended to flex on him when he was tightening or loosening certain components on his bike. This particular fellow was a heavily muscled triathlete obviously capable of applying a lot of leverage to the end of a wrench. Generally speaking, few bike repair jobs involve the application of tremendous amounts of force, and those that do can be done with the bike standing on the ground or, in the case of freewheel removal, with the wheel off the bike. A stand is most helpful when you are undertaking such tasks as adjusting your derailleurs and taking up slack in your brake cables. For jobs such as these, even the lightweight stands should prove adequate.

There is a fairly inexpensive device on the market called The Handyman Work Station. It consists of a length of pipe welded to a piece of angle steel at one end and to a hand-turned screw-down clamp at the other. You bolt the angle end to a ceiling rafter and fasten the top tube of your bike in the clamp. This simple device is ready-made for installing in workshops located in basements and garages with exposed rafters. One word of caution. Once you fasten the pipe in place, don't forget it's there. Walking into it can put a sizable bump on your forehead. Also, those of you whose bikes have oversize aluminum tubing will find the clamp on this product does not open wide enough.

Always be careful when you clamp your bike in place. If there is any danger

that the clamp might scratch the paint on your bike, wrap a soft cloth around the tube or line the jaws of the clamp with tape first. Whether you buy a manufactured unit or use your ingenuity, you will find that some method for suspending your bike off the floor will save you a lot of time and frustration when you clean, adjust, and repair your bike.

## Acquiring Tools

Before you can start working on your bike you have to acquire the necessary tools. One way to do this is to page through a catalog or browse in a well-equipped shop and buy everything that looks useful. However, this is not the approach we recommend. It is best to wait until you are ready to tackle a particular job, then acquire the tools you need to handle it. Some jobs can be done with basic tools available in any hardware store. But others call for specialized tools, made specifically for bikes.

Since bike components vary in size and structure from manufacturer to manufacturer and model to model, you have to make sure when buying a specialized tool that it will fit the component on your bike. As a general rule, it is best to buy the tool made by the manufacturer of the product being worked on. This is particularly the case with a freewheel removal tool, since a close match between tool and freewheel is critical. When it comes to crankarm removal, by contrast, a universal puller will work on many bikes. However, even here, it is probably wiser to obtain the tool made specifically for your brand of cranks.

Another basic rule in buying tools is that it is almost always better to go for quality than to attempt to save a couple of bucks. The only exception to this rule might be when you are purchasing a tool you know you will very rarely use and when second-best appears to be good enough. To ensure that you find the quality you need, make your purchases at a well-equipped bike shop. And take your bike along, or at least the part you wish to work on, so you can match the tool to the component.

Some common, multipurpose tools can be substituted for specialized tools, but should be used carefully. For example, if your crankarm removal tool is not equipped with a wrench for removing the crankarm fixing bolt, you can use a thin-walled socket of the appropriate size. And when working on your headset, you can substitute a large adjustable wrench for the headset spanner, so long as you are careful not to damage the edges of the wrench flats or chew up their surface with the rough jaws of the wrench. Also, since tools appropriate to the home shop are often too bulky and heavy to carry on the road, it is useful to find lightweight tools that can be used for a variety of road repairs—tools like small adjustable wrenches and small locking pliers.

More specific discussion of tools will be found in the various chapters when specific repair jobs are described in detail. Experienced cyclists are often quite ingenious in finding solutions to common problems and making do when the ideal tools are not at hand.

## Avoid Problems through Preventive Maintenance

These days most people are aware of the importance of following a good diet, getting adequate exercise, and of learning how to avoid or minimize stress. Increasingly, people realize that they must take primary responsibility for maintaining their own physical and mental health, that the doctor and his wonder drugs are only a secondary aid to good health. Obviously, it makes no sense to neglect your body and abuse it until it becomes a wreck, then rush to a doctor and expect him to come up with an instant cure.

This is hardly a new idea, of course. For generations people have repeated sayings like, "an ounce of prevention is worth a pound of cure." This clearly makes sense when it comes to maintaining good health. Prevention-minded people not only avoid a lot of the problems that afflict other people, they are often able to solve those problems that do occur without resorting to expensive specialists.

The same logic applies to you as a cyclist and bicycle owner. Thanks to healthy competition and advances in technology, most bicycles sold today are capable of providing long and dependable service to their owners if they are given proper care. To paraphrase the old saying, we can say that when it comes to bikes, "an ounce of preventive maintenance is worth a pound of expensive repair."

Not only is preventive maintenance cost-effective, a way to prolong the life of your bicycle and its various components, it is also much easier than making expensive repairs. Why easier? Because preventive maintenance consists almost entirely of quite simple activities. First and foremost it consists of keeping your bike clean, free of the grime and grit it inevitably picks up on the road. Cleanliness may not make your bike godly, but it sure will help it perform better mechanically.

What needs to be cleaned? how often? how? For one thing, your frame needs to be cleaned periodically to preserve its paint and thus not only its looks but its resistance to rust. In Europe many cyclists hose down their vehicles after every ride. If you find this an excessive bother, at least once a month wipe down your frame with a damp cloth. While you are at it, you may want to polish your frame with a car wax or one of the special products on the market that are made for cleaning and shining the metal parts of a bike.

Perhaps the most critical parts of your bike that need frequent cleaning are the rims of your wheels, since the grime that builds up on them is passed along to your brake pads and can reduce the effectiveness of your brakes. At least once a month, more frequently if you do a lot of riding on dirty road surfaces, clean your rims and brake pads with alcohol.

The grit and grime that makes its way into your hubs, headset, and bottom bracket cannot be so easily removed as that which builds up on your rims and frame. In this case, you must disassemble the parts, clean them, and repack them in fresh grease. However, there are preventive measures you can take such as wrapping pipe cleaners around the openings into your hubs or pulling sections of old tire tubes over the upper and lower stacks on your headset. Such techniques are described further in the chapters devoted to these parts of the bike.

If some of these recommendations sound like a lot of trouble, just remember that keeping bearings, cables, and other moving parts of your bike clean and properly lubricated not only helps them function properly, it also slows the speed at which they deteriorate and have to be replaced. This type of preventive maintenance is the best way you can take care of your bike.

Besides cleaning and lubrication, the other primary maintenance tasks on a bike are to make sure that parts are properly fastened together and adjusted. Loose fixing bolts on cottered cranks can lead to damage of expensive components that must then be replaced. Loose locknuts on headsets and wheel hubs can lead not only to damaged parts, but can also cause a dangerous loss of control of the steering of the bike. Loose mounting nuts on brake pivot bolts can allow brakes to vibrate loose from the frame, and loose cable anchor nuts can cause brake failure in an emergency.

The list could go on. Some loose or improperly adjusted parts are dangerous. Others simply lead to unnecessary wear and deterioration of components. Both types of problems can be avoided by frequent checking to make sure all parts of your bike are properly tightened and adjusted.

## Choosing Materials for Cleaning Your Bike

But what should you use to clean a bike? Water, for starters. As we said before, some cyclists actually hose down their bikes after a dirty ride. When you do this, just bounce the bike on its tires a couple of times to shake off some of the water, then let it air dry in a warm place. Treat it the same way after riding in a drenching rain. Of course, in both cases, if you have a leather saddle you may want to avoid getting it wet.

Along with the water, you might try cleaning your bike with a mild soap, such as a dish soap. Just rinse it off afterward. Of course, some parts get too greasy and grimy to be cleaned with soap and water. Chainwheels, chains, the insides of hubs, headsets, and bottom brackets—parts such as these need to be cleaned with a solvent. Which one you use should probably be dictated by how difficult the part is to clean. In general, the most agressive solvents are the most volatile, which means in part that their vapors will quickly permeate the air around you and may pose a hazard to your health. Gasoline and lacquer thinner are examples of readily available solvents of this type. Both are very effective cleaners, but also highly volatile and highly flammable. Work with these solvents only in a very well-ventilated place.

WD-40 is a well-known product that contains several different solvents mixed with a light oil. The most aggressive solvent in the mixture will quickly evaporate into the air if you leave it sitting in an open container. For cyclists, this product may be most useful in its spray form for loosening gummed-up parts in derailleurs and chains. LPS-1 and CRC 5-56 are similar products.

A relatively new product called Bike Elixir removes grease and tar and polishes metal surfaces as well. It contains petroleum distillates and is quite potent, as a sniff of the container will quickly show you, so use it only in a well-ventilated place. Though Bike Elixir is an effective cleaner, it is apparently intended for use on those chrome and painted surfaces that you want to shine. Its price makes it a poor choice for more general use.

Kerosene and paint thinner are less volatile than gasoline and lacquer thinner and are good general-purpose solvents. When working with any of these petroleum products, it's a good idea to protect your hands with rubber gloves.

One idea that has been suggested for cleaning bike parts is to go to an auto parts store and buy carburetor cleaner.

However, this is a highly potent solvent made to dissolve lacquers that build up from fuel combustion—a solvent that will eat through paint or rubber. It is also expensive. You really should not need anything so potent for cleaning bicycle parts. However, if you have one of those little carburetor cleaning kits that consists of a small tub and wire basket, you might wish to use that with a suitable solvent for giving dirty parts a brief soak before brushing and wiping them clean.

Alcohol is less harsh to your skin than most solvents and will work for lighter jobs, such as cleaning brake pads and the braking surfaces of your wheel rims.

Besides soap, water, and solvents, all you need to get your bike parts clean are plenty of rags and a few pads or brushes. Scouring pads made of synthethic materials that are kind to shiny metal surfaces are useful aids to cleaning rims and removing road tar from bike frames. Old toothbrushes can be put to good use cleaning freewheel cogs, chainwheel teeth, and chains.

## Lubricants

Along with thorough cleaning, proper lubrication of the moving parts of your bike is extremely important. There are far too many lubricants on the market for us to evaluate them all, but we do want to offer some general guidelines.

### Grease

Frequently in the subsequent chapters of this book we call for the use of medium-weight grease. This is the lubricant recommended for all bearing instal-

*(continued on page 12)*

**table 1-1** RECOMMENDED LUBRICANTS

| Part | Lubricant |
|------|-----------|
| Ball bearings | White lithium grease/bike grease |
| Bottom bracket axle | White lithium grease/bike grease (do not lubricate tapered ends) |
| Brake cable | Spray lubricant with Teflon (if lined housing) White lithium grease/bike grease (if unlined housing) |
| Brake pivot | Spray lubricant with Teflon or silicone |
| Brake spring | White lithium grease/bike grease |
| Chain | Oil with high water resistance, melted paraffin |
| Derailleur pivots | Spray lubricant with Teflon or silicone |
| Freewheel (inside) | Medium-weight oil (cycle oil or motor oil) |
| Hub with internal gears | Medium-weight oil (cycle oil or motor oil) |
| Seatpost (section inside seat tube) | White lithium grease/bike grease |
| Stem (section inside steerer tube) | White lithium grease/bike grease |
| Threads (bottom bracket, freewheel body, steerer tube, etc.) | White lithium grease, bike grease, or antiseize compound |
| Wheel axle | White lithium grease/bike grease |

**table 1-2** ## MAINTENANCE SCHEDULE

### Before Every Ride

- Make sure tires have adequate pressure
- Make certain brake quick-release is closed
- Make sure wheels are centered in frame and quick-releases firmly closed
- Check to see that brakes are centered on wheels and brake shoes are properly positioned in relation to rims
- Squeeze brake levers to see that after

initial contact they have enough travel left without bottoming out against the handlebars; adjust cable length if necessary

- Bounce bike and listen for rattles indicating parts that need tightening
- Make sure bags and panniers are secure with no loose straps to catch in wheels
- Check to see that tire pump and repair kit are securely fastened to your bike

### After Every Ride

- Brush foreign objects off tire tread and check condition of tires
- Hose down bike if very dirty; bounce off excess water and store bike in warm, dry place

- Dry off wet saddle and treat with dressing
- Wipe down wet chain and lubricate lightly

### Every Month (or more often if riding a lot)

- Wipe down entire bike with damp rag except near bearings where grit could get pushed inside
- Check for cracks in frame, rims, and cranks
- Hold front wheel between your knees and try to twist the bar and stem; if it moves, tighten the stem binder bolt
- Take off chain and soak in solvent if very dirty; otherwise, clean it in place with spray solvent and rag
- After cleaning chain, drip or spray lubricant into pivots between links

- Clean rear gear cluster with rag or stiff brush and spray solvent
- Clean chainwheels with rag
- Drip oil into interior of freewheel body while rotating it
- Lubricate interior bushings of jockey and idler pulleys on rear derailleur
- Lubricate pivot points on front and rear derailleurs
- Lubricate pivot points on brakes and levers
- Check crankset nuts or bolts for tightness

## Every Month (continued)

- Check tightness of nuts on brake bodies, brake shoes, and cable anchors

- Check tension on spokes; adjust as needed

- Check cables for kinks and fraying

- Check wheels for trueness and dish; correct if necessary

- Check chain, cogs, and chainwheels for wear; replace if excessively worn

- Check condition of brake pads; replace if badly worn or excessively hard

- Clean brake pads and rims with alcohol

- Check rack bolts and all add-ons for tightness

- Check condition of glue holding tubulars to rims

- Add two to four drops of oil to 3-speed hubs

- Clean leather saddles with saddle soap and/or treat with leather dressing

- Check toe clips for cracks; dress toe straps

- Check headset for proper adjustment

## Every Six Months

- Check the bearing adjustment on front and rear hubs

- Check the adjustment on pedal bearings

- Check bottom bracket for proper adjustment

- Check the handlebar stem and the steerer tube for rust; clean and regrease

- Apply rubber and vinyl preservative to gum rubber hoods on brakes and vinyl coverings on cable housings

- Check the seatpost and the seat tube for rust; clean and regrease

- Check, clean, and lubricate brake and derailleur cables; replace if worn or rusted

## Every Year

- Overhaul pedals
- Overhaul front and rear hubs
- Overhaul headset
- Overhaul bottom bracket
- Check internal parts of gear shift levers; clean and regrease as necessary

- Check frame alignment; take frame to professional for repair if needed

- Replace toe straps

- Replace pipe cleaners, pieces of tire tube, and anything else being used to keep grit out of bearings

lations on the bike and for threaded parts on freewheels, bottom brackets, headsets, pedals, and wheel axles. The same grease can be used to lubricate and rust-protect brake and gear cables.

The bike greases marketed by Schwinn and Phil Wood, among other bike product companies, are the type we have in mind. These greases are generally sold in tubes. If you expect to use a lot of grease, you may want to purchase a tub of white lithium grease at an auto parts store. This is similar to the Schwinn bike grease and should work just as well. Just make sure you buy white lithium grease and not automotive bearing grease, which contains molybdenum disulfide to help it handle high temperatures. This grease is too thick and sticky for use on a bike.

## Oil

Oils are used on a bike to lubricate the pivot points of brakes and derailleurs, the insides of the freewheel, and the links of the chain. The internally-geared hubs on 3-speed bikes also need a periodic healthy dose of oil.

Sturmey-Archer gear oil is an old reliable lubricant that can be used for all these applications. Schwinn also makes a good general bike oil. You should avoid the familiar 3-in-1 oil, because it is vegetable based and will gum up your bike's moving parts.

As with grease, so with oil. The automotive industry provides an alternative to the oil sold in bike shops. Ordinary 30-weight motor oil is a workable substitute. Pour it into a squirt can and apply a few drops where needed.

There is a great diversity of opinion concerning the best lubricant for a chain, one bike component that is particularly subject to the ravages of dirt and water.

The ideal chain lubricant is one that can penetrate into the tiny spaces between rivets and plates, repel water, and not attract grit. Some people swear by a paraffin treatment that involves taking the chain off the bike, cleaning it thoroughly in solvent, then soaking it in a can of melted paraffin. If done well, this treatment is quite effective. But it is a lot of trouble and must be done right to work.

Other people like to clean a chain in place with a penetrating spray like WD-40 and LPS-1, then lubricate each link with LPS-3, motor oil, or some other heavier lubricant. Phil Wood makes a product called Tenacious Oil, which is supposed to be very good for chains because of its high resistance to water.

Some of the newer products gaining popularity for use on chains as well as other bike parts are the penetrating sprays containing Teflon, such as Super Lube and Tri-Flow. There are also sprays containing silicone that offer good water resistance. Some people also use these products instead of grease for lubricating and waterproofing gear and brake cables. Whatever you choose to use, make sure it does not leave a sticky film behind. If it does, wipe off the excess from your chain and your gear cogs so they do not collect grit. Avoid using anything on your cables that gets sticky after drying, since that will produce the very friction you are seeking to avoid.

## Basic Principles of Bicycle Maintenance and Repair

Finally, we wish to summarize some of the basic rules that guide what we have to say in this book on the subject of bicycle repair and maintenance.

1. Don't wait till severe problems arise before doing anything. Preventive maintenance is the best way to take care of your bike.

2. When lubricating your bike, use plenty of oil or grease, but wipe away excess that will attract grit. However, don't wipe off dirty grease that appears on the outside of bearings until overhaul time; doing so will only shove grit inside the bearings.

3. Check threads to see that they match before installing any threaded part. Don't mismatch threaded parts. Always grease threads first, then start threading them together carefully.

4. Some repair jobs are better left to experts. Learn to recognize your skills and limitations. Learn to make wise choices as to what you can handle and what is better left to a trained shop mechanic.

# 2 FRAMES

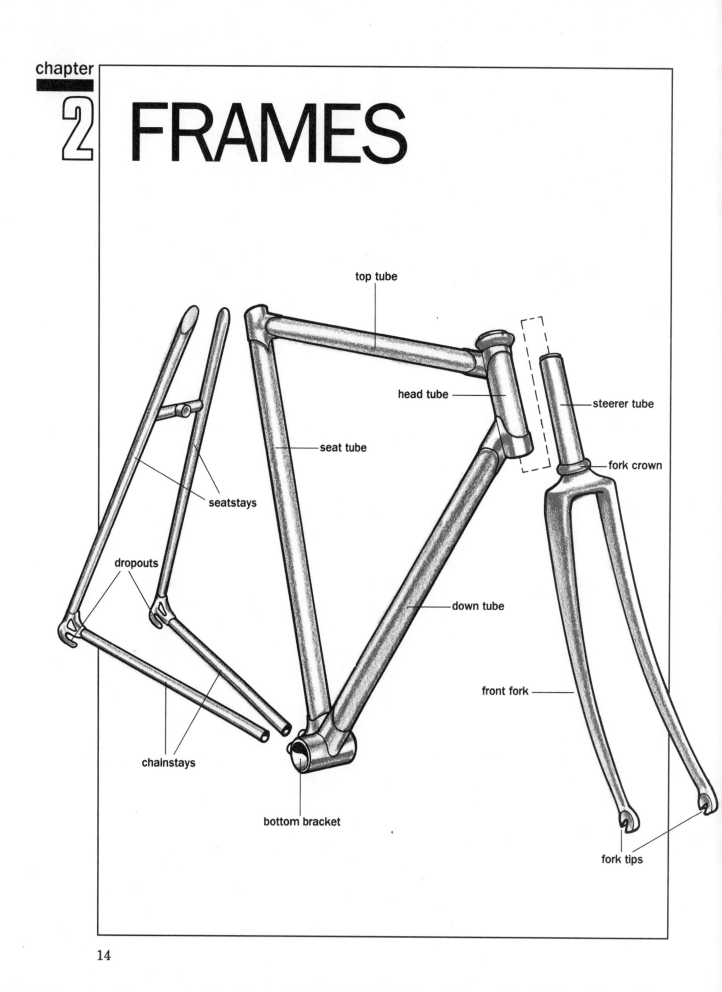

top tube

head tube

steerer tube

seat tube

fork crown

seatstays

dropouts

down tube

chainstays

front fork

bottom bracket

fork tips

Most of the chapters of this book focus on the maintenance and repair of particular parts of your bicycle. This chapter is different. Its primary purpose is to help you understand and become familiar with the heart of your bike, its frame. Not much will be said about maintenance and repair, since there are only a few things you can do to maintain your bike's frame. Frame repairs are best left to the talents of either a frame builder or a professional mechanic. Fortunately, repairs to a frame are seldom necessary. Your frame doesn't need the regular attention your drive train does, for example. Still, you shouldn't take it for granted.

The frame is the most important part of your bicycle for many reasons. It provides—by the way it locates in space your saddle, crankset, and handlebars—a geometry that positions your body for efficient pedaling. The same geometry also determines the handling, or behavior, of your bike. How stably it races downhill, its willingness to cut deeply into corners, and its ability to carry loads—all these factors are determined by the frame's geometry. Since it is impossible to build a frame that optimizes all three of these factors, trade-offs are made between them to make your bike a racer, sports tourer, loaded tourer, or an all-terrain bike. In addition, your frame's geometry, combined with its type and gauge of tubing, along with the type of tires with which it is equipped, determines how comfortably your bike rides.

So let's not underestimate the importance of the frame. Even though you can change your bike's personality to some extent by changing the parts that are hung on it, your bike's general handling and comfort, and your position on it, are determined by its frame. Therefore, it is valuable for you to learn to identify the principle parts of a typical frame and to recognize different types of frames.

## Frame Nomenclature

Your bicycle's frame is often described by its two halves, the front and the rear triangles. The *front triangle,* also known as the *main triangle,* is actually a quadrilateral. It consists of the following tubes: the *head tube,* which is located at the front of the frame and holds the headset, or steering bearings; the *top tube,* which connects the head tube and the seat tube under your saddle; the *seat tube,* which runs from the seat down to the bottom bracket; and the *down tube,* which runs from the head tube down to the *bottom bracket.* The bottom bracket holds the bearings and axle of the crankset as you pedal.

The *rear triangle* consists of the *chainstays* and the *seatstays.* The chainstays are the twin tubes that connect the bottom bracket and the two rear axle holders known as the *dropouts.* The seatstays are the twin tubes that connect the dropouts and the junction of tubes under the saddle called the *seat cluster.* Technically, the seat tube completes the triangle. However, when frame builders or bike mechanics talk about the rear triangle, they're usually referring only to the two sets of stays.

Completing the frame are the *fork* and the *steerer tube.* The fork consists of two fork blades that are attached to a horizontal piece known as the *fork crown.* At the lower end of the blades are the two front axle holders known as *fork tips* or *front dropouts.* The steerer tube rises out of the crown at the top of the blades and is normally hidden in the head tube. It connects the fork crown to the headset.

The materials used in the manufacture of your frame affect the way it feels. But as we said before, the length of the tubes and the way they relate to one another—that is, the frame geometry— play a major role in determining the way your bike behaves.

Some critical parts of frame geometry are the *fork rake,* which is the amount the front axle is offset from the centerline of the fork; the position of the bottom bracket, which is either given from the line drawn between the front and rear axles and called the *drop,* or is given from the ground and called the *bottom bracket height;* the *seat angle,* which is the smaller of the two angles formed by the seat tube and any horizontal line; and the *head angle,* which is the smaller of the two angles formed by the centerline of the head tube or the fork and any horizontal line. All of these factors combine to determine your bike's

*Illustration 2-1: The basic dimensions of a bicycle frame.*

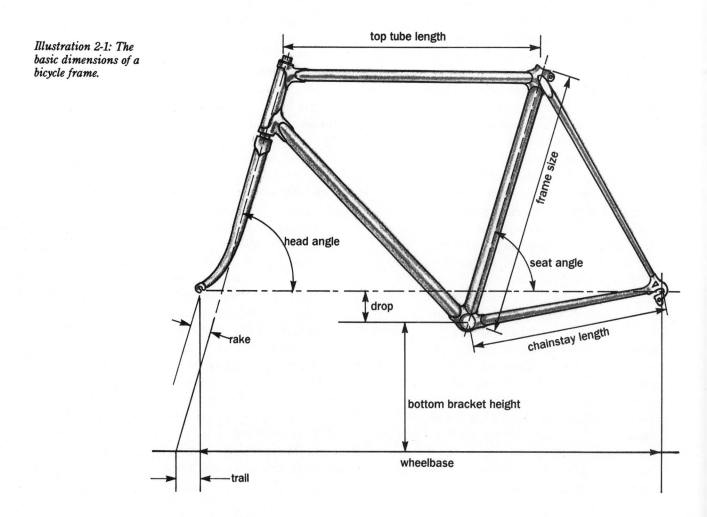

*wheelbase,* or the distance between the axles of the two wheels.

## History of the Bicycle Frame

The typical bicycle frame—sometimes called the *diamond frame* because of its shape, but more commonly known as the men's frame—has been with us for almost 100 years, even though there are many other frame designs. Ladies' and *mixte* frames (see illustrations 2-2 and 2-3) may provide easier mounting and dismounting because they don't have a top tube. But the diamond frame still provides the best combination of rigidity, strength, and light weight and is the predominant frame in use today.

Rigidity is important in a bicycle frame because a frame that is too flexible will waste some of your pedaling energy. Frames that do not have a top tube are essentially incomplete from a structural standpoint. To regain some of the strength lost because of their poor structure, ladies' frames have traditionally been constructed with heavy tubing. Not surprisingly, these bikes have also been quite heavy. In an earlier time, this wasn't a major concern, since most men's frames were also made from the same heavy, cheap tubing. But in recent years the bike market has changed considerably.

Modern technology developed over the past several years has provided less expensive ways to manufacture high-quality, lightweight tubing. At the same time, the demand for better-performing, lighter bikes has greatly increased. Technical know-how and consumer demand are factors that have pushed and pulled each other to the point where even beginning biking enthusiasts expect to purchase a lightweight bike.

*Illustration 2-2: The top tube on the ladies' frame is replaced by a second down tube, which makes mounting and dismounting the bike easier but eliminates much of its structural strength.*

*Illustration 2-3: The mixte frame is a compromise between the diamond frame and the ladies' frame. It replaces the top tube with twin lateral tubes that run from the head tube all the way back to the rear axle.*

Since a ladies' frame can't be made with light-gauge tubing, many quality manufacturers offer mixte frames (see illustration 2-3). These frames can be made of light tubing because they are structurally superior to the ladies' design. If you need a frame without a top tube for clearance reasons, a mixte frame bike provides much more rigidity and strength, and is much lighter, than a ladies' frame bike. Even so, the traditional diamond frame is still stronger and more rigid.

Just as the basic configuration of the men's frame hasn't changed in almost a century, the total of all the changes made in the bicycle frame's angles and tube lengths have been limited to about 10 percent or less during that period of time. That's because the proportions of the human body, the average bicycle wheel size, and the need for clearance between the front wheel and the rider's feet haven't changed. Given those fixed factors, the men's bicycle frame represents an excellent compromise between the factors of light weight, rigidity, body position, handling, and visibility. The small changes in frame geometry that have occurred have resulted in a secondary benefit—increased comfort.

High-strength, light-gauge steel tubing increases comfort in two ways. First, a lighter frame means less "unsprung" weight, to borrow a term from our automotive friends. That means that a lighter frame will transmit less road shock to your body. Second, light-gauge tubing is more resilient, or flexible, which enables it to absorb more of the bumps and smooth out the ride. This is made possible by its high-strength steel alloy, which is strong without being too rigid. Butted tubing, which has thinner walls in the center sections of the tubes, decreases weight even further at the same time that it increases the resiliency of the frame.

These advances in tubing design have permitted bicycle designers to make some geometric changes for more responsive handling that might otherwise seriously reduce rider comfort.

Head and seat tube angles that are steeper, that is, closer to a vertical orientation, increase steering quickness and improve hill climbing and sprinting. Unfortunately, those steeper angles also seem to feed road shock more directly to the rider. The same advantages and disadvantages accrue from shortening a frame's wheelbase.

Fortunately, compared to straight-gauge frames, butted frames allow the more modern (steeper and shorter) geometry while softening any increase in road shock with their increased resiliency.

## Frame Materials

Even though you can't change the type of tubing from which your frame was constructed, it can be very helpful to be able to identify it from the tubing sticker displayed prominently on one of the frame's main tubes. This will help you determine the value of the frame. So, before you sink a lot of money into repairing or upgrading your old bike, you can check to see if the frame is made of tubing good enough to warrant the expense. And the next time you spot a racy-looking, but unfamiliar, brand going for cheap at a garage sale, by reading the tubing sticker you can get a good idea whether it is a lemon or a bargain worth purchasing.

If there's no sticker at all on your frame, it's undoubtedly made of mild steel. That means the tubing walls are very thick and heavy. The frame will be adequate in the utilitarian sense, but will have no appreciable value of its own. Frames that read "high-tensile," "highten," or any similar term on their stickers won't be much lighter or worth much more.

The first level of quality in bike frames generally involves "high-carbon" tubing, which may also be called by a name particular to a certain brand. Examples of this are Fuji VALite, Columbus Aelle, and Reynolds 500 tubing.

Approaching the highest level of quality are steel alloy tubes such as Reynolds 501, Tange's Mangaloy and Ishiwata's Mangy-X. Frames made of these materials will be substantially lighter and better riding than all high-tensile and many high-carbon steel frames. A frame made of these materials might be worth rehabilitating, but not if you have to pay a lot for it.

Tubes of the finest steel alloys are those whose stickers indicate that they are either "chrome-molybdenum" or "chrome-moly" or "manganese-molybdenum" steel. Reynolds 531 and Columbus SL and SP are the best-known and most highly regarded brands, although True-Temper, Tange, Vitus, Ishiwata, Miyata, and Fuji all make tubing of similar quality.

But there's more to bike tubing than just its alloy. One way manufacturers market the use of a name brand of tubing is to use the expensive tubing in just the three tubes of the frame's main triangle. The tubing sticker of such a frame might state the well-known alloy followed by the words "3 main tubes." That makes a better frame than one made of "high-tensile" steel, but not as good as one constructed entirely of high-quality alloy.

Another factor of some concern is whether or not the frame's tubes are seamless. The finest grades of bicycle tubing have always been seamless; that

is, they were made from solid blocks of steel that were pierced and, through many stages, "drawn" into tubes. Seamed tubing, which is made from steel strip stock that is curved until its edges can be welded together, has always had a terrible reputation.

The bad reputation of seamed tubing arises from its use in the cheapest, lowest-quality bikes and is deserved in regard to mild steel or high-tensile tubing. However, if seamed tubing is made of chrome-molybdenum or another high-strength alloy and is subsequently drawn through the same dies used to finish seamless tubing, not only does the seam line virtually disappear from sight and touch, the strength of the seam becomes almost identical to that of seamless tubing. So don't be afraid of seamed alloy tubing. If you have it, it probably saved you $20 to $30 on the retail price of your bike.

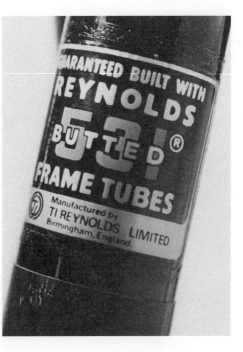

*Photo 2-1: Many bikes have stickers on the seat tube that identify the type of tubing from which the frame was constructed. This information can help you assess the value of the frame.*

Another important tubing factor displayed on many stickers is butting. That refers to the process of making one section of a tube with a thicker wall than another part of the same tube. Single-butted tubing is usually only found in seat tubes, with the thicker wall end placed in the bottom bracket shell to resist pedaling forces. Double-butted tubing has a thicker wall at both ends. Or, you can think of it as tubing that has two wall thicknesses: one thickness in the middle of the tube and the other at the two ends. Triple-butted tubing is similar, except that it has three gauges: the two end thicknesses are not the same. Quad-butted tubing not only has two dif-ferent end-wall thicknesses, the middle section also tapers from one gauge to another. Triple- and quad-butted tubes recognize that the loads at the two ends of a tube may be substantially different, requiring different strengths.

There are two good reasons for butting tubing instead of leaving it plain gauge. First, butting reduces weight by allowing lighter gauges to be used in the center sections of the tubes where there is less stress and where there is no brazing and filing such as takes place at the tube ends. (Both brazing and filing slightly weaken tubing.) Second, butted tubes are more resilient, or have more "give," which means they provide a

*Illustration 2-4: A butted tube has thin-ner walls in those parts of the tube sub-jected to less stress, unlike a plain gauge tube, which has uni-form thickness throughout its entire length.*

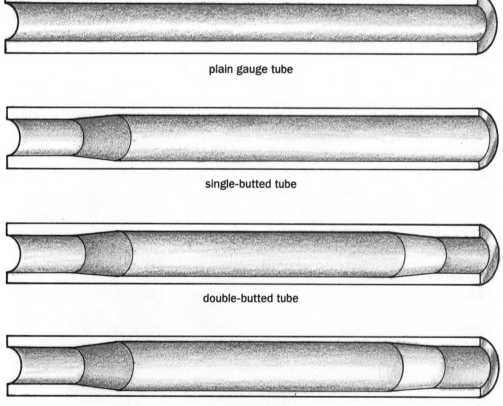

plain gauge tube

single-butted tube

double-butted tube

triple-butted tube

more comfortable ride. Don't totally discount plain gauge tubing, however. There are places, such as tandem or ATB (all-terrain bike) down tubes, where it may be superior to butted tubing. In any case, even on lightweight frames, butted tubing is found only in the three tubes of the main triangle and in the fork's steerer tube.

Recently, materials such as aluminum and composites made from graphite, boron, and Kevlar fibers have begun to appear on top-of-the-line bike models. Frames made from these advanced materials offer lighter weight and, often, increased comfort. In the future, increased use of exotic materials will bring down their current relatively higher prices.

## The Basics of Frame Geometry

Depending on the use for which a bike is designed, the seat angle, head angle, fork rake, chainstay length, and drop are varied within a narrow range of values. Small differences in the dimensions of any of these factors can make a great difference in the performance of a bike and in your performance on it.

The seat angle helps determine the comfort of your bike's ride. Steeper seat angles, like those found on racing frames, are generally associated with harsher rides and stiffer frames. This helps in hill climbing and sprinting, but not on long rides. The seat angle also helps determine your leg position vis-à-vis the crankset (see the discussion "Fitting You to the Frame" on page 25), which can influence the way you pedal. In general, steeper angles are better for

high-cadence spinning, while shallower angles are more conducive to muscling a bigger gear at a slower cadence.

The head angle is also instrumental in determining your frame's comfort level. Once again, steeper angles provide a stiffer, more efficient frame at the expense of a harsher ride, while shallower angles have the opposite effect. In addition, the head angle of your frame determines, along with the fork rake, how your bike handles. That includes stability, whether at cruising speed or in high-speed descents, and cornering capability.

As a rule, the steeper the head angle, the quicker the bike will react to your steering input, intended or not. The amount of fork rake used with a particular head angle determines the rest of your bike's handling characteristics. Larger fork rakes improve low-speed stability (up to about 15 mph) at the expense of high-speed stability. They also make a bike reluctant to lean very much in corners. In contrast, racing frames have little fork rake in order to maximize high-speed stability and cornering power. However, there are other factors besides fork rake that can affect the stability of a bike.

Loaded touring bikes have a lot of fork rake, which not only provides the comfortable ride you need for long days in the saddle, but also gives you look-at-the-scenery stability and minimizes any adverse effects on handling caused by attaching cargo to the fork. So what saves most touring bikes from being unstable on those long downhills? The extra weight of the average loaded touring bike's sturdy wheels adds extra gyroscopic stability to what would normally be a minimally stable combination of head angle and fork rake. Just don't ex-

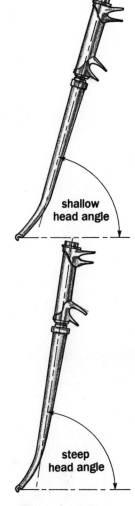

shallow
head angle

steep
head angle

*Illustration 2-5: Steeper head angles are used on racing bikes to stiffen the frame for hill climbing and sprinting, whereas touring bike frames employ shallower angles for a more stable and comfortable ride.*

pect to change your line very quickly, either in a corner or speeding downhill, on one of these bikes.

Chainstay length also affects the way a bike rides in many ways. Shorter chainstays like those on racing frames make a bike ride more harshly, but with less flexing in the rear triangle. That's especially important in hill climbing. Shorter chainstays also decrease a bike's wheelbase, and the shorter that is, the more nimble and stiff the bike feels. Loaded touring bikes, on the other hand, need longer chainstays for heel clearance with rear panniers, or rack bags. Those long chainstays also provide the softer, more stable ride a tourist usually wants.

A larger drop, or a lower bottom bracket height, is also often found on loaded touring bikes. The lower the bottom bracket, the lower the saddle and the lower the center of gravity (CG) is for the combination of the bike and its rider. A bike with a lower CG is more stable without losing any handling quickness. That's a desirable characteristic for any bike. Unfortunately, most racing events involve cornering and many racers like to pedal out of corners. For such riders, higher bottom brackets are necessary for the clearance needed between their pedals and the road. Traditional road racing bikes retain the lower bottom brackets of their touring cousins, while tight-cornering criterium racing models usually have high bottom brackets. Almost all track racing bikes have high bottom brackets.

A similar trade-off between low-CG stability and ground clearance figures into the various frame designs for all-terrain bikes. Once you get off the beaten path, you can expect to encounter some large rocks and fallen trees, not to mention deep weeds!

With these general observations in mind, let's take a closer look at the main types of bicycle use and the frame geometry appropriate to each.

## Racing

The frame of a racing bicycle is designed for stability at high speeds, easy cornering, quick steering response, and a stiff, efficient ride that minimizes energy losses. As a direct result of these virtues, the racing bike usually has poor low-speed stability, handles worse if any load is carried on the frame, requires constant attention to maintain a straight line, and very efficiently transmits even the tiniest bump in the road straight to you-know-where! You can identify a racing frame by the following measurements:

**Seat angle:** 73 to 74 degrees. Add 1 degree to that range for frames with a seat tube smaller than 21 inches (measured from the center of the bottom bracket to the top edge of the seat lug) and subtract 1 degree for frames larger than 24 inches.

**Head angle:** 73 to 74 degrees. Subtract up to 2 degrees from that range for frames smaller than 21 inches and add 1 degree for frames larger than 24 inches.

**Chainstay length:** 16 to 16½ inches.

**Drop:** 2⅜ to 2⅞ inches. That equals bottom bracket heights of 11 to 10½ inches.

**Fork rake:** 1½ to 1¾ inches for a 73-degree head angle. Subtract or add ⅛ inch for every degree of head angle greater or smaller, respectively.

## Sport Touring

Sports tourers are the midsize sports cars of the biking world. They're not all-out racers, but they're not loaded touring bikes, either. They can carry a load with racks and small panniers, but not too much. Their major attribute is their stable handling, which is predictable, if a little slow by racing standards. Sports tourers just want to have fun, so to speak, and can do just about anything well enough for you to enjoy it. Not surprisingly, the vast majority of derailleur bikes sold in the United States fall into this category. Look for the following dimensions:

**Seat angle:** 72 to 73 degrees. Add 1 degree to that range for frames with a seat tube smaller than 21 inches (measured from the center of the bottom bracket to the top edge of the seat lug) and subtract 1 degree for frames larger than 24 inches.

**Head angle:** 72 to 73 degrees. Subtract 1 degree from that range for frames smaller than 21 inches and add 1 degree for frames larger than 25 inches.

**Chainstay length:** 16½ to 17½ inches.

**Drop:** 2⅝ to 3 inches. That equals bottom bracket heights of 10¾ to 10⅜ inches.

**Fork rake:** 1¾ to 2 inches for a 73-degree head angle. Subtract or add ⅛ inch for every degree of head angle greater or smaller, respectively.

## Loaded Touring

The pack mules of the two-wheel road, loaded touring bikes exhibit great stability and straight-line tracking, even with up to 40 or 50 pounds of cargo. You can watch the scenery from aboard one of these without the constant fear of meandering either off the road or straying into traffic lanes. In addition, they're comfortable over rough roads and also come with gearing low enough to allow you to climb over any mountain. This all adds up to a bike that's perfect, loaded or not, for those whose main interest is in being there, rather than speeding on by.

**Seat angle:** 71 to 72 degrees. Add 1 degree to that range for frames smaller than 21 inches.

**Head angle:** 71 to 72 degrees. Subtract 1 degree from that range for frames smaller than 21 inches and add 1 degree for frames larger than 25 inches.

**Chainstay length:** 17 to 18 inches.

**Drop:** 2⅝ to 3⅛ inches. That equals bottom bracket heights of 10¾ to 10¼ inches.

**Fork rake:** 2 to 2¼ inches for a 72-degree head angle. Subtract or add ⅛ inch for every degree of head angle greater or smaller, respectively.

## All-Terrain

Originally called "mountain bikes," all-terrain bikes have captured the Walter Mitty in most people's spirits. With their comfortably shallow head and seat angles and fat, knobby tires, ATBs are perfectly suited to off-road riding and are loads of fun, too. West Coast models, which started the off-road movement in the hills north of San Francisco, have slightly shallower head angles for maximum stability in racing descents down California fire trails. Professional-level racers prefer steeper head angles because they provide quicker handling,

*Photo 2-2: The all-terrain bike is becoming increasingly popular as an all-purpose vehicle, one equally at home on city streets, mountain trails, and sandy beaches.*

while East Coast "rockpickers" like them because of their better low-speed, "trials"-type handling.

But only a small percentage of ATB buyers ever use their bikes off-road in the hills. The smooth ride of these "fat-tire flyers" makes them very attractive to those of us who don't enjoy being bounced hard over every tar strip on the road. ATB-derived city bikes are even more comfortable than loaded touring bikes, plus they are almost immune to potholes and broken glass. They aren't nearly as fast as a regular road bike, however.

When you shop for an all-terrain bike, you need to be clear about where and how you intend to use it. Most bike shops will recommend that you select an ATB frame 2 inches smaller than what you would pick for a road bike. If you are simply buying the bike to use for commuting, running errands around town, and occasional riding along dirt roads or sandy beaches, that formula should work fine. But if you plan to try serious off-road adventures involving log jumping and rock climbing, you should try out even smaller frames. In truly rugged terrain you need short chainstays for efficient climbing and a small frame that enables you to thrust your rear end back and down over the rear wheel for safe descents.

**Seat angle:** 69 to 71 degrees. Add 1 degree to that range for frames smaller than 19 inches.

**Head angle:** 68 to 70 degrees. Subtract 1 degree from that range for frames smaller than 19 inches and add 1 degree for frames larger than 23 inches.

**Chainstay length:** 17¼ to 18 inches, shorter (if you can find it) for really steep climbing.

**Drop:** 1¼ to 2 inches. That equals bottom bracket heights of 12 to 11¼ inches.

**Fork rake:** 2 to 2¼ inches for a 70-degree head angle. Subtract or add ⅛ inch for every degree of head angle greater or smaller, respectively.

## Fitting You to the Frame

For starters, you should be able to comfortably straddle the top tube of a bike with both feet placed flat on the ground. Next, adjust the height of the saddle so you can maintain a slight bend in your knee at the bottom of your pedal stroke with your feet held level. If your frame is the right size and you are a racer, the top of your saddle should be 6½ to 7 inches above the end of your seat tube, measured along the line of the seat tube and seatpost. If you're a long-distance tourist, the same measurement should equal about 5½ to 6 inches.

For this next step you'll probably need some help. In position on the bike, rotate your crankset backward until your right crankarm points straight ahead. With the crankarm horizontal, a vertical line passing through the pedal axle should intersect your knee about ½ inch behind its front surface. Loosen the saddle clamp and slide the saddle either forward or back to get closer to this ideal position, if it's possible.

With your saddle correctly adjusted, your arms locked straight, and your hands in position on top of the brake lever hoods, your back and the bike's top tube should form an angle that's equal to or slightly smaller than 45 degrees. Raise or lower the stem to get the correct position. If the length, or forward reach, of your bike's stem is correct, the angle formed by your arms and body with your arms straight and your hands once again on top of the brake lever hoods, shouldn't be greater than 100 degrees or less than 90 degrees. If you ride a lot, it might be worth the money to change stems if yours is too short or too long by more than ½ inch.

## Frame Maintenance

Now that you're fitted correctly onto your machine and you understand its design and function better than ever before, what maintenance can you perform to insure the long life of your bike's frame? A lot more than you might think.

One of the best ways to help your frame endure a long time, needless to say, is to avoid twisting it out of shape in an accident. A good bike frame has considerable resilience but cannot be expected to regain its original shape after being wrapped around some immovable object.

Next to accidents, the greatest enemy your frame faces is corrosion. If you drop beads of sweat onto your bike while you ride it, either indoors or out, you should thoroughly rinse it off as frequently as is practical. Salt deposits form in any kind of corner, especially underneath every kind of clamp, and continue the process of corrosion, even if the bike is dry. Braze-on parts contribute less to this severe problem than clamp-on parts, but they still trap unwanted salt. And even if your frame's paint isn't chipped, corrosion can start through the pores of the paint and spread under its surface.

Prompt attention to your frame after sweaty rides or workouts on rollers or wind trainers means a thorough, gentle water rinse. Don't use high pressure hoses or concentrated spray patterns, because they will force water, maybe also dirt, into your bike's bearings.

Paint chips can allow rust to start even on a dry salt-free frame. To prepare the surface for touch-up paint, *don't* sand the chipped area. Most manufacturers treat their frame's bare surface with a very thin phosphate coating that inhibits rust; sanding will remove it. Instead of sanding, use a solvent, such as lacquer thinner, to clean any oil from the chipped area. Then cover the chip with one or more coats of almost any type of paint that will match your bike's original color. If rust has already reared its ugly head through the hole in your frame's finish, use fine sandpaper to remove all of it before you touch up the frame.

Don't expect miracles: the main purpose of your touch-up work is to minimize rust damage to your frame until you have it repainted.

An occasional waxing, when your bike is clean and dry, will help its appearance and improve your chances of staying ahead of rust. Try using aerosol furniture wax instead of paste car wax. It's faster and provides a good shine, especially if your frame has an Imron or another urethane finish similar to those used on a lot of today's furniture!

Another household item, clear silicone rubber bathroom caulk, can help keep sweat and water out of the inside of your bike's frame. Unless the locknut on your headset has an o-ring seal, sweat can seep down the sides of your stem into the steerer tube. The resulting corrosion can sometimes require a hacksaw to remove the stem from the steerer. A thin bead of clear caulk around the base of the stem (wipe away the excess) will prevent the problem.

If you ride in the rain even occasionally, the same caulk treatment applied to the junction of the seat tube and the seatpost will prevent water thrown up under your saddle from leaking into your seat tube and collecting in your bottom bracket. Even if you have a shield protecting the bearings, the threads of your bottom bracket shell can rust, a situation that could eventually make it difficult to keep your bottom bracket cups tight.

Although the best defense against corrosion is to prevent moisture from entering your frame tubes, it may also help to fight corrosion from the inside. Anytime you have your seatpost out of the frame or your headset or bottom bracket dismantled for an overhaul, use the opportunity to spray or swab a rust-inhibitor such as WD-40 or LPS-1 inside the exposed tubes.

## Repainting a Frame

Eventually, the time will come when your battle-scarred mount needs a new finish. A repaint in your chosen color not only looks good, it also provides an opportunity to nip any ongoing rust in the bud and acquire any braze-on fittings you've been wanting.

If you cannot locate either a frame builder or a bike finishing specialist in your area, check with the nearest pro bike shop. People there can probably provide the services you need, or at least point you toward a reputable refinisher.

When arranging for refinish work, make sure that the frame will be chemically stripped of most of its old paint before being sandblasted or, preferably, glass beaded. A phosphate coating under the primer will help the new paint endure and will minimize the damage caused by the inevitable paint chips.

Catalyzed enamels and urethanes like Imron and baked enamels provide the most durable topcoats. Stay away from lacquers—they chip easily.

## Frame Maintenance: A Worthy Investment

Your bicycle's frame can accompany you for many years and tens of thousands of miles given proper consideration and care. So take heed to our maintenance recommendations. Deal with paint chips promptly, don't allow perspiration or road salts to accumulate, and once in a while treat your frame to a new paint job. You will be giving yourself a treat as well.

Every bicycle has its own special feel and its own peculiar idiosyncrasies. After riding thousands of miles, you become accustomed to your bike's behavior. If your bike has been good to you and you like its familiar feel, you may be loath to part with it even after it shows signs of aging. You cannot give up on it any easier than you can any other trusted friend. Invest a little time, attention, and money on maintaining your bike frame in good condition and it will continue to serve you well for a long, long time.

# 3 WHEELS AND TIRES

tire

tube

rim strip

spoke nipple

rim

spoke

hub

Next to the frame nothing has a greater influence on the way your bike rides than its wheels and tires. A wheel that is tight and true and fitted with a properly inflated tire of good quality makes bike riding a true pleasure. By contrast, a wheel that is loose and wobbly and surrounded by an underinflated tire of poor quality makes bicycle riding an unpleasant, if not dangerous, experience. Riding fast on such a wheel makes steering and braking difficult and is an invitation to disaster.

A well-built bicycle wheel is strong and durable, whereas a poorly built or poorly adjusted wheel is weak and vulnerable. The good wheel is not only made from materials of good quality, but is also put together in a way that maximizes the source of its strength, its spokes. The tension applied to the spokes enables the wheel to stay round and to withstand the pressures of weight and road shock.

When weight is applied to a wheel, the spokes beneath the hub lose some of their tension. If this tension is inadequate to begin with, the rim is in danger of becoming permanently deformed. A well-built and well-maintained wheel is thus a tight wheel, one whose spokes are at optimum tension. Such a wheel can better withstand pressures both from above and from the side than can a loose wheel. A tight wheel flexes less than a loose one and thus experiences less metal fatigue. It is more durable and less likely to go out of true.

Unfortunately, buying a complete bike or a set of wheels new does not guarantee that your wheels are good. Wheels on mass-produced bicycles are machine-built and often arrive at the bike shop loose and out of true. The shop mechanic may have neither the time nor the inclination to make them much better before selling them. The only guarantee of a good set of wheels is to get them from someone with a reputation for building quality wheels—or to learn to build quality wheels yourself.

## Selecting Wheels

Bicycle wheels come in an impressive array of sizes and types ranging from 12- to 28-inch diameters and ¾- to 2⅛-inch widths. The bicycle world contains two rim and tire numbering systems: the English-American standard and the European. Although many wheels are essentially interchangeable, the exact tire-to-rim fit is unique to each system.

The English standard uses two-digit numbers to indicate the approximate wheel diameter in inches (measured tread to tread), followed by a tire width number. For instance, 27 × 1¼ describes a wheel that, with its tire, is about 27 inches across and 1¼ inches wide.

The French system is metric and wheel diameter is designated by a three-digit number, the approximate diameter in millimeters. This number is sometimes accompanied by a two-digit number, which indicates the tire width. Usually a letter (A, B, or C) indicating rim width is placed after one of these numbers. So, for example, the French counterpart to the English 27 × 1¼ will be labeled 700 × 32C or simply 700C. The two tires are similar in size, but not interchangeable.

Factors that must be considered when choosing wheels include *diameter* (the "27" or "700" number), rim *width* (this dimension affects tire selection but is not formally numbered), and tire *size*.

Wheel diameter is determined by the frame designer who proportions the fork and stays for a specific size. Most bicycles made for 27-inch wheels will also wear 700C. But the only way to be sure of the interchangeability is a trial

fit. Make certain the brake pads have no difficulty reaching the rim. Unless you plan to regularly swap standard wheels with racing sew-ups (which only come in 700 size), there is no performance advantage to one size or the other.

Rim width affects tire choice. Although there are no hard and fast rules on rim-tire compatibility, most rims will fit several tire sizes. For instance, a narrow rim with an outside width of 20mm (often called a "1-inch" rim) will carry tires with widths of 19 to 28mm. In making your rim selection, anticipate the full range of riding conditions you wish to encounter. Table 3-1 shows which tires are suited for different types of riding. Find the tires you will be using, then select a compatible rim.

When selecting tires, beware that although makers can be trusted to list diameters correctly, their way of indicating width is undependable. One company's 25mm tire is the same size as another's 28. Some 26 × 1.75 labels are worn by tires that would be labeled 26 × 1.5 by another maker. So the exact size of a tire can only be determined from direct experience. The ISO international tire size system, a five-digit sequence, is potential salvation from this marking confusion. But although tire engineers all understand and adhere to it, this form of labeling rarely finds its way to consumers as a guide to tire choice.

Besides size, tires vary in many other ways, casing construction and tread pattern foremost among them. The rougher the pavement, the coarser the casing (larger, less frequent cords—down around 20 to 36 per inch) and the larger the tread pattern. Dry, loose ground calls for large, numerous tread knobs. Wet muddy conditions, on the

*Photo 3-1: Bicycle tires are available in many different sizes and tread patterns. Skinny treadless tires help racers maximize their speed while fat knobby tires help off-road riders cope with mud and water.*

## table 3-1 RIM AND TIRE COMPATIBILITIES AND USES

| Rim Category or Name | Rim Width (mm) | Rim Weight (g) | Tire Sizes | Typical Uses |
|---|---|---|---|---|
| 1″ clincher | 20 | 410-500 | 700C × 19-28mm<br>27″ × ⅞-1⅛″ | Road racing and sport touring |
| 1⅛-1¼″ clincher | 22-28 | 500-600 | 700C × 28-35mm<br>27″ × 1⅛-1⅜″<br>26″ × 1.5-1.75″ | All-purpose touring, ATB racing and touring, tandem road riding |
| 1.5-2.125″ clincher | 28-32 | 600-700 | 26″ × 1.5-2.125″<br>700C × 32-35mm<br>27″ × 1¼-1⅜″ | ATB racing and touring, Third World touring |
| Aero tubular | 16-19 | 260-350 | 18-20mm<br>150-220g | Time trials on track or road |
| Lightweight tubular | 20 | 280-350 | 20-25mm<br>220-300g | Road time trials, criteriums, and all-purpose racing for lighter riders |
| Team weight tubular | 20-22 | 395-420 | 25-28mm<br>240-350g | Training, all-purpose racing |

other hand, are best met with shorter more widely spaced knobs that do not collect mud.

On smoother surfaces such as well-maintained pavement, casings can be made of finer, more numerous threads (36 to over 100 per inch). And the tread patterns can be less aggressive. On good roads, in the wet or dry, some of the best results are obtained with entirely smooth tires. But nothing could be more counterproductive in the mud than smooth treads.

## Compatibility of Wheels and Bike

When considering a change of wheels you must not overlook wheel and bike compatibility. The factors affecting compatibility are wheel *diameter*, rim *width*, hub axle *size* and *width*, and freewheel *threading*.

The diameter of the wheel is important because it must be compatible with the brakes. Brake shoes must make solid and secure contact with the sidewalls of

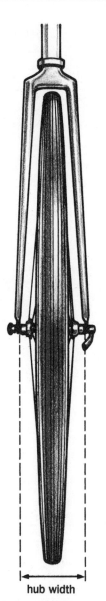

**hub width**

*Illustration 3-1: Hub width is measured from the outer edges of the two axle locknuts, a distance that should be equivalent to the space between the two fork blades of the frame.*

the rim, which serve as their braking surface. Because brakes are made in many different lengths and are mounted to frames in different locations, you cannot simply assume your brakes will reach any wheel size you might choose. For instance, bicycles equipped with 27-inch wheels will occasionally not accommodate the slightly smaller 700C size because their brake shoes cannot be lowered even 1/16 inch. With such small distances to measure, a trial fitting of the wheel you propose to use becomes very helpful. Borrow a friend's or visit a retail bike shop to test your bicycle's wheel tolerance.

Rim width is a measure of wheel strength and indicates the range of tire options. Refer to table 3-1 for suggestions on tire and rim sizes. Select a rim that is suited to the type of riding you will be doing.

Hub axle size and width must be appropriate for your bike frame. Hub width is measured from locknut to locknut and needs to conform to the space between the two blades of the fork (see illustration 3-1). Otherwise fitting your new wheel can be a real thumb buster. Most front hubs come either 95mm or 100mm wide. Exceptions to this rule include juvenile sidewalk bikes, which have even narrower hubs, and the rare tandem equipped with a front hub brake, which requires a dished wheel and a hub of 110 to 115mm in width. The same width consideration should be observed for the rear wheel where the range of sizes is much wider. Try to achieve a close fit so the difference between wheel and frame is no more than 3mm.

The goal of racing teams is to set up all their bikes with the same exact spacing for all rear wheels and frames. If all derailleurs are set up for the same freewheel space then lightning-fast wheel changes are possible. Whenever you expect to regularly use several different rear wheels on your bicycle, take the time to make each overall width and freewheel spacing the same. Damaging chain overshifts from misadjusted derailleurs can occur after wheel swaps, but they are avoidable.

Axle size, i.e., diameter, varies according to the axle type. Quick-releasing axles are thicker by 1/2mm than most nutted axles. Many bicycle frames can handle either type, but some designed for nutted hubs have dropout slots that are too narrow to permit the thicker quick-release axle. Since the convenience and popularity of the quick-releasing system is so overwhelming, you should consider filing your dropout to enlarge its slot opening. The amount of metal to remove is small, just work very carefully and do not misshape the dropout and cause the wheel to sit crooked.

Beware that the quick-release axle extension, that which protrudes past the locknut, must not be longer than the dropout is wide. On inexpensive bicycles fitted with higher class hubs this is often the case. If so, the clamping skewer will not secure the hub when tightened. The answer is to either remove the conical springs, which are only speed-fitting conveniences, or shorten the axle extensions.

After you have taken extensive measures to be sure your new rear wheel fits your frame you may be surprised to find that your freewheel will not thread on its hub. Two dimensions may be responsible for the problem. First is threading size. There are three distinct and somewhat incompatible threads found on freewheels. French threading (designated 34.7 × 1) is smaller than the others, so freewheels with this thread will be tight fits on the other two standards, English (1.370 × 24 tpi) and Italian (35 × 24 tpi). If a French-thread freewheel is forced on either of the other two, the hub will be forever transformed to French. Do not take that shortcut because in North America the French freewheel standard is disappearing. The other two threads will fit on French hubs, but loosely, so the chances of stripping the hub and losing use of the wheel are greatly increased.

English and Italian threads are almost compatible with one another. Italian threads feel larger and freewheels with this threading fit English-thread hubs easily and safely. By contrast, English-thread freewheels fit stiffly on Italian-thread hubs and a minor amount of force is required. Luckily, most hubs and freewheels these days are of the English standard and interchangeability is assured. The entire issue of freewheel threading is very confusing, and unless you know exactly what you have, check it out with a pro.

The second possible freewheel misfit involves the rear hub's right side spacing. We mentioned the desirability of matching spacing, but how should one choose which distance? Try to conform your hubs to the prevailing international standards. The right side space is measured, with the freewheel removed, from the shelf which the freewheel strikes when tight out to the last locknut edge that contacts the frame. This distance should be 31 to 32mm for 5-speed or ultra-6 spacing and 36 to 37mm for 6-speed or ultra-7 spacing.

## Special Use Wheels

Speciality bicycles often use very different equipment from our day-to-day machines. Track bicycles do not use brakes and punctures are rare on the velodrome surface. This explains why lightweight glued-on sew-up tires are so universal for track racing. For explosive events like matched sprinting, which features unpredictable maneuvering and sudden acceleration, 32- and 36-spoke wheels with sturdy rims in the 350-gram range abound. But for individual pursuit in which speed is steady and riders have the track mostly to themselves, rims can weigh as little as 260 grams and wear 24 and fewer spokes.

Massed start road racing is a rough-and-tumble world governed by weather and pavement conditions. Potholes, crashes, and punctures are facts of life so the predominant rims are of "team weight," that is from 395 to 420 grams supported by 32 or 36 spokes of full 14 (2.0mm) gauge. Under selected conditions of lighter-weight riders and better roads, as few as 28 spokes are used and rims can be as light as 340 grams.

Triathlon racing has room for all equipment. Since it is a timed, largely individual race over usually good roads, many competitors employ the lightest possible wheels and tires. Top riders often use rims and tires of the type designed for track pursuit bikes. But since the emphasis is on steady speed and not accelerations, rim and tire weight are not terribly important. A good many triathlons are won with everyday clincher rims and tires, in good condition and inflated to 100 or 155 psi.

Some of the best bicycle touring these days is on infrequently traveled rural roads. These are safer due to low traffic but they are poorly maintained. To enjoy them while carrying loaded panniers, wheels must be sturdy and tires generous. Use rims of 550-gram weights capable of carrying larger tires.

The same formula applies to tandem bikes.

# Wheel Maintenance and Repair

The best way to obtain outstanding performance from your wheels is to make sure they are appropriately designed for your riding, constructed from top-quality components and expertly built. From then on, avoiding damage is the biggest challenge. Well-built wheels do not need periodic maintenance apart from hub lubrication, unless damaged. Moreover, quality tires will last for many thousands of miles if kept properly inflated and free of puncture-producing foreign matter. Unfortunately, many wheels are not expertly designed or built. Such wheels demand more time and effort for maintenance and need to be repaired more frequently.

## Maintaining Proper Spoke Tension

Wheels built too loose, as the mass-produced ones generally are, can loosen even further with use. Wheels plagued by many limp spokes are dangerous and deteriorate rapidly. Not only are they prone to sudden collapse but their spokes fatigue much faster. Every time a wheel is used the spokes accumulate fatigue. Better spokes last much longer than inferior ones, though they all eventually wear out.

A process known as the "snap effect" causes spokes that reach zero tension during use to fatigue many times faster than those that do not. A tight wheel is able to resist severe loads more successfully than a loose wheel. Tightness also enables each spoke in the

wheel to stay above zero tension and escape the "snap effect."

Besides much longer life, a tight wheel is less likely to have individual nipples rattle loose from vibration. If you find one loose spoke and the rim is not dented at the spot, the culprit is a wheel that is simply too loose. The remedy for the problem? Lubricate all the nipples, tighten the individual loose one, and then add tension all around, perhaps one-half turn to each. Go easy on the general tightening, because as spokes reach their optimum level of tension, small twists of the nipple add tension very rapidly. Occasionally, nipples need to be glued tight, but adequate overall tension will normally keep a wheel free from further loosening.

Beware that excessive tension can create instability and make a wheel susceptible to sudden collapse. To be on the safe side, find a well-built wheel that you can use as a model. When plucked, similar gauge spokes will make a musical note that is proportional to tension. Higher is tighter, lower is looser. Make your wheel approximately as tight as the one you are using as a model, but no tighter. Your aim is not to make the wheel as tight as possible, only tight enough to prevent any spokes from loosening during use. It takes a good bit of experience to be able to sense when a wheel has reached this "optimum" level of tightness, so don't expect to automatically get it right the first time you try.

## Proper Tire Inflation

Air-filled, pneumatic tires were one of cycling's great breakthroughs. They provide traction, comfort, and protection for the rim. To deliver these advantages tires need to be properly inflated. The number one reason wheels are rebuilt is rim damage. And the number one cause of rim damage is underinflation of tires. Yes, owner laziness or inattention to proper tire pressure is an even greater threat to tires than potholes and curbs and other road hazards.

Make a regular habit of checking tire pressures and inspecting for tread damage before riding your bike. To leave the house with underinflated tires is a terrible financial risk if you are riding on expensive wheels. With no warning, a minor road hazard can cost you $50 to $100 in wheel damage.

Besides rim damage, the other big cost exacted by underinflated tires is tube pinching. When the tire is collapsed by a curb, the tube is caught between it and the rim, making a puncture likely. You can recognize a puncture caused by pinching by the telltale pair of "snake bite" holes that it typically produces.

## Avoiding Road Hazards and Rim Damage

Even though your wheels are appropriately tight and your tires properly inflated, you can still ruin a good set of rims if you hit a deep pothole or a large bump in the road while traveling at high speed. Prevention is the key. Avoid road hazards and you will escape rim damage.

Attention to the road surface has many payoffs besides wheel preservation. Debris or moisture on the road

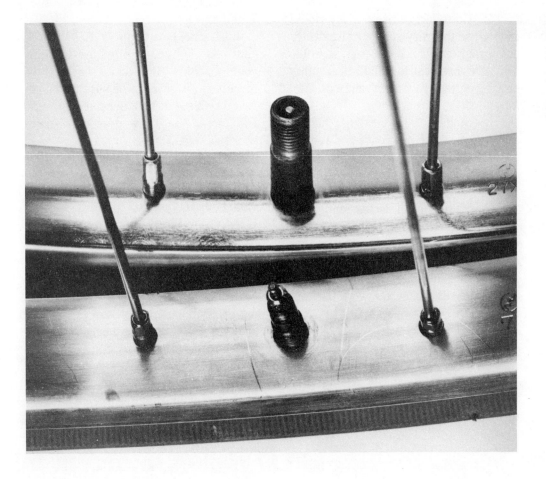

*Photo 3-2: The Schrader valve (top) is similar to valves found on automobile tires, whereas the Presta valve (bottom) is thinner and has a small nut on its end that must be loosened while the tire is being inflated.*

could cause you to tumble, especially if you hit it while making a turn. Crossing railroad tracks at an angle other than 90 degrees can be treacherous, especially if you are riding on tires with little or no tread. Be alert and learn to make quick maneuvers to dodge major obstructions and to thread your way carefully through water or debris that cannot be completely avoided.

Despite all your precautions, you may find that your wheels receive occasional dents. If so, try one of the following solutions:

**1.** Increase air pressures up to the maximum after first inspecting for any tire damage that such increased pressures might aggravate.

**2.** Go to larger tires. Many riders cannot use the very smallest tires without experiencing costly rim injuries. Tiny tires are best for small riders and/or near-perfect pavement surfaces.

**3.** Modify your riding habits. Avoid particularly bad roads and reduce speeds where pavement trouble is unavoidable.

Punctures, head winds, and dirty chains are facts of life. Wheel damage need not be. Spared from crashes, underinflation, and road hazards, an appropriately designed and well-built wheel should deliver many years of trouble-free service.

## Avoiding Spoke Damage

Spokes are regularly damaged in two ways. Something gets caught in them or the chain overshifts low gear

and lands on them. Common sense can minimize the chances of either problem occurring. However, if ever you discover one of your wheels is inexplicably out of true, check for bent spokes.

The rule with low-gear shifting is conservatism. Always shift gently into low gear when riding after a wheel change or when riding a bike whose derailleurs may be improperly adjusted. Test the gear before you reach a steep section of road where your shift will be rapid and pedaling force extreme. And when adjusting the derailleur, do not allow it to move closer to the spokes than necessary. It is better to just barely get into low gear than to occasionally throw your chain into the spokes. Once scratched, drive-side spokes are much more likely to break when they are subjected to a lot of pressure.

After experiencing a fall, having your bike tip over, or after transporting your machine in a car, shift gently through your gears to be sure that your rear derailleur has not become bent. If it has, shifting into low gear may cause spoke damage.

## Removing and Remounting Wheels

You must master this operation. Without it you are not likely to enjoy cycling. The two keys to wheel mounting ease are lubrication and proper fit. Whether your wheel is fastened to the frame with nuts or a quick-release, the removal and remounting procedure should be as easy for you as putting on or taking off your shoes. After all, wheels are your bicycle's shoes. Lubrication of the axle nuts or the quick-release lever helps the process go smoother.

Dismount your wheels with the bicycle supported. Turn it upside down; hang the saddle's nose over a branch, fence, or loop of rope suspended from a rafter; or get a companion to hold the bike while you remove the wheels. Experiment until you find the method that suits you best. With experience you can learn to remove a single wheel while supporting the bike yourself.

Front wheels are the simplest to remove. First loosen the axle. If it is held with nuts then use a wrench to loosen one side a bit, then the other, and back to the first. Nuts should be tightened or loosened gradually. Problems can arise if you try to do one all at once. A quick-release lever needs to be opened by pulling it away from the frame until it points straight out and then rotating it on around until it is parallel with the frame again. This 180-degree rotation will, like the nut loosening, allow the hub to come free from the front forks.

Before a wheel will easily lift away from a frame, however, it may encounter resistance from the brakes. If your brake shoes are adjusted close to the rim, they will probably have to be opened more to allow the tire through. Most bikes equipped with quick-release hubs also have quick-release levers for slackening the brake cable, which allows the calipers to spread enough for tire removal. If your bike is not so equipped, you may have to remove a brake shoe in order to get your tire out of the frame.

The chain makes rear wheels more difficult to remove. For derailleur bikes, begin by shifting to the smallest outside cog on the freewheel. Loosen the axle nuts gradually, or the quick-release all at once. Check to see that the brakes are widened to permit tire clearance. Now give the wheel a sharp blow from behind. If it is ready to be removed this blow will jar the axle forward in the dropout slots, hopefully all the way out.

Once the axle is out of the dropouts the wheel is free. With derailleur bikes, the rear derailleur's upper body must be grasped and twisted back (clockwise) so the wheel can exit. Now the only encumbrance is the chain and it must be unlooped from the wheel. This can only be accomplished by lifting if off manually. No problem, just do not wipe your face with the same hand before cleaning up.

Most of the difficulties encountered when replacing wheels are caused by a mismatch between frame and wheel. It is worthwhile letting an expert adjust your frame if necessary to allow your wheels to fit properly. Otherwise, every time you dismount or replace a wheel, you will find yourself caught up in a first-class wrestling match.

## Tire Mounting and Tube Repairs

Tire removal is a deceptively easy task, well within the abilities of anyone who can ride. Since punctures are largely unpreventable it is vital every cyclist learn how to remove a tire, repair the tube, and replace both. Success depends on five factors, the last and most important of which is correct procedure.

*1. Rim and tire size.* These must, of course, match. A difficult fit is rarely caused by mismade rims and tires. Rim makers almost never err by more than 1 percent in diameter. Major tire companies are scrupulously careful to match their tires to prevailing rim designs. The most likely mistake you will make is to try to mount a too-narrow tire on a wide rim. Although their diameters might match, the tire's inadequate width will crowd the tube and resist installation.

*2. Rim design.* Some rims are easier to fit with tires than others. There is no easy way to second-guess a rim's tire tolerance. The biggest factors seem to be overall diameter and the difference between the rim's inner trough and its upper edge. When fitting a tire the mounted bead sits in the center trough of the rim, while the remainder is lifted over the rim edge. The difference between these two provides the slack needed for installation. The larger the difference, the easier the fit. To get the most benefit from this slack, use the thinnest rim strip possible. No rim is safe without a rim strip or liner of one sort or another to protect the tube from the ends of the spoke nipples. However, the thinner the material used for this liner, the simpler it is to mount tires.

*3. Tube size.* Whenever possible, use a tube one size smaller than the tire. For instance, use a 1-inch tube with a 1⅛-inch tire. The more compact the tube, the simpler it is to insert and the less crowding will occur as the tire's last tight section is lifted onto the rim.

*4. Talc.* This much overlooked substance is a necessity for smooth tire manipulation. A tube without talc tends to stick to its tire and is much harder to force into position. Sprinkle some into the palm of your hand and draw the partially inflated tube through it. Then dust the inside of the tire by putting some talc into the bottom and rotating the casing while spreading the talc with a soft brush. With many tires the use of talc spells the difference between success and failure.

*5. Procedure.* The last critical factor is procedure. Without skillful procedure, even the best matched components refuse to cooperate. As with any endeavor, attitude plays an important role. Tire mounting often catches us at bad moments, especially after unwelcome flats. The embarrassment of delaying a group ride or the disappointment of being late to work is enough to make most people cross-eyed with impatience. Keep cool and be cheerful, if possible. Work smoothly and efficiently and you will soon be on your way again. For complete step-by-step instructions for tire and wheel mounting, and tube repairs, see the repair sections at the end of this chapter.

When dismounting your tire remember to be sure the tube is *completely flat.* Once the tube is deflated press the beads of the tire together and away from the rim edge, down into the center trough, as shown in illustration 3-2. Here you can find the slack to lift one section of tire over the rim edge with tire levers. Using two or three levers in sequence, continue to lift sections of the tire off the rim, one side at a time. When the tire is entirely off the rim on one side you can reach in and pull out the tube. To remove the valve stem the loose bead must be lifted over the valve hole. Leave the other half of the tire on the rim.

Inflate the tube until the puncture reveals itself with a gentle hissing

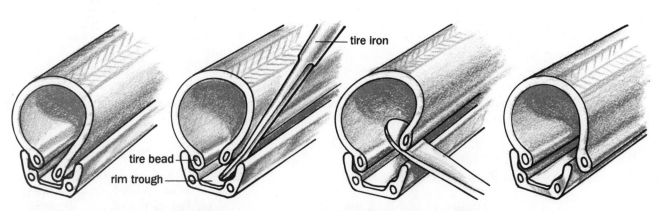

*Illustration 3-2: When removing a clincher tire, deflate the tube and push the tire bead off the shoulder of the rim into its center trough, then use a tire iron to lever the bead over the side of the rim.*

sound. Mark the spot with a pen. Success in gluing rubber patches is owed to thorough cleaning of the tube and use of fresh vulcanizing cement. Clean the tube with a solvent like alcohol. Then buff the area with light sandpaper, which is usually provided in the patch kit. Apply plenty of cement, which should be thin and runny. If the solution is thick and gummy it will barely work. Smear the cement out over a generous area, larger than the patch you plan to use. Once the shiny wet surface of the cement dulls, apply a second coating. After it dries the patch can be fixed.

Most patches come with a protective backing. Peel it off, then roll the patch, sticky side down, onto the double-coated tube and press it firmly to eliminate any air bubbles. Put a spot of talc on the repaired area to keep it from sticking to the tire. Do not wait to remount the tube, for its repair will be strong by the time you are ready to inflate the tire.

Check the condition of the tire by running your fingers around the inside. Any bits of wire, thorns, or glass must be removed before inserting the repaired tube or else you will probably experience another puncture right away.

Put a small amount of air into the tube so it will insert easily, sit straight, and avoid being caught under the tire's bead. Fit the stem of the tube first by lifting the tire bead back and away, exposing the valve hole. Once the tube is back in place, let most of its air out and begin working the bead of the tire back onto the rim.

Try completing the job without the use of tire levers, in order to minimize the chances of your pinching the tube. Begin remounting the bead opposite the valve hole so the last difficult section will occur at the valve. This ensures the maximum possible slack in the tire bead. The valve's base interferes with the bead, and its presence at the end allows you to lift the tube up and away from the tire's tightest section.

With the tire replaced on the rim, take a breather. Start inspecting the bead seat by pushing the tire away from the rim, one side at a time, and looking down into the rim. Make sure the tube is not visible. If the tube is caught under the bead the tire will not inflate evenly and may blow later. If everything looks right, add 20 to 30 pounds of pressure and rotate the wheel to see that the tire is sitting uniformly. Bulges at low pressure can be explosive at high pressure. If the tire looks straight, inflate to full pressure. If not, lubricate the beads with soapy water and reinflate or simply dismount everything and try again.

## Mounting and Repair of Tubular Tires

Tubular, or sew-up, tires are glued to the rim with a special contact cement. This bond is critical to riding safety. If the bond fails, a fall is almost certain. The success of the cementing procedure depends greatly upon the rim and tire being clean before bonding. So begin tubular mounting by wiping the rim with a solvent such as alcohol. If in doubt, wash the tire with detergent water and allow both to dry before proceeding.

Fit a new tubular to its rim first *without* cement. This permits the tire to stretch and gives a vital forewarning about the difficulty you will face when cement is applied. Start by putting a bit of air in the tire so it has a shape, but no pressure. Then set the wheel vertically on the ground in front of you with the valve hole on top. Insert the valve through the hole and grasp the tire to either side with your hands. Place each section on the rim and advance your hold down the side, lifting each section of the tire onto the rim.

Bending over the wheel, continue to mount the tire while watching the valve to see that it remains straight. If it becomes crooked, pull the tire harder with one hand to correct. As your hands near the bottom of the wheel the tire will become tight. You must use your body weight to stretch the tire into place. The last difficult section will be conquered by lifting the wheel off the ground and rolling that tire section away and then onto the rim.

Move around the wheel, straightening the tire and then add full air pressure. Let the tire sit for awhile—preferably overnight, but at least for 10 or 15 minutes—to give it time to stretch. Dismount the tire and apply cement to it and the rim separately. Allow each to dry and then add a light second coating to the rim. Before the second coat dries, mount the tire exactly as before. You will know you did a good job of gluing if, when eventually punctured, the tire is nearly impossible to remove from the rim.

Repairing tubulars is slow but easy work. When possible, locate the puncture while the tire is still on the rim. Inflate the tire and listen for leaks. If you cannot hear air escaping, perhaps you will feel it on your face. Look closely for a hole or cut in the casing that is the point of the puncture. Once you locate it, mark the spot so you can find it again quickly after you get the tire off the rim.

Unfortunately, some leaks are difficult to pinpoint. This is especially true of holes caused by the pinching of the tube when a tire hits a pothole or similar obstacle. If you cannot locate the precise point of the problem by one of the above methods, pull the tire off the rim and try another method.

If you have a slow leak, you can try pumping up the tire and immersing it in water, watching for bubbles. Unfortunately, air bubbles sometimes travel inside the tire casing before emerging into the water, so this method is not foolproof.

The most certain way of pinpointing the tire leak is to isolate one section of the tire at a time and see if any air escapes from the rest of the tire. If not, then you know the problem lies in the isolated section. You can try blocking off a section of tire by squeezing it between your hands. A more elaborate way is to clamp a couple of short 2 × 4 blocks around the tire, section by section. Once you have located the source of the problem, you can begin your repair.

A tubular tire has protective tape over the stitching that holds it together. This tape is bonded to the tire with liquid latex, not rim cement. Cut the tape and pull it back to expose about 6 inches of stitching at the location of the puncture. Use a sewing seam ripper to cut the stitching threads. Pull the tire open and remove the thread remnants. Carefully pull aside any protective gauze to expose the tube. Lift it out and look for the leak. Patch the leak using the same methods used with ordinary tubes.

While you have the tire open, you should look inside to see if any pieces of the object that caused the puncture are embedded in the casing. Remove any offending material. Also check to see if any casing threads are cut. Such damage must be reinforced with a casing patch. Cut your own patch out of a piece of old tire or strong canvas or nylon. A generous size is best; overlaps of 2 inches or more are suitable. Sheer pressure will keep the casing patch (or "boot") in place so there is no need to cement it.

Sprinkle a little talc into the casing to help the tube slide back into place. Pump a little air into the tire, if it is needed, to help the tube position itself properly, then straighten the inner tape. You are now ready to restitch the tire around the tube, but take special care to use the exact same holes as were originally used for this. You don't want to weaken the casing by cutting new holes through it. A simple overhand stitch will work fine, or you can use a sewing awl of the type used by leather workers to reconstruct the original cross pattern. Use strong thread or even dental floss in a pinch, overlapping generously at the ends to prevent unraveling. Glue the rim strip back in place with liquid latex. This is the same material used to coat and protect the tire's sidewalls after extended use dries them out. Now you have a perfect spare tire.

The residue of rim cement left on the tire means it will achieve a decent bond with the rim when installed on the road. A brand-new, never cemented spare tire is dangerous. So use a repaired tire as your spare. It is best to transport it in a simple pouch or old sock to protect it from light.

These days clincher tire technology has reached new heights and tubulars are no longer the "kings of the road." Still the greatest virtue of tubulars, as yet unchallenged, is their rims. Because cement is the bonding agent, the tubular rim need not provide a protruding lip for tire mounting. Most of the rim's mass is employed to support spoke tension and resist dents. The result is a much lighter rim. Tubular rims are 25 to 35 percent lighter than comparable clinchers. This is a difference hard to match and makes tubulars the tires of choice in situations, such as track racing, where eliminating unnecessary weight from the bike is particularly beneficial.

## Basic Wheel Repair and Maintenance

All wheel maintenance and repair can be undertaken either with your wheel mounted in your bicycle or on a trueing stand. To work on a bike-mounted wheel, suspend the bike from rafters, fasten it in a repair stand, or simply upend it so the wheels can turn freely.

Wheels should be cleaned at least once a month. The tires should be inspected for cuts and bruises and gently scrubbed with a soft bristle brush and soapy water. Take care to keep the solution away from the hub bearings. The rim, hub, and spokes can be wiped down with a clean cloth lightly dampened with a solvent such as kerosene. Again, keep the solvent away from the hub's bearings. Brake pad material, which accumulates on the rim, can interfere with braking performance and is tough to dislodge. Use an abrasive pad or mild-grade steel wool to remove this residue.

After extended exposure to the elements, spoke nipples may resist turning, making corrections in spoke tension difficult. So, before undertaking adjustments to your spokes, lightly lubricate the nipples with penetrating oil. Place oil on the spoke where it enters the nipple and between the nipple and rim.

Turn the wheel and feel the tension of each spoke. Locate broken spokes or any that are completely loose. These, of course, will require attention. Closely observe the rim to discover bends, wobbles, or dents. A wheel can wobble for several reasons. You must identify the source of the problem before you can remedy it.

*1. Loose hub bearings.* If the wheel is wobbling on loose bearings, it will be impossible to true until the hub has been properly adjusted. Remove any looseness for the sake of the trueing session. Any desired play can be reintroduced into the hub after the wheel is straight. See chapter 4 for instructions on hub adjustment.

*2. Incorrect spoke tension.* If the wheel is untrue, spoke adjustments can often make it right. Keep the following points in mind whenever you begin to true your wheel:

a. You need not remove the tire to true the wheel but you ought to release most of its air pressure. Otherwise the turning nipple may cut through the rim strip and puncture the tube.

b. Beware of spoke windup while you turn the nipple. This can occur when inadequately lubricated or damaged threads cause the spoke to twist with the nipple instead of threading into the nipple. Check for this by feeling the spoke with two fingers while turning the nipple. Back off to unwind the shaft if necessary.

c. Pliers and crescent wrenches are no substitute for a close fitting spoke wrench. A damaged nipple is undesirable and often cannot be removed without cutting and replacing its spoke. A spoke with a frozen (rusted) nipple must be replaced.

d. Work in small increments. By adjusting nipples only one-quarter turn at a time you can avoid making overcompensations in spoke tension. Larger adjustments can be made when you have enough experience to know when they are appropriate.

e. The tension in neighboring spokes on the same side of a wheel should be similar. Pluck them to compare their sounds. Large differences suggest incorrect building or rim damage.

f. If, to correct a wobble, you attempt to tighten a spoke that cannot be further tightened, or loosen one that is already slack, then you may be faced with a bent rim. If the spokes cannot correct the bend, you can attempt to forcefully rebend the rim and try again. Chances are the rim will simply have to be be replaced.

*3. Broken spokes.* Broken spokes must be removed and replaced as soon as possible. It is usually best to replace the nipple as well. If the wheel is otherwise undamaged the replacement will be very easy. With a rear wheel, the gear cluster may need to be removed. The new spoke, whose length is precise and specific to your wheel, is threaded through the hub and brought up to the nipple. It may be bowed considerably for installation as long as sharp bends near the elbow are avoided and it is straightened afterward. Tighten the new spoke until its tension resembles its neighbors (pluck and compare sounds). Then tighten further, if necessary, to straighten the rim at that point.

This process is usually as simple as retuning a radio station after the dial is mistakenly brushed. Tighten and loosen only the new spoke until the rim runs true. On some very light or excessively tight wheels, a broken spoke leaves a kink in the rim that the new spoke cannot correct. Sometimes the wheel is lost, though often it is salvageable.

*4. Dents and bends.* Small dents that widen a rim contribute to choppy braking action but can be eliminated by a gentle squeeze with a smooth jaw vise. Avoid overcorrection by squeezing only a little at a time. Spoke readjustments can also help hide the damage. Small dents to narrow clinchers can often be remedied by grabbing the bent rim bead seat with a narrow-jawed crescent wrench, levering out and up.

Larger dents are serious business and require expertise. One way to undent a "flat" spot in a rim is to release the spokes at the point of damage and suspend the wheel off the ground with that position down. Slip a $2 \times 4$ block of wood about 1 foot long between the spokes over the spot and strike it with a hammer, pounding the dent away from the hub. You may want to first carve the wood to the shape of the rim where they contact.

Keep pounding until the rim is very slightly bulging. But beware, it may take less force than you expect, so begin with light blows. Some lightweight rims will fail when subjected to this treatment, so do not assume success. If the correction is more than ½ inch or the rim ends up with cracks or wrinkles, the result may be unstable and therefore unsafe.

Sideways bends are tricky to fix. A typical cure for a small local bend is to release some of the spoke tension at the bend and then remove the wheel from the bike or trueing stand. Kneel on the ground and lay the wheel on its side before you with the bent section facing down and positioned nearest you. Lean over the wheel and grasp the rim 8 to 10 inches to either side of the bent section, pressing it to the ground. By applying some of your body weight the rim can be forced back into shape. If you're lucky you may be able to retension the spokes and reuse the wheel.

## Emergency Wheel and Tire Repairs

When is a wheel or tire too far gone to be repairable? Never say never! If a mishap disables your bike it is time for emergency measures. Tire damage is the most likely inconvenience. When you discover that your tire casing has a cut too large to allow the tire to hold the tube at pressure, you can use an internal reinforcing patch. In an emergency, such a "boot" can be made of scraps of clothing, high-fiber paper such as currency, or whatever is available. The less suitable the reinforcement, the lower the resultant pressure. If the casing damage is near one of the tire's beads, the repair needs to be made from a long piece of cloth that wraps around the tube next to the inside of the tire and circles around the tire's beads so that it will be held between the tire and rim when the tire is reinflated. Carry such a piece of reinforcement in your tool kit, something like a 5-by-10-inch rectangle of tough nylon.

Broken spokes must be removed as soon as detected or, at least, wrapped around a neighboring spoke to prevent tangles. If the damaged wheel will not clear the brakes or frame, then some on-the-spot trueing might help. A spoke wrench is almost essential, but other metal grabbers like crescent wrenches and pliers can do the trick. Position the spoke to be adjusted near the frame stays or fork. Use your hand to pull the rim in the direction of the spoke that needs to be tightened, grasping the rim and frame together and squeezing. With such a deflection the spoke will become slack and easy to turn.

In the case of complete wheel collapse, little can be done besides rebuilding. If the wheel assumes a very symmetrical "potato chip" shape, try bouncing it back to normal. Lay the wheel on the ground and kneel over it holding opposite edges of the rim in both hands. Grab the high spots and press them down forcefully. Occasionally this will cause the wheel to spring back to rideable condition. If so, consider yourself lucky. This procedure may get you home, but the wheel still needs rebuilding.

If a skid or crash bends one section of rim badly out of true, a temporary repair can sometimes be effected by inserting that section in a narrow slot and bending it back into line by levering the rest of the wheel. Such slots can be door jambs, sewer gratings, and spaces between boulders and trees. Use your imagination!

Whether you use such drastic methods or simply phone home is your decision. But bicycles are tools of survival and many irreverent and impromptu repairs have kept them on their way.

## Wheel Construction

Wheel building is impossibly complex unless you start with the right parts. Above all, have an expert select matching hub, spokes, and rim. Arrange the parts and inspect them for flaws of any kind. If you use thread compound, apply it to the loose spokes. Now is the time to insert the spokes in the hub, one-fourth at a time.

1. *Lacing.* The spokes are connected one "round" at a time. The wheel consists of four rounds, each inserted into the hub flanges from a different direction. In a 36-spoke wheel each round contains 9 spokes. Start by holding the hub in front of you, axle pointing down. If you are working on a rear hub, the gear side should be down. Drop 9

spokes into the top flange, using every other hole. Have a seat and hold the rim around the hub, balanced on a bench in front of you and/or on your knees. Orient the rim so the valve hole is opposite your stomach.

Lift one of the spokes and stick it through the hole to the left of the valve hole and attach its nipple loosely. This hole should be drilled a bit offset to the top of the rim; it is intended for spokes from the top hub flange. If the holes are drilled some other way, then bad luck. You will have to seek another lacing method. Luckily 98 percent of all modern rims are drilled with the left hole offset up. Now take the spoke next to your first and insert it into the rim leaving three rim holes empty between it and the first. Attach the nipple and proceed to insert and attach the rest of these spokes.

Flip the rim and hub over so the second flange is on top. Look carefully from the top to the bottom flange and notice that the holes are not drilled in line with one another. They are offset so that a spoke dropped straight through one hole will hit the other flange directly between two holes. The first spoke in this second round will be dropped into the hub hole, which is next to the first spoke inserted in the first round and one hole away from the valve. This spoke (the tenth, if you are lacing a 36-spoke wheel) should be lifted up into the rim hole next to spoke number one and away from the valve hole. Attach its nipple and then insert the remaining spokes of round two. This time do not flip the wheel for the next round.

Drop the spokes set aside for round three through the remaining spoke holes in the bottom (first) flange of the hub. After this comes the only complicated part of the lacing procedure. Lift the rim up off your lap so it sits vertically, just as on the bike. The round three spokes should all fall sideways, hanging loosely by their elbows. If not, help them to do so. Lay the wheel down flat again, but the opposite way so that the round three spokes are on top. Holding the rim still, twist the hub relative to the rim, away from the valve hole. If you twisted correctly, then both spokes number one and number ten (for a 36 wheel) will be parallel and will exit the rim moving away from rather than over the valve hole.

Each round three spoke will travel in the opposing direction from the round one spoke with which it shares the upper hub flange. Now is the time to arrange the correct cross pattern. In the case of cross three, each spoke will pass over two and under one round one spoke before entering its rim hole. The first spoke cross occurs right at the hub. Grab any loose round three spoke and direct it over two and under one round one spoke, then insert it into the first available rim hole. Loosely attach the nipple and go to the next. Do not worry if the spokes seem a stiff fit in the hub. It is an inconvenient but healthy sign.

Round four is a repeat of three. Without flipping the wheel in your lap, drop the remaining spokes into the open holes in the bottom flange. Lift the wheel up vertically so the loose spokes can fall down. Then lay the wheel down the opposite way so the round four spokes are now on top. Lace each to the remaining rim holes following the same cross pattern as before.

*2. Initial tensioning.* With all spokes attached it is time to mount the wheel in a trueing stand or bicycle so your hands will be free. Oil the nipples with some mild lubricant so they will turn easily. Now tighten each until the last spoke thread is just showing. While the wheel is still loose, bend the spokes near the elbows so they conform to their new directions. Press the outside spokes toward the hub with your thumb or a mallet.

If you are using the correct spoke length the wheel ought to still be loose. Tighten each nipple one-half to one turn and check tension. Repeat this uniform tightening until the spokes begin to feel snug. Only with minimum tension can the next step, trueing, be undertaken.

*3. Trueing.* Now the wheel must be straightened in both radial and lateral directions until it is as true as you want the finished product. We call this point of supreme straightness at minimum tension "ground zero." Once achieved, layers of tension can be added with little disturbance of the trueness. Any other procedure is full of risks and delays.

True the wheel side to side by tightening and loosening pairs of spokes in the center of the undesired wobble. Always work on the wheel's worst spot, rotating after each correction to discover which is still the worst. Treat each wheel section as an independent pie-shaped part. Do not worry about adjusting spokes opposite the problem, just those directly at the spot.

After some patient, one-quarter turn trueing try some roundness corrections. Adjust high and low spots by tightening and loosening opposing pairs of spokes to raise and lower the rim. Work in one-half turns for this dimension. Once about one dozen corrections are made, go back to side-to-side trueness. Alternate between trueness and roundness, patiently making small corrections. Like silver that is being polished,

the wheel will begin to show the results of your patient efforts. Once the wheel is very true it is time to add tension.

If the rim is disjointed, it will show at this point. If the discontinuity is extreme, then lay the wheel on its side and press the joint on the ground in the direction that will correct it. Once the wheel is tight, this procedure will be extremely difficult to execute.

The wheel's side-to-side symmetry should be quite good, but needs checking. By using a dishing tool or your frame, reverse the wheel and watch to see if the rim is in the same place regardless of hub direction. A dished wheel will always present its rim at the same spot whether the hub is in forward or backward. Correct any asymmetry by tightening only one side of the wheel to draw the rim nearer to one or another of the hub's locknuts as needed.

*4. Adding tension.* A true wheel at low tension is a very cooperative subject. Add one-half to one turn of tension all the way around. Check trueness and make a few corrections to it, then add more tension. Continue to add tension until the total is similar to another wheel with which you can compare. Pluck the spokes and listen. Remember that in a rear wheel it is normal for the left side to be considerably looser than the right. Whenever tightening a nipple its spoke tends to wind up a bit. So after turning, back off a bit so the spoke can unwind. If you do not, the hidden windup will be released while riding, spoiling the wheel's straightness.

*5. Prestressing.* To begin the final step, grab parallel sets of spokes on opposite sides of the wheel, left and right, in each hand. Squeeze each pair firmly to stretch and stress the spokes. This technique will set up the elbows for greater fatigue life and stretch all the parts so hard that use will not cause loosening. If the wheel becomes unacceptably looser, then add tension. If it goes wildly out of true, it is possible there is too much tension in the wheel. Retrue it and try again. If it's unstable a second time, try loosening it before a third stress step. The wheel is ready to ride after reaching appropriate tension and resisting prestressing with little untrueness. Whenever in doubt, show your wheel to an expert.

Remember that a builder's goal is to build a wheel that runs straight but also has a high uniform tension. The best wheel is not necessarily the straightest but the most equally reinforced by its spokes. Do not just be a wheel truer, be a tension equalizer! If unsure of which adjustment to make, pluck the candidate spokes and loosen the tightest and tighten the loosest. Steps taken to equalize tension nearly always contribute to a better wheel.

Wheel repair and building is a vast and detailed science. The brief tips offered here ought to get you off to a good start. But never tire of asking questions and seeking additional information. And don't forget to enjoy the fruits of your labors. Good rolling!

**1**

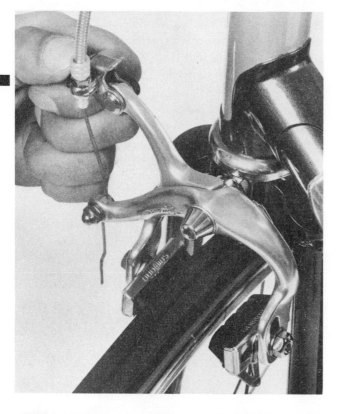

**2**

If your bike is equipped with quick-release hubs, removal of the front wheel is quite simple. First, open your brake quick-release lever to spread the caliper arms wider so your tire can pass between the brake shoes without hanging up. (Photo 1)

When locked, your quick-release lever should be parallel with your bike frame. Grab the lever and twist it in a 180-degree arc away from the frame and on around until it is parallel with the frame again. (Photo 2) Your wheel should now be loose enough to drop out of the frame. If not, give it a push or a tug to force the axle out of the dropouts.

If your wheel is fastened in your bike frame with nuts, fit a wrench of the proper size on one of the nuts and loosen it slightly. Then move the wrench to the other side of the wheel and loosen the other nut in the same way. Or put a separate wrench on each nut and break both free at the same time.

Loosen each nut just enough to allow the wheel to drop out of the frame. Watch your axle as you rotate the nuts to make sure you are not altering the adjustment of your bearing cones and changing their position on the axle. When you fasten the wheel back on your bike, you want the same amount of axle protruding from each side.

If your bike is not equipped with quick-release hubs, chances are it also lacks a brake quick-release. In this case, you may have to loosen the cable anchor nut on the brake body and allow the cable to slip a little. This will enable you to spread the calipers further apart so the wheel can drop free.

Another way to create the room you need is to remove a brake shoe. (Photo 3) Whichever method you use, don't forget to properly adjust and tighten these parts after you have replaced your wheel.

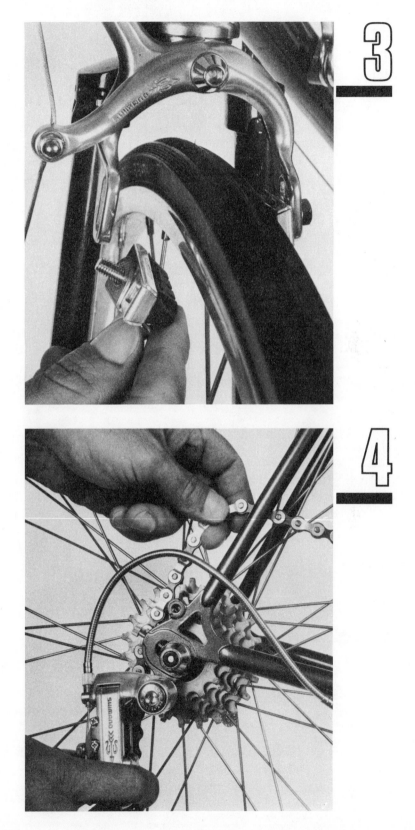

A rear wheel is a bit more complicated to remove because of the chain and the freewheel cogs. First, shift gears so that your chain is on both your smallest chainring and smallest rear cog. Next, spread the brakes and loosen the wheel in the same manner you would for the front wheel. Then, either lift the chain off the rear cog or push the idler pulley of the rear derailleur forward to help free the chain from the cog. (Photo 4) Give the back of your wheel a sharp rap, if necessary, to dislodge it from the frame. Slip the wheel down and out, disentangling it from the chain as you proceed.

Replace your wheels by following the same procedure in reverse order. Push the rear derailleur idler pulley down and forward to take tension off the chain while you slip the wheel inside the chain and pull it up into place in the frame.

Center each wheel in the frame and tighten it in place. If your wheel is fastened with nuts, tighten each the same amount until both are snug. If you have a quick-release, make sure that when you push the lever into the locked position that it is quite tight and cannot loosen accidentally. Fine-tune your quick-release adjustment by turning the nut on the opposite end of the skewer before locking the lever.

Rotate the quick-release lever so that when open it points forward and when locked it points toward the back of the bike. This will eliminate the possibility of the lever accidentally catching on something and loosening while you are riding.

Lastly, give your brakes a final inspection to make sure everything is in working order. Make sure all bolts and fasteners are tight.

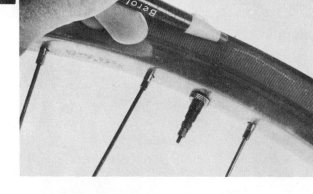

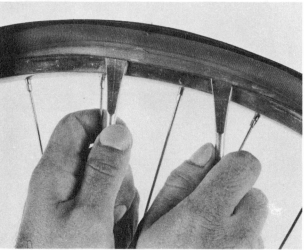

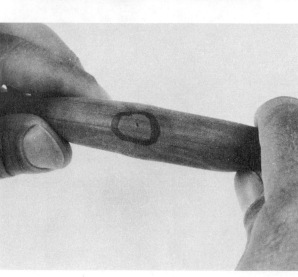

Whenever a tire goes flat and needs repair, don't ride on it any further. Push or carry your bike to where you can make the repair, then remove the wheel from the bike while you repair the tire.

Before taking the tire and tube apart, mark the tire next to the valve stem to establish the relationship between the tire and tube. (Photo 1) This will make it easier later to locate any foreign matter still embedded in the tire casing.

If any air remains in the tire, let it out by pressing on the valve. Start your tire removal on the side of the rim opposite the stem to minimize chances of damaging the stem. Squeeze the sides of the tire toward the trough at the center of the rim to produce some slack, then hook a tire iron under the edge of the tire and pull it over the rim. But first, make sure your tire irons have no sharp edges that could further damage the tube. The best tire irons are shaped a lot like spoon handles. There are also good plastic tire tools available that are less likely to damage a tube than many of the metal ones.

Move a few inches along the rim and hook a second tire iron under the same bead of the tire and pull it over the rim. (Photo 2) If necessary, use a third tire iron. Once you get several inches of the tire diameter over the rim edge you should be able to pull the rest of it over the rim by hand.

When one entire bead of the tire is free from the rim, you can easily remove the tube for repair. There is no need to take the tire completely off the rim at this point. Just push it over to one side while you remove the tube. Lift the tube's valve stem out of its rim hole, being careful not to damage it, then slip the remainder of the tube out of the tire and pull it away from the rim.

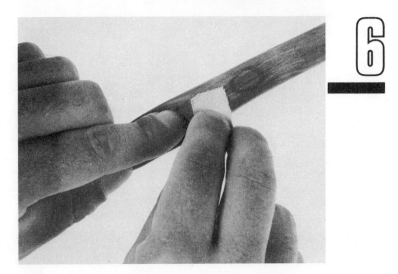

Pump some air into the tube and try to pinpoint the puncture by listening to or feeling the escaping air. Or, if a container of water is available, immerse the tube in water and watch for air bubbles.

Draw an imaginary line through the center of the tube, dividing it into inner and outer halves. If the puncture is in the inner half, the part that faced the wheel rim, the tube is not worth repairing. Also, if you find two small holes near each other, indicating the tube was pinched by the rim, it is not worth repairing.

When you locate a repairable puncture, mark the tube at that point. (Photo 3) Pull the tire off the wheel and lay it down. Spread the tube over the tire so the two are in the same relationship they had on the wheel. Line up the stem valve with the mark you previously made on the tire. Then check both the inside and outside of the tire casing at the point of puncture. (Photo 4) Remove any remnants of the offending object.

If you are unable to locate a puncture in your tube, check the valve stem. Tubes on underinflated tires can shift position, allowing the rim to cut into the side of the stem. If your stem is cracked or cut, you will need to replace the tube. (Photo 5)

Spread the tube on a table and clean the area around the puncture with alcohol. Then take a piece of sandpaper or a metal scraper of the type included in many tire repair kits and rough up the puncture area. (Photo 6)

Coat the roughed area of the tube with a fine, even layer of rubber cement. Make sure there are no globs of cement in one place because they will prevent your patch from sealing properly. After spreading the cement on your tube, allow it to air dry for 15 minutes. (Photo 7) Spread a second thin

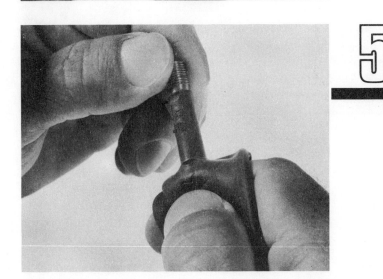

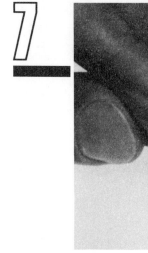

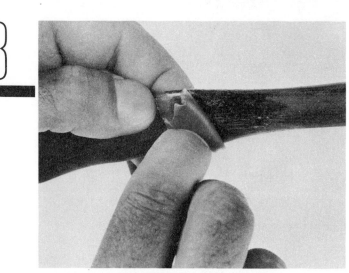

coat of cement over the area to make sure you have good coverage. Let that coat dry the same length of time as the first before putting on the patch.

Take a patch out of your repair kit. If it is larger than needed, cut it to a size that will cover the puncture and make good contact with the area all around it. Peel off the protective coating from the sticky side of the patch and fasten the patch in place on the tube. (Photo 8) To make sure you get a good seal, fasten one tip of the patch first, then roll the patch on, pressing down hard to force out any air bubbles. (Photo 9) Inflate the tube enough to give it shape, then give it a light coating of talc. The easiest way to do this is to put a little talc in your hand and pull the tube through it. The talc will make it easier for the tube to be moved into its proper place inside the tire and will minimize the possibility of its being caught between the tire bead and rim.

Push one bead of the tire back onto the rim leaving the other bead and most of the casing hanging off the rim while you replace the tube. Temporarily push the second bead of the tire over the rim at the stem hole and roll it back over the first bead to uncover the hole. Fit the valve stem of the tube through the hole, then pull the compressed section of the second tire bead back over the tube and off the rim. Then, beginning at the stem area, work your way around the rim, tucking the tube back inside the tire. (Photo 10)

Once the tube is in place, let the air out of it while you work the second bead of the tire onto the rim. It is a good idea to start this process on the side of the rim opposite the stem and end at the stem. This way you will be able to get the maximum possible slack in the tire when you need it for forcing the final few inches onto the rim. However,

on very skinny tires you may find it difficult to roll the final section of bead over the rim and seat it properly because of the thickness of the tube around the valve stem. If so, pull a section of bead back off the rim, take care of the stem area before the bead gets excessively tight, and finish the job at a different location on the rim.

Avoid using tire irons to force the tire back onto the rim. You should be able to do it with your hands alone. If you use tire irons, you risk pinching the tube and damaging it. To get the slack you need for the final part of the process, go around the tire squeezing the two beads together so they will drop down into the trough in the middle of the rim. (Photo 11)

When you get to the last section of tire you may find it quite difficult to force it onto the rim. Make sure you have given yourself all the available slack, then grasp the tire with both hands and using a vigorous twisting motion of the wrists, try to roll the stubborn bit of bead over the edge of the rim. (Photo 12) If this technique does not work for you, push the bead onto the rim bit by bit with your thumbs, until it is almost completely in place. The final 2 or 3 inches should be easy to roll over the edge.

Once the tire is on the rim, work your way around each side of the rim, checking to make sure the tube is not caught between tire bead and rim. If it is, the tube will get pinched and the tire won't seat properly when you inflate it. If everything looks OK, pump 20 to 30 pounds of pressure into the tube. Check to make sure the stem is still straight and that the tire is seating properly. If everything appears to be in order, continue pumping until you bring the tire up to the pressure recommended by the manufacturer. ▲

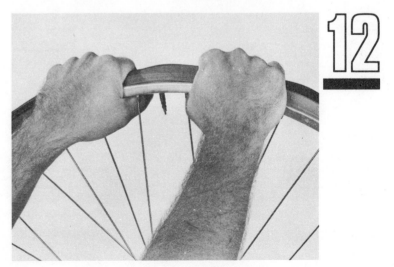

When a tubular tire goes flat, stop riding on it immediately. Take the wheel off your bike and pump a little air in it to see if you can locate the puncture while the tire is still on the rim. If you can, you are in luck. Mark the spot and proceed with the removal of the tire from the rim. If you cannot, you will have to resort to more elaborate search methods after you pull the tire off the rim.

If the tire was glued on properly, it will not come off the rim easily. Try gripping one section of the tire with both hands and rolling it over the side of the rim, pushing on its underside with your thumbs or palms. Once you get a section loose, it will be easier to get a good grip for pulling the rest of the tire off the rim. (Photo 1)

Pump some air back into the tire, then hold it near your ear and listen for a leak. Even if you cannot hear anything, you may be able to feel the escaping air hitting your face. Or, if you'd like, immerse the tire in a pan of water and watch for escaping air bubbles. Once you see, hear, or feel escaping air, search for evidence of a puncture in the tire. Until you actually locate a cut or puncture you cannot be certain where the problem lies, because air can travel out of a hole in the tube and move several inches inside the tire before emerging.

The most foolproof way of isolating a leak is to clamp off a small section of tire, then pump air into the tire. If no air escapes, then you know the problem lies in the section you have isolated. If air does escape as before, loosen the clamp and move it along to another section of tire. When no air escapes from the unclamped part, then you know the problem lies within the clamped section. Take off the clamp and inspect that section closely until you discover the source of the leak.

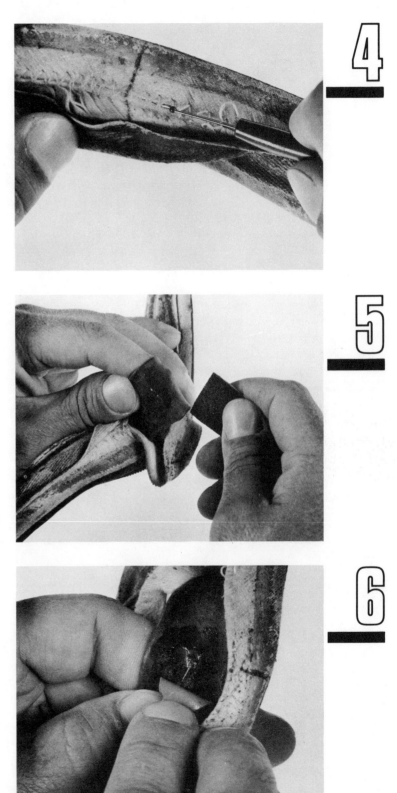

Some tubular tire repair kits contain pieces of wood to use as clamps. But you can easily devise your own. Take a couple of scrap pieces of 2 × 4 lumber and tighten them around the tire using a large C-clamp or the jaws of a bench vise. (Photo 2) The smaller the pieces of wood used, the more frequently you'll have to reposition them, but the more narrowly you can pinpoint the source of the leak.

It is important that you know precisely where your tube needs repair before you cut the stitching, because you want to keep to a bare minimum the area you have to cut and later restitch.

Once you have located your puncture, lift up a few inches of seam tape in that area. (Photo 3) The seam tape covers your tire's stitches and is bonded to the tire with a latex glue. This is a different glue than the glue used to mount the tire to the rim. When the stitching is exposed, make a distinct mark across the seam to help you line up the edges of the tire later for restitching.

Take a sharp knife, a razor blade, or (best of all) a sewing seam ripper and cut enough stitches to allow you to pull out the section of tube you need to repair. (Photo 4)

Pull out that section of tube, clean the puncture area with alcohol, then rough it up with fine sandpaper. (Photo 5) Spread a thin layer of rubber cement over the area and let it dry until it loses its glossy appearance (about 10 to 15 minutes). Then spread a second thin layer of cement over the area and let it dry.

Find a patch of the appropriate size or cut one to size and peel off the protective backing from its sticky side. In order to get a good seal, place one edge of the patch on the tube first, then roll the remainder of the patch on over. (Photo 6) Sprinkle a bit of talc

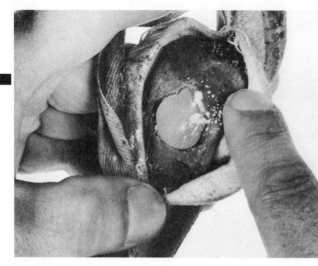

over the patched area to prevent the tube from sticking to the tire. (Photo 7) Check both inside and outside the tire to locate and remove any foreign material remaining that may repuncture it once it is inflated and back in use. If any threads of the tire casing have been severed, cut a piece of strong canvas, nylon, or old tire casing and insert it inside the casing over the damaged area. When the repaired tube is inflated it will hold the patch in place.

Push the tube back into place inside the tire. A little talc will help it slide into the proper position. Straighten the inner tape over the tube, then pull the edges of the casing together, lining up the two halves of your mark.

Restitch the tire using the original holes. Creating new holes will only weaken the casing. Just be sure you begin by overlapping the old thread for several holes on either side of the repair area. If you have a talent for stitching you may want to try to duplicate the original thread pattern in the tire. However a simple overhand stitch will work adequately. (Photo 8)

Tubular tire repair kits provide thread, but any strong thread should work. Some people prefer dental floss to the type of thread found in most kits. Just tie a small knot in the end of your thread like you would if sewing on a button and tie off the other end when you complete the stitching. Fasten the seam tape back over the seam with liquid latex.

Carefully scrape the old glue off your rim and tire, then clean the rim with a solvent. After the rim is dry, it is ready to receive a fresh coat of glue. However, if you have never put a tubular tire on a rim before,

you may want to practice putting it on without glue first.

Set the rim down on a clean floor with the stem hole at the top of the circle. Insert the stem through the hole and begin at that point to stretch the tire around the rim, working in both directions at once. (Photo 9) When you get to the last difficult section, lift the rim off the floor and simultaneously stretch and roll the final part of the tire over and onto the rim. (Photo 10)

Now work your way around the rim, checking to make sure the tire is on straight. When it looks right, inflate it. If the tire was difficult to get on, let it sit for awhile, perhaps overnight, to stretch a little. Then deflate the tire and remove it from the rim for gluing.

Run a bead of glue all the way around the rim. (Photo 11) Apply a lighter coat to the seam tape of the tire. Put a small plastic bag or a piece of plastic over your hand and use one of your fingers to spread the glue around. (Photo 12) After 15 or 20 minutes, apply a second coat of glue in the same way.

Before this glue dries, proceed with the tire mounting. When you set the rim down, be sure the floor is clean because you do not want to contaminate the glue. Also, do not set it on any surface that might get soiled by the glue. You do not want to contaminate either the glue or the floor.

Roll the tire onto the rim as you did before, then check to make sure it is on straight and properly centered. Partially inflate the tire and put it on your bike. Spin it around to make sure it is well centered on the rim. If everything looks OK, inflate the tire to full pressure and let it sit overnight before being used. ▲

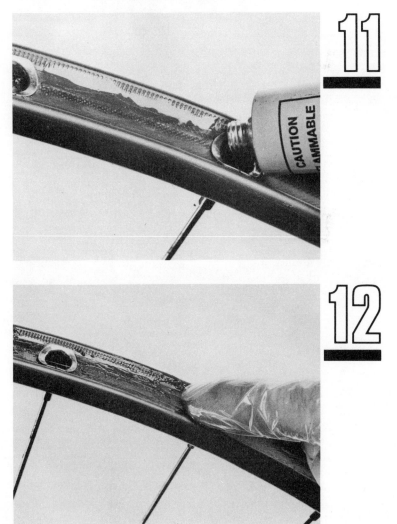

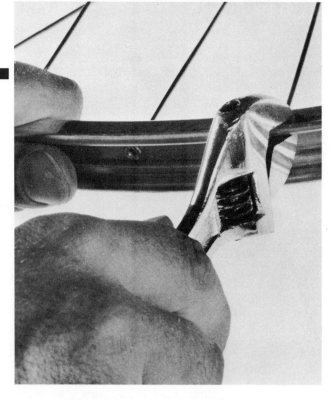

One of the most important things you can do to maintain your wheel rims in good condition is to clean them regularly. The road grime that builds up on all rims interferes with good braking performance and should be removed.

Begin your rim maintenance by washing down both the rims and the tires with soapy water. Break up the residue that remains on the rims with a solvent such as kerosene and fine steel wool or an abrasive pad made of material that will not scratch metal. (Photo 1)

Take care not to get the kerosene on your tires or brake pads. Use a milder solvent such as alcohol to clean the grime off your brake pads.

Not only do rims get dirty, they also frequently get scratched or dented. If the dents are not too severe, you may be able to squeeze them out. Remove the tire from the rim and fasten the dented section of the rim between the jaws of a smooth-jaw vise. Tighten the vise to squeeze out the dent.

You may be able to straighten a minor bend in the edge of the rim with the help of a small adjustable wrench. Just screw the jaws of the wrench down snugly against the rim and lever the rim in the direction needed to straighten it. (Photo 2)

Large dents or bends that result from a crash are more of a challenge to correct. There is no guarantee you will be successful, but it is usually worth the effort to try to salvage an expensive rim.

First you must remove the tire from the wheel and the spokes from the affected area, then you can choose whether to go for push or for pull. If it is push, then tie the rim to a limb of a tree or hang it from a rafter with the bent section pointing down. Lay a block of 2 × 4 lumber across the smashed-in area and hammer down on it to force the rim back out into its proper shape.

The alternative approach is to set the rim vertically on the ground and run a heavy stick or a length of lumber over the dented-in area. Position your feet on the stick, one foot to either side of the rim. Bend your knees, grasp the upper part of the rim with your hands, then straighten up, pulling the rim back into shape. (Photo 3)

Sideways bends can be handled in a similar manner. However, in this case you may not need to remove any spokes, but only to take the tension off of those found at the trouble spot. If you have a big bulge at one spot you can set the edge of the rim on a workbench table top and try pounding it out with a mallet.

If the bend is over a fairly large area, place one hand 8 to 10 inches on either side of the problem area, then push the rim down against a piece of lumber or against a tree trunk to try to eliminate the bend.

This process can also be reversed. Hold your knee against the bulge in the rim and your hands several inches to either side. Pull back on the rim to pop it back into round. (Photo 4)

If you are lucky, one of these techniques will eliminate the unnatural tension in the rim, and you can use spoke adjustment to bring it back into usable shape. But if not, at least you tried. Replace the rim with one that is dependable, keep your rims strong through proper spoke tension, and try your best to avoid potholes and trees. ▲

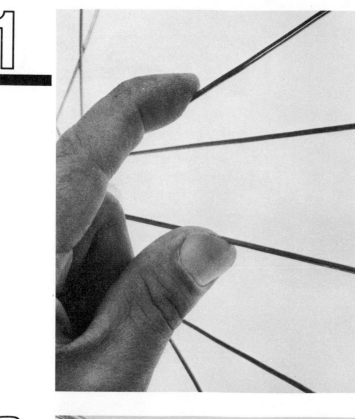

The spoked wheel is a marvelous invention. When properly built and maintained, it is incredibly strong; when improperly adjusted, it is very vulnerable to damage.

Spokes do not demand a lot of maintenance. Primarily, all you can do for them is make certain they are properly tensioned. Periodically, work your way around each wheel plucking on each spoke to make sure it is not loose. You can spot a loose spoke both by the way it feels and also by the way it sounds when plucked. (Photo 1)

When you locate a loose spoke, use a spoke wrench to bring it up to a level of tension that is similar to that of its neighbors. After you have tightened all of your loose spokes in this manner, you should check your wheel for trueness and make further adjustments to your spokes as needed. Consult the instructions beginning on page 66 for more details on this process.

Wheel trueing is made easier and more precise when it is done in a special trueing stand. But if you do not have access to such a stand, you can use your brake calipers to help you check your wheel. Tighten the calipers until the brake pads almost touch the rim, then spin your wheel around. By sighting between your brake pads and the rim, you can see whether or not it needs horizontal trueing.

Vertical trueness can be checked by fastening a straightedge to the frame or the brake body just above the wheel. Spin the wheel and sight along the straightedge to see if it is out of round. For a more accurate check, remove your tire from the rim so the straightedge can be fastened just above the rim edge.

When a spoke breaks, it is best not to ride any further on the wheel. Instead, push

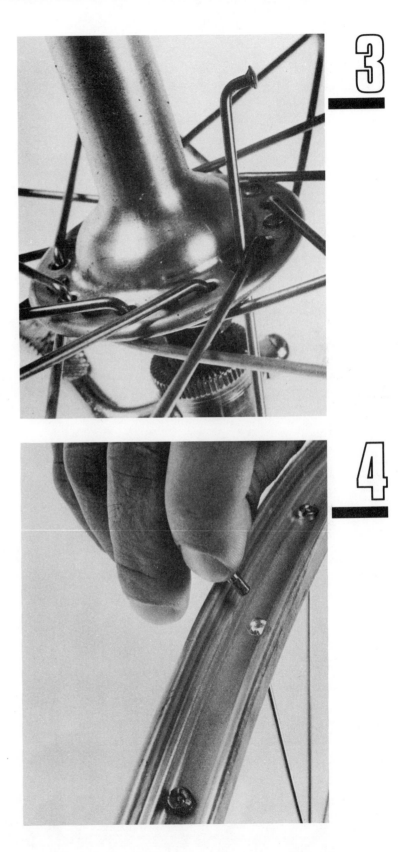

**3**

**4**

your bike to a place where you can replace the spoke. But if you must ride the bike, first weave the loose spoke end around an adjacent spoke and then ride slowly to your destination.

Replace the spoke with one of the same size. (Photo 2) You should also replace the nipple at the same time. To do that you must remove the tire from the rim. Lift up the rubber strip that covers the tops of the nipples and take out the old nipple. Drop a new one in its place.

Remove the broken spoke and run the new one through the hub flange in the same direction as the old one. You can determine the correct way to insert the new spoke by the fact that adjacent spokes go through the flange in opposite directions.

Pull your new spoke through the flange until its curved end is seated, then weave it through the other spokes, following the pattern of the old one. If in doubt, follow the pattern of the second spoke to either side of it. (Photo 3)

Before threading the new spoke into its nipple, apply a small amount of oil to its threads. This will make it easier to thread the spoke into the nipple and will help prevent it from freezing in the nipple over time. (Photo 4) Then thread it on and use a spoke wrench to bring it up to tension.

It is important when working on spokes to use a wrench of the correct size. If the wrench flats on a nipple get worn round, you will have a difficult time adjusting that spoke. Also, before adjusting any of the old spokes, it's a good idea to spray a little penetrating oil at the points where the spoke enters the nipple and the nipple enters the rim. Rotate the wheel so that the oil will flow down into the threads after you spray it on. ▲

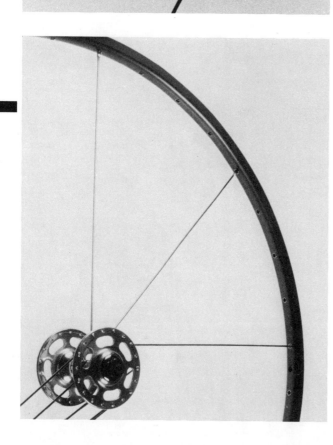

Whether you are building a 32-, a 36-, or a 40-spoke wheel, begin by dividing your spokes into four equal groups. Now sit down and hold the hub in front of you with the axle pointing down. If it is a rear hub, turn the gear side down. Drop the first group of spokes down through the upper flange, inserting one spoke through every other hole.

Pick up the rim and suspend it between your lap and the edge of a bench in front of you or simply balance it on your knees, then twist it around so that the stem hole is opposite you. Drop a nipple through the spoke hole immediately to the left of the stem hole and fasten one of the spokes to it. (Photo 1)

Now moving left or counterclockwise around the rim, skip three holes and put a nipple in the fourth spoke hole. Look back at the hub to locate the spoke immediately to the left of the first one attached and fasten that spoke to the nipple in the fourth hole. (Photo 2) Continue in this manner all the way around the rim until the entire first group of spokes is attached to the rim, with a spoke in every fourth hole. Screw each nipple only a little way down each spoke, just enough to securely hold it.

Now rotate the hub counterclockwise so that the original spoke slants away from the stem hole in the rim. That's the direction in which the first round of spokes must slant in the completed wheel. (Photo 3)

Flip the wheel over and sight down from what is now the upper flange to the flange below that contains the spokes. Notice that the spoke holes in the two flanges are not directly in line but offset from one another, so that a spoke pushed straight down through a hole in the upper flange will hit between two holes in the lower flange.

Locate the hole in the upper flange, which is immediately to the right of the hole

containing the original spoke in the lower flange. Drop your first spoke in the second group down through that hole. Now skipping one hole between each spoke, drop the remaining spokes in round two down through the upper flange.

Drop a nipple through the rim hole immediately to the right of the one containing the original nipple used, that is, the second hole to the right of the stem hole. Fasten the first spoke in round two to that nipple. Now working to the right or clockwise around the rim, drop a nipple through every fourth hole and fasten the next available spoke to it. (Photo 4) Continue clockwise around the hub and rim until all the spokes in round two are fastened to the rim.

Before flipping the wheel over again, drop the third group of spokes down through the remaining holes in the bottom flange so that they enter and exit the flange in the opposite direction from the spokes already present there. Now as you start to turn the wheel over, stop when it is vertical and force the new group of spokes to turn sideways on their elbows so they won't fall back out of the flange when you lay the wheel down.

Now lay the wheel down with the loose spokes on top. Each spoke in this round will run to the left, in the opposite direction from those installed in the first round. This is the time when you must commit yourself to a cross pattern. If you choose to use the popular cross three pattern, each spoke in this third group will cross over two round one spokes and then under a third before being fastened to the rim.

Grasp any loose spoke and pull it to the left across the first two adjacent spokes and under the third one, then fasten it to a nipple inserted through the first available rim hole. (Photo 5) Notice that the first crossing of

spokes occurs right at the edge of the hub flange and the second crossing still quite near the hub. Don't worry about the fact that you have to bend the spokes as you lace them or that they feel stiff when you are fastening them. After the wheel is laced and tensioned, the spokes will straighten out and find their proper place.

After you have finished lacing all the spokes in round three, drop the final set of spokes through the remaining holes in the lower flange. Raise the wheel up into a vertical position while you seat the spokes in the hub flange and bend them at their elbows toward the rim. Then turn the wheel the rest of the way over and lace up these spokes following the same pattern as you did in round three. (Photo 6)

Once all of your spokes are fastened to the rim, you can begin to bring them up to tension. Fasten the wheel in a trueing stand and put a little oil on all the spoke threads to help the nipples turn easily.

At the outset you want to treat all the spokes equally, so begin by turning all the nipples down until you can see only the final circle of thread on the end of each spoke. At this stage you will find it easier and faster to turn the nipples with a screwdriver inserted into their heads.

When you can no longer use visible spoke threads as a reference point, start working your way around the rim, turning the nipples with a spoke wrench to tighten the spokes. Work in increments of one-half turn of the nipple each time. (Photo 7)

As tension begins to build up on the spokes, check to see how well they are

seated in the hub flanges. You may need to press on the spokes near the hub to help them straighten out more quickly after they bend at their elbows. When the spokes finally begin to look straight and feel snug, you are ready to true the wheel. See the following repair section for details on this process.

Once the wheel is true, your next task is to bring it up to optimum tension. Unfortunately, there is no way to precisely describe what this is. An expert wheel builder can sense when that point has been reached. The best the rest of us can do is to locate a well-built wheel and compare the sound and feel of its spokes when plucked to that of the wheel on which we are working.

As your wheel gets tighter, keep in mind that turns of your spoke wrench have an increasingly dramatic effect on the level of tension in your spokes. So work in small increments. Each time you complete a round of tensioning, check your wheel again for trueness and make any adjustments needed. Also keep in mind that as you turn the nipple, the spoke tends to twist a little. So after each turn of the wrench, back it off a little to eliminate this spoke windup.

The final step in building a tight wheel is to grab parallel sets of spokes, one pair in each hand, and squeeze them to prestress them. (Photo 8) If this causes the wheel to become too loose, then add more tension. If the wheel goes badly out of true, you may have too much tension on the spokes. Retrue the wheel and try again. If it will not stay true, then reduce the overall tension in the wheel, true it, and stress it a third time. ▲

**1**

**2**

Wheel trueing can be done most accurately with the tire off the wheel so the outside perimeter of the rim can be closely checked for roundness. But if the tire is on the rim at the time you wish to true your wheel, simply let out most of its air to minimize your chances of puncturing the tube while twisting a spoke nipple.

Mount your wheel in a trueing stand and adjust the calipers so that their tips are close to the sides of the rim. (Photo 1) Spin the wheel and readjust the calipers to move them as close as possible to the rim without hitting it at any point in its revolution.

Start the trueing process by working your way around the wheel, beginning at the stem or some other reference point, plucking each spoke in turn to see if any are unusually loose. (Photo 2) Bring each loose spoke up to a level of tension similar to that of its neighbors.

Spray a little penetrating oil where the spoke enters the nipple to help the nipple turn and use a spoke wrench of the proper size so you will not round over the sides of the nipple. As you tension each spoke, place one or two fingers on it to make sure it does not turn along with the nipple. If it does, back off the adjustment to eliminate this windup and try again. Tension caused by spoke windup will be released when you use your wheel, ruining your adjustment.

Now spin your wheel to check for horizontal trueness. To pull the rim to the right at any point, tighten the spoke or spokes that run from the right side of the hub to that point and loosen the adjacent spokes that run from the left side of the hub. Reverse the procedure to pull the rim to the left.

Tighten and loosen opposing spokes the same amount and work in small increments of one-quarter to one-half turn each time. (Photo 3) After working all the way around the wheel once or twice you should have the wheel fairly true horizontally.

At this point you should check for vertical roundness in the wheel. If your tire is on the rim, you can check this by hooking a caliper over one of the inside edges of the rim, spinning the wheel, and looking for high and low spots. If the tire is off the rim, set the caliper, or other gauge provided on your trueing stand, near the outside edge of the rim, then watch for changes in the distance between the gauge and the rim as it spins. (Photo 4)

To eliminate high spots in the rim, tighten the spokes that meet the rim at those spots and to eliminate low spots, release some of the tension on the spokes in those spots. This time you should tighten or loosen the spokes in pairs, one right side and one left side spoke in each pair.

Remember, when you add or subtract tension from any section of the rim, you are affecting the tension on other parts of the rim as well. So work in small increments and recheck the trueness of the rim frequently. Alternate between horizontal and vertical trueing until you see only very minor variations in the rim's movement in either direction as it spins. ▲

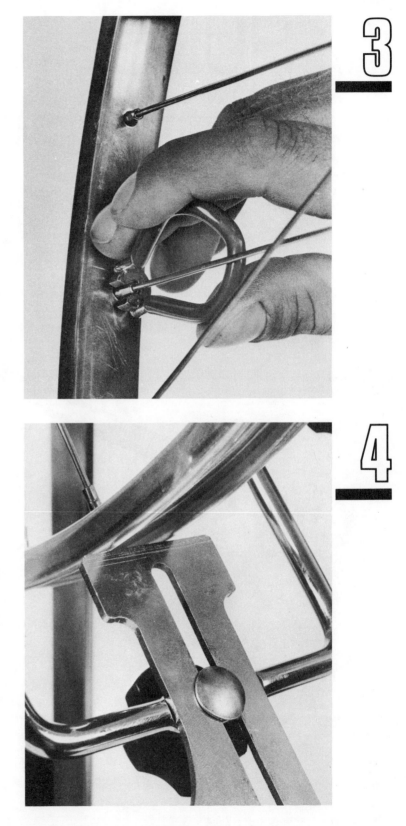

# 4 HUBS

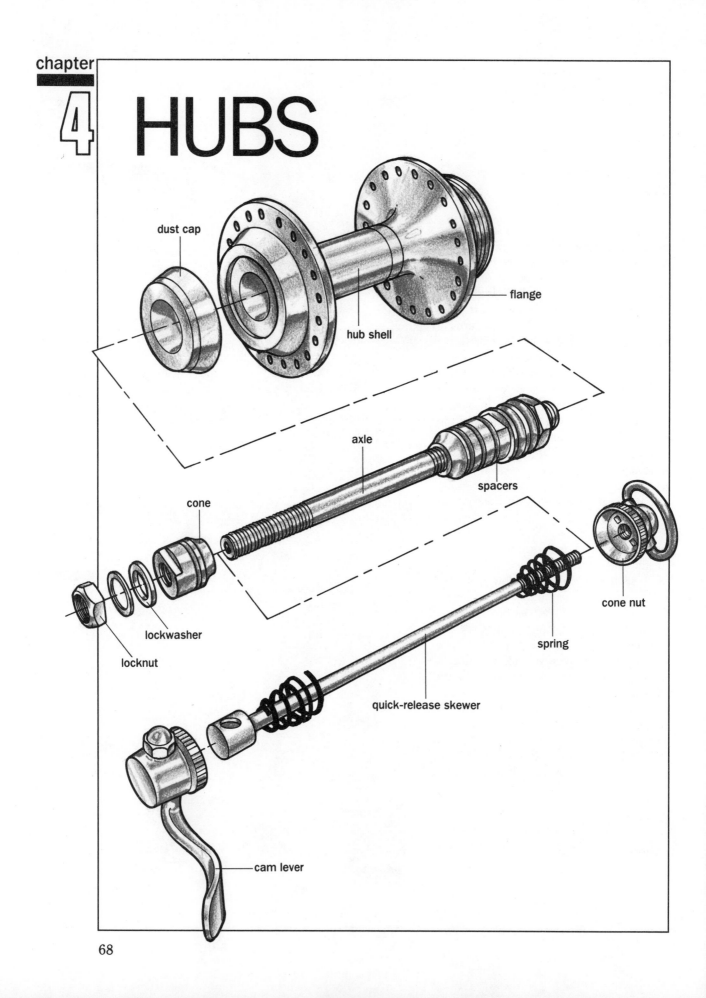

dust cap

flange

hub shell

axle

spacers

cone

lockwasher

locknut

cone nut

spring

quick-release skewer

cam lever

68

Every bicycle, no matter how big or small, no matter if it has fifteen gears or just one, has two wheels. At the center of each wheel is a hub, at its circumference a rim and a tire. Spokes serve as connecting links between the hub and the rim, the center and the circumference. Small as they are, the hubs are an extremely critical part of the wheel system. They hold the wheels in the frame and allow them to spin.

The wheels are a vital part of your bicycle—the very term "bicycle" means "two-wheel." They are also one of the most vulnerable parts of your bike, the location for a lot of problems commonly associated with bicycles. Tires wear out or go flat, rims dent, and spokes break. But fortunately, there are comparatively few problems with hubs. With reasonable care many hubs can carry you through several sets of tires or rims.

You should feel no hesitation about working on your hubs, because the mechanisms inside are very simple. There is no reason why you, with a little instruction, cannot understand how they function and service them yourself.

## Hub Construction

It's best if you understand how a hub is put together before you begin to disassemble one. Most hubs are of the conventional adjustable cone and race variety. Hubs of this design come in all price ranges and are easily serviced. Replacement parts are readily available.

The largest part of any hub is the shell. The shell is the part to which the spokes are attached and encases the working parts—that is, the axle and bearings. The part of the shell that holds the heads (the flared ends) of the spokes is called the flange.

Flanges come in different sizes depending on the intended purpose of the wheel. The conventional wisdom is that the larger the flange the stiffer the wheel. For most applications this rule applies. If you want a comfortable wheel you should use a small flange hub, for a stiffer wheel use a large flange. The actual strength of a wheel is determined more by the type of spokes, rim, and spoking pattern employed than by the size of the hub flange.

Hubs are often described by the type of flange they have. You may hear people refer to them as high-flange, large-flange, low-flange, or small-flange hubs. Sometimes you will hear someone refer to medium-flange hubs, though they are comparatively rare.

Inside the shell of a hub are two bearing races, one at each end. The bearings roll on the surface of the races and are held in place by the cones. The bearings also roll on the surface of the cones. Because of the special shape of the race and the cone, the bearings roll in a circular path. The cone fits on the axle and is held in place by a series of washers and a locknut.

The axle on a front wheel hub fits into slots cut into the tips of the front fork and on a rear hub into slots in the rear fork called "dropouts." A hub is held in place on a bicycle frame either by means of an axle and a pair of axle nuts

*Photo 4-1: The flanges to which spokes attach differ in size on different hubs, which is why hubs may be characterized either as high-flange or low-flange.*

or by a quick-release unit consisting of a hollow axle, a skewer rod, springs, a cam lever, and a cone nut. Axle nuts must be tightened and loosened by means of a wrench, whereas a quick-release mechanism permits wheels to be locked in place or removed without any tools.

### Sealed-Bearing Hubs

Presently there are a number of hubs available, often called "sealed-bearing hubs," that, instead of the conventional race and cone system, use precision-bearing cartridges. The bearing assembly is a premanufactured unit and is fitted into the hub shell with bearing adjustment preset.

Many of these hubs are not user-serviceable and have to be referred back to the manufacturer or to bicycle shops with special tools for maintenance. Hubs with this kind of sealed bearing usually

don't have any place to attach a wrench to the axle. If you suspect that you have hubs of this kind, consult your bicycle dealer before attempting to service them.

In addition to these nonserviceable hubs there are some that use cartridge bearings but still can be serviced by the consumer. If you unthread a cone and find that the bearings are not loose but packed in a covered cagelike device, stop. These hubs vary in how much work you can do and how easily the parts are replaced. We recommend here too that you check with your local shop before attempting to service them.

## Checking Hub Adjustment

To check your hub's adjustment you will have to remove the wheel from the bicycle. The front wheel is easy to remove. Unbolt the axle or flip the quick-release lever to the open position and drop the wheel out of the forks.

If you have caliper brakes you may have to open the caliper arms a bit to get the tire past them. Some caliper brakes have a quick-release mechanism, a small lever that, when thrown, opens the caliper to permit the tire to go past. If your brakes don't have such a release lever you will have to loosen the brake cable anchor bolt to open the caliper arms. If you loosen the cable be sure to retighten it after you install the wheel and before you ride your bike.

To remove the back wheel you have to contend with the gears. Shift the the chain onto the smallest cog on the freewheel and the smallest chainring on the crankset. Loosen the axle nut or the quick-release lever. While holding the rear of the bicycle off the ground, pull

back on the body of the rear derailleur and push the rear wheel down and forward. You may also have to loosen the brake to get the rear wheel out.

Once the wheel is off the bicycle, grasp one end of the axle with the thumb and index finger of your most sensitive hand. Spin the axle several times. Does it feel rough and seem to catch in pits as you turn it? If it does, it's too tight. If your hub does not feel too tight, then check it for looseness. Grasp the axle again, only this time shake it up and down and from side to side. If you can feel the axle moving in these directions, it's too loose.

If your hub failed either of these tests, if it is too tight or too loose, it should be adjusted. To continue to ride on it while it is out of proper adjustment will subject its parts to unnecessary wear and will prevent you from getting

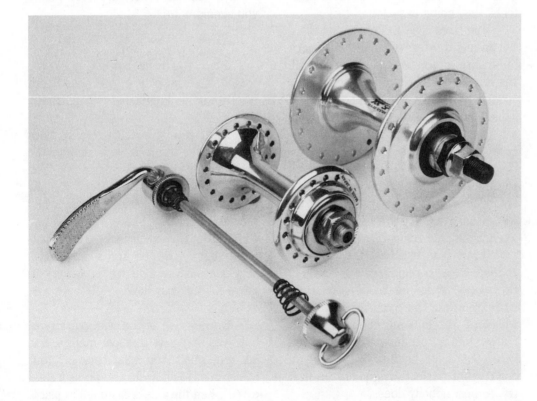

*Photo 4-2: Some wheel hubs are equipped with solid axles onto which conventional nuts are threaded, while others have hollow axles through which runs a removable quick-release skewer.*

the type of performance out of your bike that you should expect.

## Hub Adjustment

When you adjust your hubs the wheels should be off your bike. However, you do not need to remove the hubs from the wheels. The only time that is necessary is when you are replacing a hub, a rim, or a set of spokes.

You will need some tools specially suited for hub adjustment: wrenches to fit the axle locknuts as well as wrenches for the cones. A cone wrench is a special wrench that is made very thin so that it can be fitted on the flats of a cone while a regular wrench is on the adjacent locknut. Regular wrenches are too wide to fit side by side in this way. You can get cone wrenches from your local bicycle shop. They range in size from 12mm to 17mm and, unless they are professional tools, they come in sets.

The front axle locknut is usually a 13mm and the rear a 15mm, but check to be sure. If you wish, and are careful, you can use an adjustable wrench for the locknut. If you have professional-grade hubs you may need two sets of cone wrenches because the axle locknuts require a cone wrench rather than a regular wrench. Check your hubs before you buy the cone wrenches to be sure they are needed. For these instructions we will assume that you are using one cone wrench and one regular wrench.

If you plan to adjust the rear hub you will have to remove the freewheel. See page 120 for instructions on freewheel removal. Once you have the freewheel off you can begin the adjustment. Follow the procedure recommended here, but don't be intimidated if you don't get it perfectly right on the first try. Almost nobody does.

For ease of handling, lay the wheel flat on your workbench. Put the cone wrench on the upper cone and another wrench on the axle locknut above it. Tighten the cone and the locknut against each other by turning the cone counterclockwise and the locknut clockwise. This locks one side of the axle so that it can't accidentally loosen while you are adjusting the hub or riding the bike. You may lock either side of the front hub in this way, but should do this on the derailleur side of the rear wheel so that fine-tuning your adjustment can be done at later times with the freewheel in place.

After locking the cone and locknut on one side of the hub, turn the wheel over and put your wrenches on the cone and locknut of the other side. While holding the cone, turn the locknut counterclockwise to loosen it.

Before you make the final adjustment to your hub, there are a few points you should note:

**1.** If you have bolt-on axles you should have no play in the adjustment prior to tightening the axle to the frame.

**2.** If you have quick-release axles you will have to make allowance for the pressure of the quick-release skewer. The adjustment of the cones will initially need to be a little loose, because when the quick-release skewer closes and compresses the axle it makes the adjustment slightly tighter. You should feel a little play in the axle when you try to move it with your hand.

**3.** Because of the wide variety of hubs you may have to experiment to find out how much you must back off your adjustment to allow for the pressure exerted when the axle is fastened in place.

**4.** Once the locknut is loose, gently turn the cone clockwise until it comes into full contact with the bearings. Back off the adjustment between one-eighth and one-quarter turn. Now tighten the locknut while holding the cone in place. Check the adjustment of the hub in the same manner as before.

**5.** If you have a quick-release hub, you will want to check to be sure the hub is not excessively loose after the quick-release has been closed. The only way to check is to put the wheel in the bike, lock the quick-release, and then try to move the rim from side to side. If you can feel any play (it sometimes feels like a clunk), then the hub adjustment is too loose. If the hub is not properly adjusted, repeat the procedure until you get it right.

If you try repeatedly and simply cannot find the magic line between loose and tight, leave your adjustment slightly on the tight side. It may loosen a bit with subsequent use. But don't settle for less than perfection in your adjustment until you have made careful and repeated attempts to get it just right. The time you spend learning to make sensitive adjustments to your hubs will be rewarded when you move on to adjustments of your headset and bottom bracket. So look at your early attempts at hub adjustment as valuable training in general bicycle repair and maintenance.

## Hub Overhaul

Your hub adjustment should be checked and any needed changes made twice a year. But to ensure long life of your hubs you should perform a complete hub overhaul at least every other year. If you ride a lot, typically more than 3,000 miles a year, your hubs should be overhauled every year. But if for some reason your hubs were completely submerged in water—this often happens on all-terrain bicycles—they should be overhauled at the first opportunity.

Only hubs that don't use precision or shielded bearings need this periodic overhaul. Hubs that use shields to protect the bearings from contaminants may be able to go much longer without an overhaul.

If you wish to overhaul your hubs you will need the cone wrenches and regular wrenches used in the hub adjustment. In addition to that you will need the following items: a large flathead screwdriver or tire iron, grease, and new bearings of the appropriate size and number. The grease you use should be medium weight and not have a vegetable base.

Why do you need new bearings? Because ball bearings change from spheroids to ellipsoids in service. (A spheroid is like a ball and an ellipsoid is like an egg in shape.) As your bearings gradually change from spheroids to ellipsoids, they manage to retain an orientation that allows them to behave like spheroids in the hub.

Once you remove the bearings from the hub, however, you will not be able to get them properly oriented again. And without the correct orientation it will be impossible to properly adjust the hub. If you rebuild a hub and use the old bearings you will find that the hub will loosen after the first adjustment. It can take as many as five adjustments until all the bearings have realigned themselves.

Bearings are not very expensive to replace. So avoid the hassle and use new ones. Just keep in mind that you need to install bearings of the same size and in the same quantity as you are currently using. So, unless you have already recorded that information, you will have to disassemble your hub to check the size and number of the old bearings before purchasing new ones.

Begin your hub overhaul in the same way as an adjustment. Here are the basic steps to follow:

**1.** Place the wheel horizontally on the floor or a table top. Use your hub wrenches to tighten the cone and locknut on the derailleur side of the rear hub against one another. (Either side of the front hub will do.) This locks one side of the axle so that it cannot accidentally loosen later while you are adjusting the hub or riding the bike. Leaving this locknut and cone in place on the axle during the overhaul makes it easy for you to reassemble the hub later.

**2.** Now flip the wheel over so you can reach the cone and locknut on the other side of the hub. Use your cone wrench to hold the cone still while you turn the locknut counterclockwise to loosen it.

**3.** Remove the locknut, the lockwasher under it, and then the cone. It is best to do this with the other end of the axle resting on a table top to prevent it from falling out and bearings spilling on the floor.

**4.** Now carefully remove the axle assembly. You should do this over a rag or paper towel to catch the loose bearings. Use the large flathead screwdriver or the tire iron to remove the dust caps. These are the small caps that fit into the openings at the ends of the hub shell.

Their function is to surround the cone and thus prevent dust and dirt from getting into the bearing grease. Some people prefer to leave these caps in place during a hub overhaul. There is nothing wrong with this and it eliminates the need to correctly reinstall them later. The only drawback is that leaving the dust caps in place makes it more difficult to clean the races.

**5.** Thoroughly clean all the parts in solvent. Inspect the cones and the races to see if they are pitted or cracked. Roll the axle on a smooth countertop to see if it wobbles. Replace any parts that are cracked, pitted, or have other signs of excessive wear.

On some top-of-the-line hubs, the races can be replaced. If you wish to replace your races check with your bicycle shop to see if the parts are available. If they are, you should also consult the shop on how to replace them, since specialized procedures and tools are required. You may prefer to have the shop replace the races for you.

**6.** If you need to replace the cone you left on the axle you will have to remove it the same way you did the other one. But, before you remove it, make a note of how much axle was protruding past the end of the locknut. When you install the new cone, grease the threads of the axle before threading on the cone. This not only helps get the cone on, it will prevent the axle from rusting under the cone. When you lock the cone and locknut together try to get the same amount of axle protruding as there was before.

**7.** Now that all the parts are cleaned and the broken ones replaced you are ready for reassembly. First, heavily grease the hub races. Don't worry if a little grease gets into the axle shaft or on the dust cap lip. Reset the dust cap. Try to get the edge of the cap even with the edge of the hub shell lip. If the cap is crooked it may rub on the cone when the wheel is spinning. Be careful with the caps because they can be bent easily.

**8.** Install the bearings in the races. The grease should hold them in place. Be sure you get the proper number and correct size of balls in each side.

**9.** Grease the entire axle shaft and the cone and insert it into the hub. Be careful not to knock any bearings off the races as you are moving the axle into place.

**10.** Grease the cone and thread it on the axle. Slide the lockwasher over the cone and thread on the locknut.

Now that you have the hub back together, you must adjust it. But before you make the adjustment, remember the differences between bolt-on and quick-release axles mentioned earlier. There should be no play in the adjustment on a bolt-on axle after the locknut has been tightened. But because of the pressure exerted on the axle by a quick-release fastener, you should start with a slightly looser adjustment on this type of axle.

In both cases, while the locknut is still loose turn the cone down on the bearings until it comes into full contact with them. Then back it off as needed for your correct adjustment—between one-eighth and one-quarter turn for bolt-on axles, more for axles of the quick-release type. As we said before, don't be

surprised if it takes you several tries before you get it just right.

Also remember, if you have a quick-release hub you will want to check to be sure the hub is not excessively loose after the wheel is back on your bike and the quick-release lever is shut. If you feel any play when you move the rim from side to side, you must take the wheel off the bike and alter your adjustment, then replace the wheel and check it again. Be patient and before long you will develop a good sense of what the proper adjustment is with the wheel off the bike.

OK, let's say you've tried a bunch of times and you can't seem to get the hub adjustment right. It's always either too tight, too loose, or it clicks when you spin the axle. One possible explanation is that the grease got contaminated with grit. If this has happened, you will simply have to take your hub apart and clean everything again. If in doubt, it is best to just go through the whole overhaul procedure a second time.

If you've done all this but still can't seem to find a happy medium between tight and loose bearings, run your adjustment a little on the tight side. Your bearings might loosen a bit as some of the grease works its way out during use, but they won't tighten. And remember, it is always a good idea to check periodically to make sure none of the locknuts has worked its way loose, thus allowing the adjustment to loosen as well.

## Some Special Tips

If you want to make your hubs more resistant to water and dirt you can do so by slipping rubber o-rings over the ends of the axles and pushing them up against the openings around the cones. You can purchase these rubber o-rings at hardware or auto parts stores. Other "poor man's seals" that work well are pipe cleaners and butcher's twine. Simply wrap a pipe cleaner or tie a piece of twine around the area next to the cone to keep out contaminants. But add one of these seals only after you have completed the hub adjustment process.

If your hubs have small holes in the dust cap you can use the holes to quickly repack the hubs with fresh grease. You will need a grease gun with a needle injector to get grease into the hole. Stick the end of the injector into the hole and pump grease in until the dirty grease is forced out of the bearing through the opening around the cone. When clean grease starts to appear simply wipe away the dirty grease and the hubs are ready to roll.

If you have new quick-release hubs that feel silky smooth with no play in the axle, they are probably adjusted too tight for actual use. The adjustment you feel is actually for the manufacturer's quality control checks. You will need to add some play to compensate for the compression that will be caused by the quick-release skewer when you mount the new wheels on your bike. If you don't do this, your hubs may suffer premature wear.

## Shopping for New Hubs

If you are considering purchasing new hubs you should take the following factors into account:

1. *Flange height.* The height of the flange will affect the feel of the bicycle. The larger the flange the more you will feel the road shock. However, this is only important if you ride the bike for long periods of time. If you ride the bike only a half hour at a time there is no need to consider this factor.

2. *Sealed or conventional bearings.* If you wish to be able to repair your hubs without returning them to the dealer or manufacturer you should purchase hubs with conventional bearings.

3. *Availability of replacement parts.* It doesn't do much good to buy expensive hubs if three years later you have to replace them because replacement cones aren't available.

4. *Freewheel threads.* This is important only if you plan to use your old freewheel. If you are buying a new freewheel be sure to buy one with the same threads as are found on your hub. Some hubs, like the Shimano cassette hubs with built-in freewheels and the Maillard Helicomatic, have special freewheel requirements. Be sure you understand this before buying these hub sets.

5. *Axle width.* A different width (length) of axle is needed for 5-, 6-, or 7-speed freewheels, since the more cogs on the freewheel the more space it takes up on the axle. If you know how many speeds and the brand of freewheel you plan to use, be sure to inform the bicycle dealer when you are purchasing your new hub so that you are sure to get an axle of the appropriate size.

Learning to overhaul and adjust hubs is not difficult and is a good way to get started maintaining and repairing your bike. Once you experience the payoff from your effort in smooth-rolling wheels, you will want to move on and master other areas of bicycle maintenance as well.

Remove the wheel from your bike (see page 48). Set the wheel upright on a workbench. If you'd like, remove the axle nuts or the quick-release skewer and nut, though this is not necessary. Grasp the axle with your fingers and spin it back and forth. (Photo 1) If you feel any binding in the bearings, your cone adjustment is too tight.

If binding is not a problem, then check for looseness. Try to move the axle back and forth, with the hub being held steady. If you feel any play, your adjustment is probably too loose. However, if your wheel has a quick-release mechanism, you have to take into account the compression it places on the axle. A hub that feels a little loose off the bike might feel OK on the bike. The only way you can be sure is to remount the wheel, then check to see if the axle still seems loose.

A hub that is either too tight or too loose should be adjusted. Before the adjustment is made, the cone on one side of the hub should be firmly locked in place. Place a cone wrench on the wrench flats of that cone and an ordinary, open-end wrench on the adjacent locknut. Squeeze the two wrenches together to lock the cone in place. (Photo 2)

Now flip the wheel over and reverse the process on the other side. Hold the cone still with a cone wrench while you loosen the locknut above it. Thread the locknut up the

axle to get it out of your way while you adjust the cone. (Photo 3) With the locknut out of the way, back the cone off until there is no binding, if that was the problem.

To find the right level of adjustment, slowly and carefully tighten the cone until you feel it make full contact with the bearings, then back it off between one-eighth and one-quarter turn. (Photo 4) Thread the locknut back down against the cone, then use a pair of wrenches as before to tighten the locknut against the cone.

Twirl the axle between your fingers again to check the adjustment. If it still does not feel right, loosen the locknut and try again. Repeat the procedure until you get the adjustment right.

If you cannot get your hub to adjust right, that is a sign you may have bearing damage and need to give the hub a complete overhaul.

Before you can adjust your rear hub in the manner described, you will first have to remove your freewheel (see page 120). When the freewheel is off, lock the cone and nut on that side of the hub and adjust the cone from the other side. If you have previously followed this procedure and are certain the freewheel side of your hub is properly locked, you can leave the freewheel on and simply adjust the cone on the other side of the hub. ▲

If your hub is equipped with a quick-release mechanism, thread the nut off the end of the quick-release skewer and pull the skewer out of the axle. (Photo 1) Be careful not to lose the cone-shaped spring that had to come off the skewer when you pulled it out of the axle. Put that spring back on the skewer and partially thread on the nut so these parts will not get lost. Set the quick-release assembly aside while you proceed with the hub overhaul. If you have an ordinary nutted axle, you will have to remove at least one of the nuts in order to remove the axle from the hub.

Fit a cone wrench on the wrench flats of the cone and an ordinary box wrench or open-end wrench on the adjacent locknut on one side of the hub. (Photo 2) Turn the cone wrench counterclockwise and the other wrench clockwise to tighten the cone and locknut against one another. It will not be necessary for you to remove these parts from the axle during the overhaul unless the cone turns out to be damaged and in need of replacement. Leaving one cone in place will simplify hub reassembly and ensure that you end up with the proper amount of axle on each side of your hub.

Move your wrenches to the other side of the hub. Hold the cone still with the cone wrench while you turn the locknut counterclockwise with the other wrench to loosen it. Once it is loose, thread the locknut all the way off the end of the axle. If you have a nutted axle, you must remove the axle nut on this side before you can remove any other parts.

After taking off the locknut, slip the lockwasher off the axle as well. Now thread the cone off the axle, being careful not to spill and lose any bearings. (Photo 3) If there

is any rust on the axle or the threads are slightly damaged, you may have to hold the opposite end of the axle still with your other hand while removing the cone. In any case, it is a good idea to hold the axle in place within the hub to prevent bearings on the opposite side of the hub from falling out of position while you remove this cone.

Once the cone is off, you can remove the axle from the hub. (Photo 4) If you do this carefully while holding the wheel upright, the grease inside the hub should prevent the bearings from falling out. Nonetheless, you would be wise to spread paper towels, newspaper, or a large rag under the wheel during this part of the process to catch any errant bearings. When the axle is out of the way you can then remove all bearings from both sides of the hub. Clean the bearings, inspect them for signs of improper adjustment and possible damage to your races, then count them so you will know how many new ones to purchase.

Even if your bearings all look good as new, you really ought to replace them. Used bearings are never perfectly round and are hard to readjust after they have been removed. New ones are inexpensive, so count the old ones and take a sample with you to the store so that you will be able to purchase new ones of the right size and number. You may want to buy a few extra bearings as spares in case you lose some while reassembling your hub.

Remove the dust caps from the hub shell using a tire iron or a flat-tipped screwdriver. (Photo 5) This will make cleaning and inspection of the bearing races easier. Clean all the parts in solvent and check the cones and races for pits or signs of excessive wear.

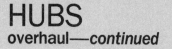

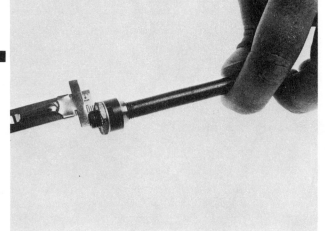

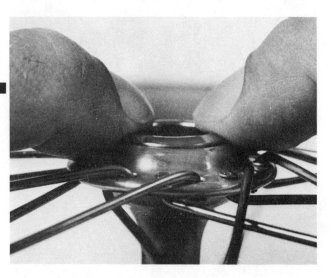

Replace any cracked, pitted, or excessively worn parts. Consult your bike shop for assistance if you need to replace worn races.

Roll the axle on a level surface to see if it wobbles. If it does, that indicates that it is bent and needs to be replaced. Take the axle with you to the bike shop to get the proper replacement.

If your cones are excessively worn and need to be replaced, you must remove the one remaining on the axle. But before loosening the locknut, measure and record the position of the cone on the axle so the new one can be threaded to the same location. (Photo 6)

When you have all the parts you need, and a container of medium-weight grease, you are ready to reassemble your hub. First, fit the dust caps back on the hub shell, taking care to seat them properly so the cones can be correctly adjusted. (Photo 7)

Grease the axle well. If you took both cones off the axle, put one of them back on and carefully thread it down to its proper position. (Photo 8) Replace the lockwasher and the locknut and lock the nut against the cone as previously explained.

Pack plenty of grease into the bearing races on both sides of the hub, then insert the correct number of new ball bearings into one side of the hub. Line the bearings up as well as you can around the race so the axle can pass through without pushing any of the

little balls out of the circle. (Photo 9) The grease will help hold the bearings in position while the axle is being replaced.

Insert the axle through the hub in such a way that the end with the cone on it ends up on the side with the bearings. Press the cone against the bearings and slowly twirl the axle back and forth to make sure the bearings are properly spread inside the race. Then lay the wheel down so the bench top will hold the cone against the bearings for you. Now insert the remaining bearings into the upper side of the hub. (Photo 10)

Put the second cone on the upper end of the axle and carefully thread it down until it makes full contact with its new bearings. Lift the wheel up into a vertical position so you can check the bearing adjustment. Twirl the axle a bit to make sure the bearings are properly spread apart, then adjust the cone so that you feel neither binding nor looseness in the hub. (See page 78 for hub adjustment details.)

When you have the adjustment right, slide on the lockwasher, then thread on the remaining locknut. Hold the adjustable cone still with a cone wrench while you tighten the locknut against it. Slide the quick-release skewer back through the axle and thread on its nut. Or, if you have a nutted axle, replace any axle nuts you may have removed. Now remount the wheel on your bike. ▲

# 5 CRANKSETS

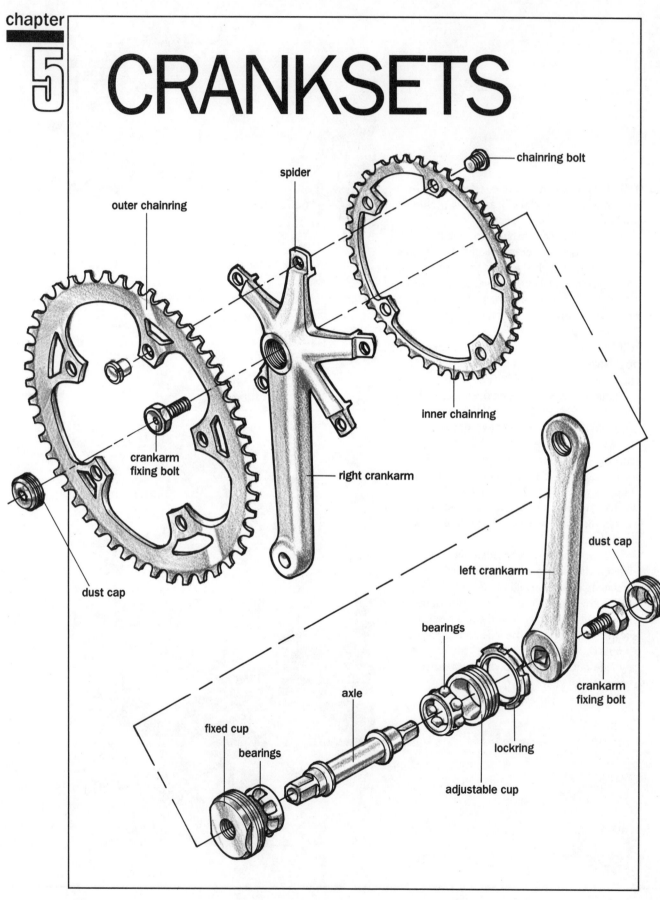

chainring bolt

spider

outer chainring

inner chainring

crankarm
fixing bolt

right crankarm

dust cap

left crankarm

dust cap

bearings

crankarm
fixing bolt

axle

lockring

fixed cup

bearings

adjustable cup

The crankset is one of the largest components on a bicycle. Next to the frame it is the most eye-catching. There are many kinds of cranksets but they all do the same job; they support the pedals and transfer leg power from the pedals to the chain and the rear wheel. Since the crankset not only transfers your pedal power but also supports your body weight when you pedal while standing, it must be very strong.

There are three general kinds of cranksets: (1) one-piece cranksets, (2) cottered cranksets, and (3) cotterless cranksets.

Most cranksets consist of a right and left crankarm, a bottom bracket assembly (this includes the axle, cups, and bearings that are held inside the frame), and one or more chainrings. The right-hand crankarm is the one that has the chainrings or sprockets attached to it. These chainrings attach to the crankarm via the arms of what is called the "spider." The spider arms radiate from the bottom bracket axle outward. Some cranksets integrate the spider with the chainrings, while others make the spider part of the right crankarm and the chainrings separate pieces. The ability to separate the chainring from the spider makes it easy to replace worn or damaged chainrings.

One-piece cranks are found primarily on juvenile bicycles and inexpensive adult bicycles. These cranksets integrate the bottom bracket axle and the crankarms into one piece. One-piece cranksets are generally made of steel, which makes them very durable, but they are also quite heavy.

Cottered cranks use two separate crankarms that mount onto an axle. The cranks are held on the axle by means of cotter pins, which are inserted through holes in the crankarm that are lined up with grooves on the ends of the axle. Generally, either a hammer or a special press is used to seat the pins firmly, then nuts are fastened to their ends to hold them in place. Most cottered cranksets are steel, though some have aluminum alloy chainrings.

Cotterless cranks are the most popular cranksets for use on high-quality adult bikes. The crankarm in one of these sets has a square tapered hole that fits onto the end of an axle, which is also square and tapered. The arm is held in place with either a nut or a bolt, depending on whether the tapered axle ends have threaded studs on their tips or are hollowed out and threaded on the inside. Most cotterless cranksets use aluminum alloy in both the crankarms and the chainrings. Cotterless cranks come in a multitude of styles and offer a wide selection of crankarm lengths, chainring sizes, and bottom bracket combinations.

## The Bottom Bracket

The bottom bracket consists of the axle, which has cone-shaped bearing races near each end, two cups, and two sets of bearings that are mounted in the bicycle frame and support the crankarms. The part of the bicycle frame in which the bottom bracket is housed is called the bottom bracket shell. A cup is threaded into each side of this shell. The cups, along with the bearings, support

*Photo 5-1: In a cottered crankset, the crankarm is fastened to the axle end by means of a pin, which is hammered or pressed into place, then held tight with a nut and washer.*

the axle and the crankarms attached to it while allowing them to spin.

The main function of the bottom bracket is to spin. However, while the axle spins, it must also carry the torsional and lateral loads produced when pedaling the bicycle. In order to minimize power losses and wear, the bearing adjustment within the bottom bracket must be properly maintained. A bottom bracket axle should spin smoothly, without either binding or looseness, on bearings that are properly protected. Grease is used not only to lubricate the bearings, but also to protect them from both dirt contamination and moisture that can cause rust.

Sealed-bearing systems are the latest word in bottom brackets. These units require little or no service because their bearings are protected with seals that prevent the grease and the bearings from becoming contaminated with grit

from the road. In fact some of these systems cannot be serviced by the user, but must be returned to the manufacturer if a problem ever develops. Other sealed-bearing bottom brackets can be serviced but require special (and expensive) tools. Some units, however, can be serviced with standard tools. But since each is a unique design you will have to consult your owner's manual to find out how to service the unit.

To function properly the bottom bracket assembly requires periodic maintenance. How often maintenance is performed is dependent on the number of miles ridden, the environment, and the kind of bottom bracket. Bicycles that are ridden only on sunny weekends at distances of 30 miles or less may require a bottom bracket overhaul every two to three years. Bicycles that are used every day, regardless of the weather, should be overhauled at least once a year. Competition bicycles may require it twice a year or more. This preventive maintenance can save many dollars by catching minor problems before they have a chance to become major failures.

## Changing Your Cranks

If you want to change the crankset on your bicycle you will have to consider several factors.

What kind of bottom bracket do you have? If you have an oversized bottom bracket used for one piece cranksets you can only use one-piece cranksets unless you buy a conversion bottom bracket assembly. However, these conversion kits are intended primarily for BMX (bicycle motocross) bicycles and you may have trouble fitting a double chainwheel crankset to them since they were intended for single chainwheel use.

Cottered and cotterless bottom brackets, on the other hand, thread into the bottom bracket shell the same way. So, if you have a bike with a cottered crankset you can change to a cotterless unit, so long as you change everything. That is to say, you can't use an axle from a cottered bottom bracket assembly with a set of cotterless crankarms. The axle and the crankarms will simply not match.

The major consideration to take into account when changing bottom bracket assemblies is the threading of your bottom bracket shell. Most bottom brackets come in English, French, or Italian threadings. You will have to get the correct one for your frame; they are not interchangeable. Your frame's origin is not always a true indicator of its type of bottom bracket threads. If you have a set of calipers and a thread gauge you can measure your cups yourself and

*Photo 5-2: Many new bottom bracket assemblies contain sealed-bearing systems, some of which cannot be serviced by the user.*

87

check them against table 5-1 to determine the threading and type of bottom bracket you will need. Otherwise, take one of the cups or the entire bicycle to a bicycle shop to find out what kind of threads it has.

## table 5-1
# BOTTOM BRACKET THREADING

| Bracket Type | Thread Dimension |
|---|---|
| English | 1.370″ x 24 tpi* |
| French | 35mm x 1.0mm |
| Italian | 36mm x 24 tpi* |

*Threads per inch.

Another factor to consider for bottom brackets is the width of the bottom bracket shell. The two most common sizes are 68mm and 70mm. Most French- and English-thread bicycles have a bottom bracket width of 68mm, while 70mm is standard for most bottom brackets equipped with Italian threads. Sometimes the axle is stamped with a 68 or 70 to tell you the width of bottom bracket for which it was designed. But the only way to be certain of the width of your shell is to measure it. To do this you should first dismantle the bottom bracket so you can accurately measure from one side of the empty shell to the other.

Most cranksets have a bottom bracket designed specifically for them. If you want to mix the crankset of one manufacturer with the bottom bracket of another you should check with one of the manufacturers as to the compatibility of such a matchup. Sometimes it works and sometimes it doesn't. You can also ask your bicycle shop to check *Sutherland's Handbook for Bicycle Mechanics.* This handbook is a standard reference tool in most bicycle shops.

Most replacement cranksets are made of aluminum alloy. This is good since aluminum cotterless cranksets are quiet, light, durable, and trouble-free when installed correctly. So when purchasing a crankset, be sure to get a model with interchangeable aluminum chainwheels. Some inexpensive cranksets come with steel chainrings. Compared to aluminum, steel rings are heavy and very noisy when shifting.

Generally, the higher the price of the crankset the higher the quality. Inexpensive aluminum cranks have the right crankarm swaged onto the spider. A swaged fitting is similar to a rivet, one piece of metal is bent in such a way that it holds firmly to another piece of metal. But a fitting of this type can loosen with age. In better cranksets the arm and the spider are forged from a single piece of metal.

As you go up the price scale in cranksets, you find systems made of lighter and stronger materials. The machining processes get more precise, which translates into systems that allow better and quieter shifts and chainrings that last longer. You will have to weigh the benefits against the costs to determine the level of quality you are willing to pay for.

You will also have to decide what chainring sizes you want. Some cranksets offer a wider range of possibilities than others. For more information on an individual crankset's range you will have to check the manufacturer's literature. For advice on how to determine the size chainrings that best suit your riding ability and needs, consult chapter 16 on gearing.

One basic decision you will have to make is whether you want a double or a triple chainwheel set. The double is standard fare for racers and most sport riders, but many people prefer the gearing flexibility gained with a triple. Triples can add a low range of gears well suited to loaded touring and steep climbs. But if you don't expect to do much of this type of riding, the third chainwheel may be useless for you. So think carefully about your gearing requirements and make your decision accordingly. Just be sure before you make your purchase that the crankset you select will accept the chainwheel sizes you plan to use.

There is also the matter of crankarm length to consider in selecting a bottom bracket. The standard length is 170mm, the one most readily available and most commonly used. But crankarms are available in 2½ millimeter increments, from 165mm to 185mm.

There are a few theories concerning arm length. Most relate the length of the crankarm to the rider's leg length. Longer arms aid uphill riding because they offer greater leverage, but they are more difficult to spin, so they limit leg speed. For a long-legged rider this isn't a problem, the longer thigh muscles benefit from the added crank length. For shorter riders, this can hamper riding form on the bike. Long arms may enhance the climbing ability of such riders, but the rest of the time their riding will suffer.

So if you are tall (over 6 feet), climb a lot, and tend to push big gears rather than spin, long cranks are for you. Otherwise you should stick to 170mm, or shorter, if you have short legs.

## Preparing a Bottom Bracket

Before installing a new bottom bracket assembly, you should have your frame tapped and faced. Tapping prepares the inside of the bottom bracket shell. A special thread-cutting tool called a tap is run through the threaded parts of the shell. The tap cuts the threads to the proper shape and depth and also makes the threads on the left-hand side concentric with the threads on the right-hand side.

Facing tools are used to prepare both ends of the bottom bracket shell. These special cutting tools smooth the outer edges of the bottom bracket shell and make them parallel to each other as well as perpendicular to the centerline of the threads. This allows the cups to tighten properly in the frame so that they won't back out while you are riding the bike.

You probably won't be able to tap and face your bottom bracket yourself since it is impossible to do without the correct tools, and the tools are very expensive. The standard tool set used to prepare a frame is the coveted Campagnolo tool kit, which sells in shops for approximately $1,800. The kit is a selection of mills, dies, and taps as well as other special hand tools to completely prepare the frame. There are less expensive frame tool kits available, but they all have price tags that discourage ownership by a single individual as opposed to a commercial shop.

*Photo 5-3: The Campagnolo tool kit has all the tools needed to prepare a frame to receive a new bottom bracket or a new headset.*

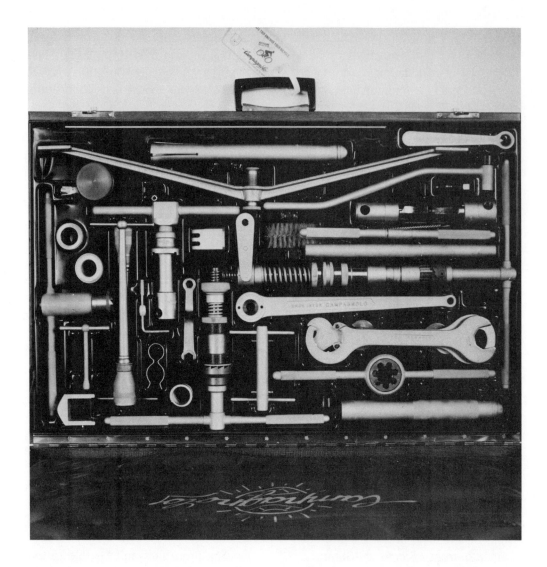

Of course, it will also cost you a bit of money to have this work done in a shop. Still, if you are installing a high-quality crankset (one that costs more than $60) you should have your frame properly prepared first. It is a one-time cost and will help your crank parts last longer.

## Overhauling a Crankset

Before beginning a crankset overhaul you should make sure you have the necessary tools and supplies to complete

the job. You will need a crankarm extractor, an adjusting cup tool, and a lockring tool. The particular type of tool needed in each case depends on the type of crankset you have. You will also need grease, preferably a medium-weight lithium grease, and ball bearings of the appropriate number and size. If you have not previously noted the latter information, you will have to dismantle your bottom bracket, extract and count all the bearings, then take some samples along to the bike shop before you can buy new ones.

You may want to remove the pedals from the crankarms before you remove the crankarms from the bike. This will make it easier to feel what is going on when you pull on the crankarms to check your bearing adjustment. Also, if for any reason you should wish to remove the pedals from the crankarms after they are off the bicycle, you will have a very tough time doing so because it is very difficult to get enough leverage.

To remove the pedals, you will need either a 15mm or 16mm wrench. The right-hand pedal, the one on the side with the chain and sprockets, has a right-hand thread and threads out counterclockwise. The left-hand pedal has a left-hand thread and threads out clockwise. In each case, rotate the arm with the pedal you wish to remove until it points toward the front of the bike. Fit your wrench on the pedal so that it runs back alongside the crankarm, then push down. If you keep the bicycle from moving, the wheels will provide the resistance needed to keep the cranks from turning while you loosen the pedal.

Once the pedals are off you are ready to remove the crankarms from the bottom bracket axle. If you have an old-fashioned cottered crank, remove the arms by loosening the cotter-pin nuts and forcing out the pins. You don't have to purchase special tools for this job. The traditional tools of choice for removing cotter pins are a wrench to loosen the nut, a hammer and punch to drive out the cotter, and a block of wood to support the crank while you are pounding on it. Commercial cotter-pin presses are available, but cost more than individual bike owners generally want to pay. Some people have created their own homemade presses with such things as locking pliers and heavy-duty C-clamps, but the hammer approach is the one

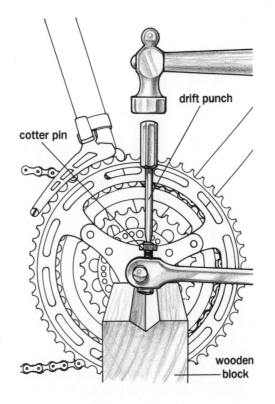

cotter pin

drift punch

wooden block

*Illustration 5-1: The traditional method for removing the cotter pin from a crankarm involves the use of a hammer and a punch. Support the crank with a wooden block or length of pipe to prevent bearing damage.*

most commonly used. Whatever method you use, plan on buying a new set of pins, since the removal process usually damages the old pins.

A specialized tool is needed to remove the arms from a cotterless crankset, though the process is much easier than driving out cotter pins. Don't try to take your crankarms off by any method other than using a tool made for the job. There are universal crankarm removal tools on the market that will work, but the wisest choice is to use the tool made by the manufacturer of your crankset, since it will be the one most certain to fit.

If there is a dust cap covering the fixing bolt or nut that is holding your crankarm on the axle, you will have to remove it before getting at the bolt. This is true unless your crankset is equipped with one of the one-step removal systems. In these systems the dust cap is left in place during the crankarm removal process. A hole in the dust cap allows you to insert an Allen wrench into the head of the bolt. As you unscrew the bolt, it pushes against the back of the dust cap, forcing the arm off the end of the axle.

On most systems, however, the dust cap is there simply to protect the threads inside the crankarm into which the crankarm extractor will fit. These dust caps will either have a narrow slit in them or a hole shaped to receive an Allen wrench. If the latter, remove the dust cap with a wrench of the appropriate size. If the former, use a wide, flat-bladed screwdriver or a quarter. In either case, take care not to damage the dust cap as you remove it.

Once the dust cap is out of the way, you can remove the fastener that is holding the crankarm on the axle. Cotterless bottom bracket axles come in two types (see illustration 5-2). One type has a threaded hole in each end, and bolts, aided by washers, are used to hold the crankarms in place. The other type has a

threaded stud at each end and uses serrated nuts that need no washers to hold the arms in place. Use a crankarm bolt wrench or a shallow-walled socket to remove the crankarm bolt. Some crankset manufacturers make a tool that has a bolt wrench at one end, a crankarm extractor at the other, and wrench flats in the middle for gripping and turning the tool.

Before you thread the crankarm extractor into the crankarm make sure the center section of the extractor is backed all the way out. Then thread the extractor in until the threads of the tool have gone all the way into the threads of the arms.

Now turn the center section of the tool clockwise until it begins to push against the axle. Continue turning the tool to force the crankarm off the end of the axle.

Once the arms are removed, check the adjustment of the spindle. Is it loose? Does it spin smoothly or does it bind? How much dirt is clinging to the area around the axle? These may be indicators of problems to look for inside the bottom bracket.

Now that the arms are off the bike, wipe off the dirt from around the bottom bracket area. This is also a good time to disassemble the right crankarm and clean the chainrings. But when you reassemble the crank, make sure that the chainring bolts are tight. Otherwise, you might get some undesired squeaking. To insure that the chainring bolts are tight and to facilitate their future removal, lubricate the threads of the bolts with oil before assembling them.

Next the lockring must be removed, preferably with a lockring spanner. Some spanners are unique to a particular brand of bottom bracket, while others, such as hook spanners and plier-

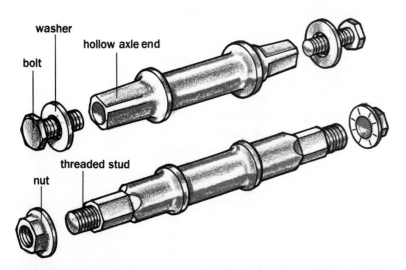

*Illustration 5-2: There are two types of cotterless crank axles. One has a hollow axle end threaded to receive a bolt, the other has a threaded stud on the end of the axle that receives a nut.*

type spanners, are more universal. Once again, tools made to match with a particular brand of component are generally the surest fitting, but not all manufacturers have such tools. You may have to use the universal kind. If you don't have any lockring spanner, a hammer and punch, used with care, can be used to drive the lockring off. Some lockrings have peculiar notch spacings and may require a hammer and punch, since even the universal tools won't grip the part adequately.

Remove the lockring by turning it counterclockwise. Work cautiously, the threads of the ring and the cup are prone to producing metal shards that easily imbed themselves into fingers.

Now the adjusting cup must be removed by being turned counterclockwise. Usually a special spannner is needed for this also. Many of the better bottom brackets match a pin spanner with a series of six pin holes in the adjustable cup. Some cups have notches and a few have a hex fitting suitable for an appropriately sized wrench. Here again, some companies make special spanners for their adjusting cup, and these will insure the best fit. But there are also a variety of universal pin and notch spanners available.

When removing the adjusting cup, be careful in case the bearings are not in a retainer. Place a rag or a piece of paper under the bottom bracket to catch any bearings that might drop out. Once the adjusting cup is out, you can remove the axle, bearings, and dust sleeve. Not all bottom brackets have the latter, which is a plastic sleeve that prevents dirt and debris in the frame tubes from entering the bottom bracket shell and contaminating the bearings.

For the time being leave the fixed cup in the frame. Clean and examine all the bottom bracket components that you have removed, as well as the bottom bracket shell and the fixed cup. Use solvent and either a rag or a small brush to remove any contaminants and as much grease as possible.

Look at the adjusting cup race for any pitting or excessive wear on the scored line around the surface of the race. This is the path of the bearings. Carefully check the axle at the shoulders for the wear line and examine it carefully. Inspect the fixed cup also, possibly with the help of a directable light source, such as a flashlight. Look at the ball bearings. Check to make sure that none have cracked or broken. See if the retainer is intact. If either the balls or the retainer are damaged, make sure that none of the broken parts are clinging inside the frame in such a way that they may drop into the bottom bracket after reassembly.

If any of the components are heavily worn or damaged, it is best to replace them. They will adversely affect the bottom bracket adjustment and cause additional wear to the other bottom bracket components.

At this time it is best to replace all the ball bearings, even if they don't appear worn. This is because load and wear distort the bearings, transforming them from spheroids into ellipsoids. Since they wear into this new configuration gradually, all the bearings are oriented properly and act similarly to roller bearings. But if you try to reuse the bearings after taking them out and cleaning them, they will not reorient themselves correctly and several readjustments will be necessary. Good bearings are inexpensive and will make adjusting the bottom bracket easier.

If the fixed cup is worn and needs to be removed it is best to have the task performed at a bicycle shop that has a special fixed cup tool. In some cases it is possible to lock the fixed cup in a vise and spin the frame off of it. This method will work if the flats of the fixed cup are large enough to grab. However, proceed very carefully. If you slip you may damage the cup or your frame. The fixed cup, especially if it has right-hand (i.e., French or Italian) threads, must be locked down very tightly to keep it from working loose. Most home mechanics cannot get enough leverage to remove this part. If the special fixed cup tool is needed to remove your fixed cup, it will also be needed to properly lock it or its replacement back into your frame.

If you must remove the fixed cup, remember that British-thread bicycles use left-hand threads on the fixed cup, meaning the fixed cup spins out clockwise. All others, except for some rare Swiss threads, unscrew in the counterclockwise direction.

### Tapping and Facing

If you have removed both cups from the bottom bracket, you may want to have the bottom bracket shell tapped and faced. As described earlier, tapping cleans and cuts the threads to their proper dimension. This makes threading in the cups easier. It also makes both sets of threads concentric, that is, cut on the same axis. This allows a finer adjustment than is otherwise possible. The facing tool shaves the outer edge of the bottom bracket shell so the lockring and the fixed cup seat are parallel to each other and perpendicular to the axis of axle.

Custom frame builders tap and face bottom brackets as a matter of course, but many fine stock frames have never

been faced. If you have such a frame you may want to have a bicycle shop tap and face it for you. It is a one-time expense that will provide you with years of easier and more precise bottom bracket adjustments.

## Installation

Now that the bottom bracket parts have been removed, cleaned, and any worn parts replaced, it is time to reinstall everything.

If the fixed cup was removed, grease both its threads and those in the bottom bracket shell before threading the cup back in. Be sure that the fixed cup is locked down very tightly, preferably using a tool designed for fixed cups.

Apply a liberal amount of medium-weight grease to the fixed cup's bearing race. If medium-weight grease is unavailable, lightweight grease is preferable to heavy. Applying the grease will require reaching through the bottom bracket. Be careful not to let any dirt or metal from the bottom bracket contaminate the grease. Once the race is greased, the ball bearings will have to be installed. If the bearings are in a retainer, pack the retainer with grease and insert it into the cup. If the bearings are loose, you will have to stick each bearing into the cup individually, relying on the grease to hold them in place until the axle is installed.

### Caged Bearings versus Loose Bearings

If you buy bearings that come in retainers, don't be afraid to use them. The retainer conveniently holds the bearings while you work with them.

Many people argue that the retainers add friction. Well, they do. But try to be realistic; the amount of friction that is added is unimportant to 99.9 percent of the riders in the world. Even many racing team mechanics use the retainers because they make bottom bracket overhauls go more quickly.

One of the most difficult things to do is to explain which way a retainer fits into a cup. Only one way works. Assembling the bottom bracket with the retainer in backward prevents proper adjustment and, used that way, will ruin something. Many a mechanic has been distracted just long enough to slide a retainer on backward only to discover the error when he tries to eliminate the side-to-side play later while adjusting.

Look at a retainer. The metal frame that holds the balls looks like a C in cross section. The open side of this C should face in toward the shoulder of the axle. Thus the open sides of the two retainers will face each other when properly installed in the bottom bracket.

Next insert the dust sleeve. It prevents contaminants from falling into the bottom bracket shell from the frame tubes. These sleeves are available from almost any bicycle shop for about a dollar, otherwise you can fabricate one out of a flexible piece of plastic cut to the proper width and rolled to fit into the bottom bracket. Make sure that the sleeve is wide enough to meet the inner edge of both cups, but not wide enough to interfere with the bearings. Also, allow a little extra length so that once the piece of plastic is rolled up, the ends overlap slightly.

Some people like to apply a thin film of grease to the outside of the dust sleeve. This can sometimes make later removal easier.

Now apply a liberal amount of grease to the whole surface of the axle, especially at both bearing shoulders. Grease applied to the inner section of the axle will serve to retard corrosion. Take a close look at the axle. Most likely one tapered end is slightly longer than the other. If so, insert the longer end into the bottom bracket first so that it emerges through the fixed cup on the drive side of the bike.

Pack grease into the adjusting cup as you did the fixed cup and install its set of bearings, then screw it into the bottom bracket shell until you feel the bearings pressed snugly against the axle shoulders. Thread the lockring onto the adjusting cup and lightly tighten it by hand. Now spin the axle back and forth to make sure the bearings are not binding. Also, try moving the axle up and down to check for looseness. If you need to alter the adjustment, back the lockring off a little and use your wrench or spanner to turn the adjusting cup until the axle spins smoothly but without play. Once you have the adjustment the way you want it, use your lockring spanner to turn the lockring down very tight.

As you tighten the lockring, watch the adjustable cup. It may start to turn along with the lockring. If so, you can trying holding it still with the other tool. However, if you are using a pin spanner, it may not be able to resist the force of the lockring without breaking off a pin. If that looks like a possibility, you should try another approach. Loosen the lockring and adjustable cup together, then hold the lockring still while you back the cup off a little further. Now tighten them both together and see if you end up with the correct adjustment.

Be patient. You may have to experiment before you find the best method to get the adjustment you want. Just remember, when you are fine-tuning your adjustment don't try to move the adjusting cup with your pin tool without first loosening the lockring. If you try to do this it is very likely you will break the tool.

Some people like to put a crankarm on the axle to check for any looseness in the axle adjustment. This is a good idea since it can often give the extra leverage needed to detect very small amounts of play. If your adjustment always seems to be either a little too tight or a little too loose, and you simply cannot find the magic place in between, leave it on the tight side. Once the excess grease works its way out of the bearings, it should be about right.

Reinstall the crankarms. Cottered cranks should have the cotter pins running opposite each other. If viewed while sitting on the saddle and the crankarms are at 6 and 12 o'clock, one cotter-pin nut should be facing forward and the other should be facing to the rear of the bike. To tighten the cotter pins you have to use a cotter-pin press or a hammer. Trying to fully tighten them by means of the nut on the cotter pin will strip the threads on the pin. If you use a hammer, give the back end of the cotter pin several sharp blows and tighten the nut until it is snug. Give the pin a couple more raps with the hammer and retighten the nut. Then, after your first ride, check to see if the nut is still tight. Check again after a couple hundred miles.

To reinstall a cotterless crankarm, put the arm on the axle, thread on the nut or bolt, and tighten fully. Expect to use a good bit of force. Don't put all your weight behind it, but snug the nut or bolt down firmly. If you have a torque wrench to gauge your force, tighten it to between 25 and 30 inch-pounds.

One common practice you should avoid is greasing the axle tapers before installing the cotterless crankarms. Every major crankset manufacturer recommends that the axle tapers be free of lubricant. Failure to keep them clean could result in the crankarms working their way up the flats until the arms bottom out against the ends of the axle. But, don't forget to retighten the crankarm bolts after your first ride, and to check them periodically thereafter.

## Removing Chainrings

Most cranksets have removable chainrings. The way to get them off is to loosen the bolts, usually five in number, that hold them in place. Sometimes these bolts require a 10mm or 11mm wrench, but increasingly chainrings are being equipped with bolts that require a 5mm Allen wrench. To loosen many of these Allen-head bolts you need a special wrench, called a chainring nut spanner, to hold the nut on the back side of the chainring. These are available through bicycle dealers, but if you can't get one, a large flat-bladed screwdriver will sometimes work in its place. You discover that the chainring bolts are very tight and that you have to slide a small piece of pipe over the Allen key to get enough leverage.

## Maintenance

There is very little maintenance that can be done on a crankset short of a complete overhaul, but there are a few preventive measures you can take. We have already suggested that you check the tightness of your cotter pins or your crankarm bolts at the end of the first ride after their installation. It is also good to recheck it at least once every six months. If you ride a long time with loose crankarms you can do them and the axle ends irreparable damage. Once you are sure the arms are tight, check the pedals as well.

When you check the crankarms, tug on them to see if there is looseness in your bottom bracket. If you discover any, then you need to readjust your adjustable cup. You should be able to take care of that without removing the crankarm again.

## Damaged Parts

If the crankarms get bent, due to an accident or whatever, only steel ones can be bent back into shape. Aluminum crankarms should be replaced if bent.

Bent spiders can be straightened in many cases, even on aluminum cranksets. The same is true for aluminum or steel chainrings. Straightening a chainring is not too difficult if you have the right tool. However, straightening a bent crankarm is a job best left to a bicycle shop. Without the proper tools and knowledge you might further damage the components.

A high-quality crankset can last for a very long time. The bearings should be replaced at each overhaul and eventually the chainrings do wear down, but the crankarms, the bottom bracket axle, and the cup should need to be replaced only because of an accident or negligence. With minor care you can count on your crankset to give you many thousands of miles of service.

# CRANKSETS
## crank adjustment

From time to time you should grab the crankarms on your bike with your hands and tug on them to check for looseness, either in the crankarms themselves or in the bearing adjustment inside the bottom bracket. (Photo 1) If you discover that the crankarms are loose, tighten them immediately. Even if they never feel loose, at least once every six months give them a preventive tightening.

Cottered crankarms are held in place by cotter pins that have nuts threaded on one end. To tighten these crankarms, give the head of each cotter pin a sharp rap with a hammer, then use a wrench to tighten the nut.

Before you can tighten a cotterless crankset, you must remove the dust cap. A dust cap with a slit across its face can be removed with the aid of a wide-bladed screwdriver or a large coin, such as a quarter. (Photo 2) Some must be removed with an Allen key.

Once the dust cap is out of the way you have access to the fixing bolt or nut that holds the crankarm on the end of the axle. Special crank bolt spanners are made for turning these bolts. A thin-walled socket wrench of the correct dimension will also work. Some crankarm removal tools are also designed to double as crank bolt spanners. Such tools must be turned with the aid of an ordinary open-end wrench. Use the appropriate tool to snug up your crankarm fixing bolt, then replace the dust cap. (Photo 3)

When you flex the crankarms, if you feel any play in the bearings, adjust them immediately. You should be able to do this without removing the crankarm. However, it will be easier if it is out of the way. To remove the crankarm, follow the instructions found on page 100. To adjust bottom bracket bearings, the lockring does not have

to be removed, only loosened. That can be done by using a lockring spanner to turn it counterclockwise. (Photo 4) Don't spin the lockring all the way off, just loosen it enough so that it does not hinder the movement of the adjustable cup. Some adjustable cups have pin holes, others have notches or wrench flats. Use a tool appropriate to your particular cup to turn it clockwise to eliminate the play in the bearings. (Photo 5)

Work carefully. You may need to move the cup just one-eighth of a turn or less to get the adjustment you need. Check frequently by grabbing a crankarm and moving the axle around. When you get the adjustment to a point where there is neither binding nor play in the bearings, retighten the lockring to hold the cup in that position.

As you tighten the lockring, watch the adjustable cup. It may try to move along with the lockring, spoiling your careful adjustment. If it does, hold it still with your spanner or wrench while tightening the lockring. (Photo 6)

One word of caution here. If your cup tool is a pin spanner it is possible to break the tool by putting too much pressure on the pins. Pay attention to how much pressure it takes to prevent the cup from moving along with the lockring. If a lot of force is involved, you should resort to a different technique. Calculate how far tightening the lockring moves the cup out of adjustment, then loosen both the lockring and cup. Hold the lockring still while you back off the cup adjustment enough to compensate for its expected later movement. Then when you retighten the lockring the cup should end up in the right place.

If you removed a crankarm, replace it. Tighten the crank bolt, then thread the dust cap back in place. ▲

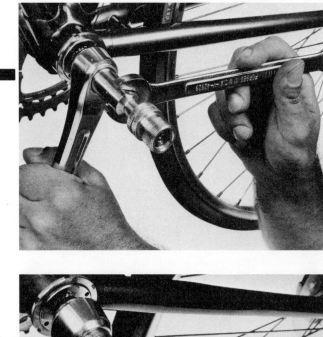

**1**

**2**

**3**

Before beginning to overhaul your bottom bracket, make sure you have all the tools and supplies you will need. For tool options, review the discussion beginning on page 90. Also, if you know in advance what type and how many bearings you will need, you can have them at hand before you begin work.

Decide now if you will want your pedals off of the crankarms anytime during the overhaul. If so, take them off now, while the cranks are still on the bike.

It is also a good idea to remove the chain from your bike to get it out of your way while you work. Unless you have a chain fitted with a master link, use a chain tool to push a pivot to the far side of one of the links. (Photo 1) Separate the links and remove the chain.

Each of your crankarms should have a dust cap protecting the threads used in the crankarm removal process. Dust caps are easily damaged, so treat them gently. Turn each dust cap counterclockwise to remove it, using a wide-bladed screwdriver, a large coin, or an Allen wrench, whichever fits it best.

Inside the crankarm you will see either a nut or a bolt that is holding the arm onto the axle. If your crankarm extractor has an end made to fit this fixing bolt, use that, along with a wrench of the proper size, to turn the bolt counterclockwise. (Photo 2) Otherwise, use a special crank bolt spanner or a thin-walled socket to loosen the bolt.

Thread the fixing bolt all the way out of the axle and set it aside, along with its washer. If you have the type of crank that is locked in place with a nut, rather than a bolt, you will find that the nut has serrated edges and there is no separate washer. The technique is the same for removing either type.

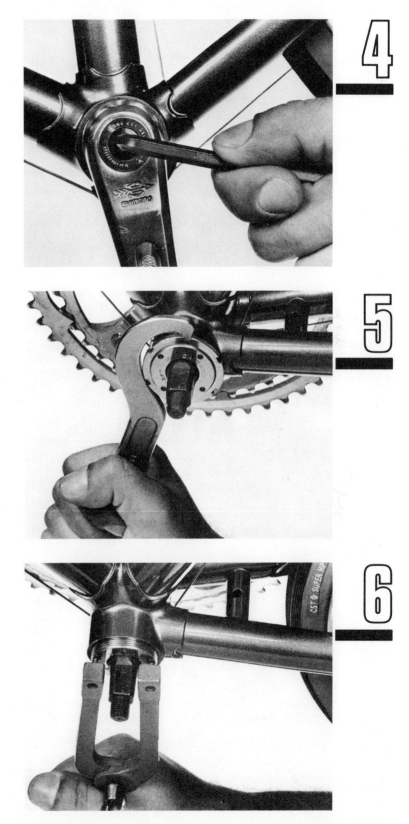

Now take a good look at your crankarm extractor. As you twist the movable part, a rod that runs down the center of the tool moves either in or out. Adjust the tool so that the rod retreats as far back inside as it can. Now thread the end of the tool inside your crankarm.

As you begin to insert the tool, make certain its threads mesh with those inside the crankarm. Thread the tool in as far as you can, then place a wrench on the wrench flats and advance the inner rod forward until it butts against the end of the axle. (Photo 3) Continue turning in the same direction, pushing the rod against the end of the axle and pulling the crankarm off the axle.

There is a new type of cotterless crank available that features an integrated bolt and dust cap removal system for the crankarm. In this design, the dust cap and crankarm fixing bolt are both used in the crankarm removal process. An Allen wrench is inserted through the dust cap into the head of the crank fixing bolt. As the bolt backs out, it pushes against the dust cap, forcing the crankarm off the axle. (Photo 4)

Remove both crankarms from the axle. Then take a C-spanner and loosen the lockring found on the left side of the bottom bracket by turning it counterclockwise. (Photo 5) Spin the lockring completely off the bike.

Now take your pin spanner and turn the adjustable cup counterclockwise until it is threaded almost all the way out of the bottom bracket shell. (Photo 6)

Unless you know that your bearings are held in a retainer, it is a good idea to turn your bike on its side and spread paper towels or rags under it to catch any of the little balls that might be inclined to roll away. Though you will be replacing these bearings, you

need to keep track of them so you can inspect them for signs of wear that indicate potential damage to other parts. You need to make an accurate count of how many replacement bearings to buy.

Hold the axle in place with one hand to trap the fixed cup bearings while you remove the adjustable cup with the other hand. (Photo 7) Once the adjustable cup bearings are out, remove the plastic dust sleeve, if one is present, along with the axle and the bearings from the fixed cup side. (Photo 8)

Clean the metal parts with a solvent and a rag or stiff brush. Don't forget to thoroughly clean inside the fixed cup and the bottom bracket shell. (Photo 9)

After you have cleaned all the parts, you need to inspect them closely for signs of damage or excessive wear. Look at the adjustable cup. You will see a score line running in a circle where the bearings made contact with the race. (Photo 10) What you want to look for are any irregularities in the surface of the race along this line. Is one part of the line worn more heavily than another? Are there any pits along the line that might cause a bearing to snag?

Inspect the fixed cup in the same way. Since it is still in place on the bike, you may need the help of a flashlight or lamp to see clearly.

Now take a good look at the axle. Look for the wear line along each shoulder where the bearings make contact. Are there any pits or signs of excessive wear there?

Clean and examine all the old ball bearings. Are any of them cracked or chipped? If the bearings are caged in a retainer, is the retainer still intact and free of damage? If there are any broken parts, check inside the bottom bracket shell one more time to make

sure no metal fragments are clinging to the frame. You don't want them hanging around to do damage after you have reassembled the bottom bracket.

Any parts that are excessively worn or damaged should be replaced. If in doubt, take the part to a knowledgeable bike mechanic for a second opinion. If your fixed cup needs replacing, we advise that you have it done at a bike shop. It is very difficult to adequately tighten a fixed cup without the special tool made for the job, a tool too specialized and expensive to be worth your purchasing. (Photo 11)

If you have not already purchased new bearings, collect and count the old ones so you will know how many to buy. Take a sample along with you to the bike shop so you can match the size. If you have caged bearings, take one of the old retainers to the shop to get two new ones to match.

Begin the reassembly of your bottom bracket by packing plenty of medium-weight grease into the fixed cup. Then push a suitable number of ball bearings into the grease, which should hold them in place until the axle is in place.

Caged bearings must be installed in the correct way. To determine what that is, take a close look at a set. Note that individual balls are separated from one another by small metal fingers that form somewhat of a C shape. When the retainer is correctly installed, the cup shape or open side of the C formed by these fingers faces in toward the center of the bottom bracket. Or, to put it another way, the individual metal fingers of the retainer curl toward the inside of the bottom bracket. (Photo 12)

Once the bearings are in place inside the fixed cup, the axle can be replaced. This

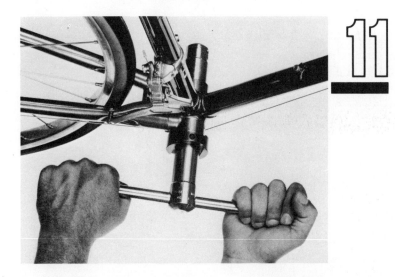

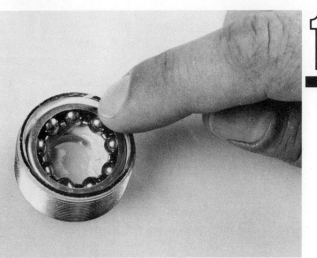

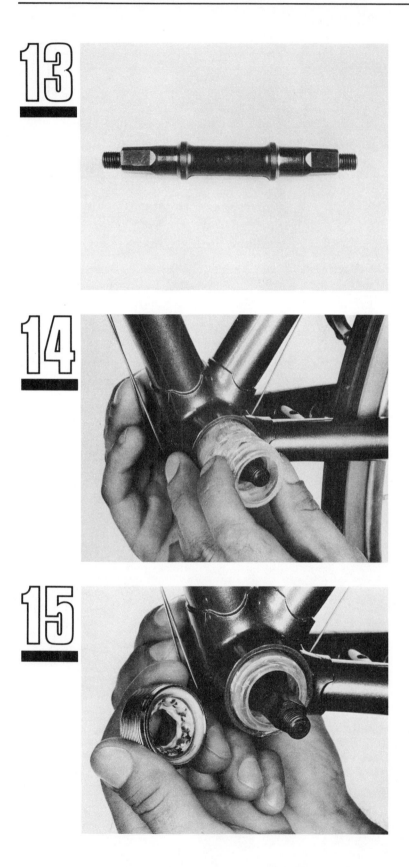

too has to be turned in the right direction, since the ends of most axles are asymmetrical. The difference may not be obvious at first glance, but on most axles the distance between the tapered end and the adjacent bearing race is slightly greater on one side than on the other. (Photo 13) If the manufacturer's name is on the axle, install the axle in such a way that if your bottom bracket were transparent you could read the name while sitting on the bike. Otherwise, make sure the longer end is on the drive side where the extra length is needed to compensate for the space taken up by the chainwheels.

If you have a plastic dust sleeve, clean off all the old grease and grime and coat it with fresh grease. Hold the axle in place on the fixed cup side while sliding the sleeve in over it. (Photo 14)

Pack the adjustable cup with grease and insert the bearings. Once again, if you are using caged bearings, be sure you put them in the correct way. Put a little grease on the threads, then carefully screw the adjustable cup back into the bike frame. (Photo 15) Turn it with your hand part of the way, then use your pin spanner to further tighten it.

Thread the adjustable cup clockwise into the frame until you feel solid contact against bearings. Back the cup off about one-eighth of a turn, then grasp the axle and twirl it back and forth to check the adjustment. If you feel any binding in the bearings, then the adjustment is too tight. Use your pin spanner to back the cup out a tiny bit, then check the adjustment again. (Photo 16)

After you are sure the adjustment is not too tight, try moving the axle up and down. If you feel any play in it, then the adjustment is too loose. Twist the cup clockwise a short

distance and check again. When you feel neither looseness nor binding in the bearings, screw the lockring back on.

Try tightening the lockring down without using a tool to hold the cup still. If the cup insists on turning with the lockring, try holding it still with your pin spanner while turning the lockring. (Photo 17) If you feel a lot of force being put on the pin tool, quit using it or it may break. Loosen the cup and lockring together, then hold the lockring still while you back the cup out a bit more. Now tighten both together and see if your adjustment is correct.

Even if you had no problem with the cup turning, check the adjustment again after tightening the lockring, since that procedure may alter your cup adjustment. When you are satisfied with the adjustment, replace the two crankarms. Be sure you DO NOT put any grease on the end of the axle. Push an arm on the end of the axle, then tighten the nut or fixing bolt to pull the arm into place. (Photo 18)

When both arms are tight, tug on them to check again for looseness in the bottom bracket and twirl them to check for binding. If you are not satisfied with your adjustment at this point, you may be able to alter it without removing a crankarm again. Loosen the lockring, adjust the cup as needed, then retighten the lockring. Once everything is OK, replace the pedals, if you removed them earlier, and the chain.

Finally, don't neglect to replace the dust caps. They protect the threads inside your crankarms, which you will need to use the next time you overhaul your bottom bracket. ▲

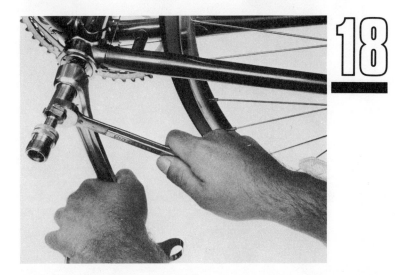

The primary maintenance you can perform on your chainwheels is to keep them clean. A lot of grease mixed with road grime is passed onto the teeth of the chainrings by the chain. The abrasives in this grime cause the chain and chainrings to wear out at a faster rate than they otherwise would.

Therefore, at least once a month—preferably more often, especially if you do a lot of riding in wet and dirty terrain—take a rag and wipe your chainrings clean. Dampen the rag with a little solvent, if you need to, or use a stiff brush to loosen the grime so it can be wiped away. (Photo 1)

Of course, it does little good for you to clean your chainrings if you never bother to clean your chain. The two work together, get dirty together, and wear out together, though not necessarily at the same rate. Thus, every time you clean your chainrings, you should also give your chain a thorough going over. For details on chain cleaning and lubrication, see page 132.

Sometimes a chainring gets bent in a crash or two chainrings are so close together that when the chain is on the smaller one it rubs against the larger one. The solution to the first problem is obvious: you need to straighten the bent area. To solve the second problem, you need to bend the larger chainring slightly away from the smaller all the way around its circumference.

Both these repairs can be accomplished with the help of a chainwheel bending tool. (Photo 2) This is a simple tool, one that is less expensive than most specialized bike tools. However, bending a chainring is one of those jobs that you may prefer to leave to an experienced bike mechanic. If the problem is

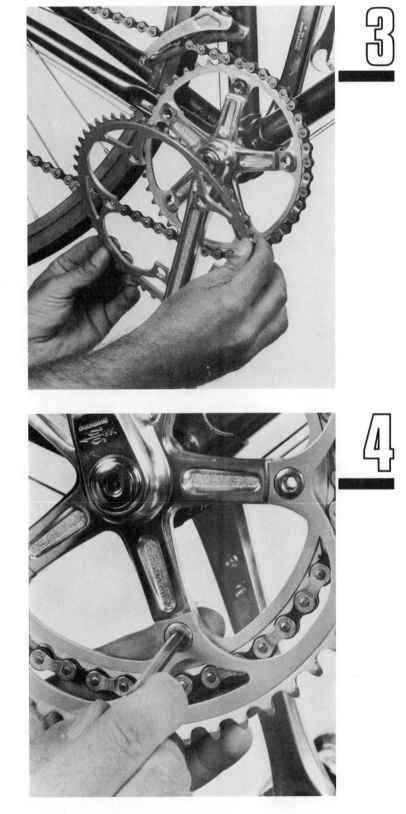

quite severe, you are better off just replacing the chainring.

If you see shiny cuts on the sides of the chainring teeth, this is a sign that you are riding in gear combinations that force the chain into extreme angles. One extreme occurs when you ride with the chain on the large chainring and the largest inner cog. Another results from the chain being shifted onto the inner chainring and the outer (i.e., smallest) rear cog. Such gear combinations are simply best avoided.

When you start riding with a new chain and new chainrings, the teeth of the rings should mesh perfectly with the links of the chain. Over a period of time, the teeth on the rings will gradually become thinner as they wear down. Meanwhile, the plates on the chain will gradually cut into the sides of the pins or rivets, causing the chain to slightly increase in length. As long as the chain and chainrings wear at the same rate, their performance should be satisfactory. However, this is not likely to be the case. Eventually, both will wear out and will need to be replaced.

Replacing chainrings is actually an easy process. Normally, they are fastened by bolts to a five-armed spider that radiates out from the base of the right crankarm. Simply remove the five bolts holding the ring in place and slide it off the crankarm. (Photo 3) Slide on a new ring and bolt it into place.

As a preventive measure, you should check periodically to make certain that all your chainring bolts are tight. You may even wish to carry the necessary wrench along with you in a small tool kit when you travel on your bike. (Photo 4) ▲

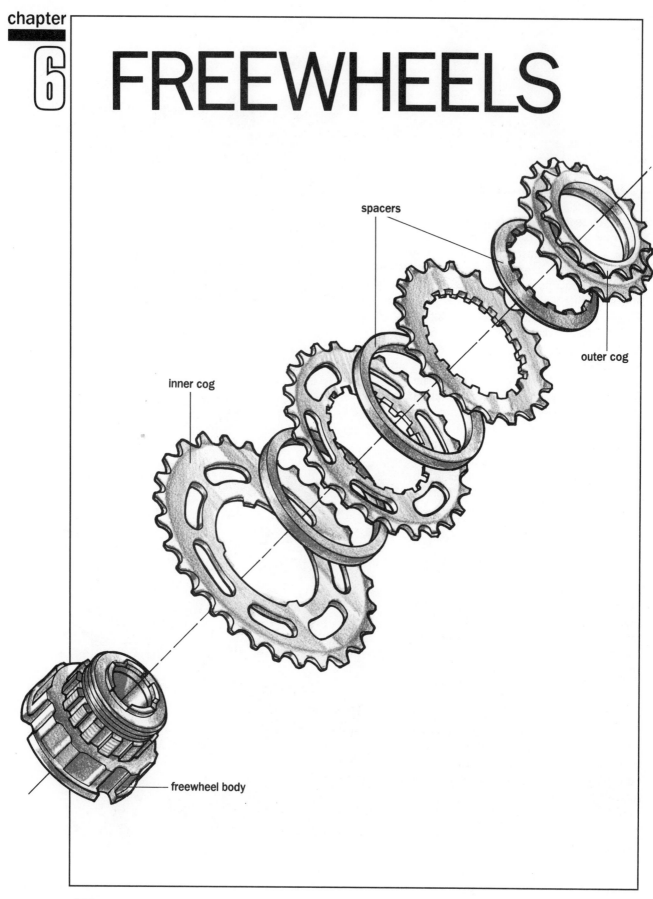

spacers

outer cog

inner cog

freewheel body

## Selecting the
## Right Freewheel

In the earliest days of bicycles there were several ways of getting the power from a cyclist's legs to the wheels of the bicycle. They all had one common inconvenience: if the wheels were spinning, so were your pedals, and your feet. Though this "fixed gear" system allowed you to contribute the strength in your legs to the braking process by resisting the forward movement of the pedals, it never made for very comfortable or very safe riding. Such a system is, however, still used on present-day track bikes because of the added control that it offers racers, whose bikes are not equipped with brakes.

The freewheel, so named because it frees the rear wheel from the connection to the cranks when you stop pedaling, has made road bikes safer and much more comfortable to ride. The modern freewheel is a ratcheting device that connects the hub of the bike's rear wheel, via the chain, to the pedals. The freewheel is equipped with one to seven cogs, depending on how many speeds are desired.

Freewheel cogs—or sprockets as they are sometimes called—are disks with teeth on them. The number of teeth on the cog, combined with the number of teeth on the chainwheel, determines the gear ratio of the bicycle's drive system at any given time. The more cog and chainwheel combinations you have, the greater the number of available gear ratios and the greater the variety of terrain on which your bicycle can be ridden.

There are many manufacturers of freewheels. Most of them use similar designs and produce freewheels adequate for the average user. But, if you have a special need or application you may want to turn to one of the more exotic freewheels.

Campagnolo makes what are perhaps the most exotic and specialized racing freewheels ever built. Constructed completely of aluminum, Campagnolo freewheels are only 25 percent the weight of ordinary freewheels—which are made of steel—but strong enough for the rigors of bicycle racing. They are best for long road races and time trials. Service and maintenance of these freewheels requires special tools that are available only from Campagnolo.

Maillard makes a very popular freewheel system used extensively on French bicycles. Because it is readily available and reasonably priced it is an excellent choice for the average user. Maillard also markets the Helicomatic freewheel/hub system. The Helicomatic freewheel and hub can be used only with each other since they incorporate a set of helical splines in place of the usual threads. Thus, if you have a Maillard Helicomatic freewheel and you need to replace it, your options are quite limited. Maillard also makes an exotic, very light, all-magnesium freewheel that uses standard threads.

Normandy makes another freewheel system popular on European bicycles. Very durable, this system can be found on many French, Italian, English, as well as American-made bicycles.

Regina freewheels are found primarily on Italian bicycles. The Regina system used to be as popular as the Nor-

*Photo 6-1: A freewheel is built up with a combination of cogs of different sizes and spacers that hold the cogs evenly apart.*

Winner freewheels have been extremely popular due to their simplicity and durability. The Winner freewheel system has been especially popular because it can be built with ratios ranging from 12 to 34 teeth in 5-, 6-, and 7-speed combinations. All this can be done on the same freewheel body simply by changing the combinations of cogs and spacers. Many bicycle tourists like the SunTour freewheels because of the availability of the large (34 to 38 teeth) cogs, which provide the low gears needed when carrying heavy touring loads.

Zeus, Spain's freewheel manufacturer, builds freewheels aimed primarily at the racer. While not as exotic and expensive as the Campagnolo freewheels, their limited choice of cogs makes Zeus freewheels best suited for racers.

## Freewheel Ratios

As we have already indicated, the combinations of cogs possible on freewheels vary from model to model and manufacturer to manufacturer. Whether you are buying a stock combination or building up a custom freewheel, you should check the manufacturer's literature or speak to your local bicycle dealer to find out what combinations are available and possible for the model you are considering. If you find a freewheel that either comes with or can be built up with the combination of cogs you desire, you should still check on the availability of replacement cogs. This might influence your decision on whether or not to make a purchase.

Some companies furnish cog boards to dealers. These boards hold all the sizes of cogs available and provide instructions on how to build up the gear

mandy, but began to be displaced somewhat in the late 70s and early 80s by inexpensive Japanese freewheels. However, the Regina CX system remains popular for racing bikes.

Shimano, the world's largest bicycle parts manufacturer, makes several lines of freewheels. The quality and durability of all the Shimano freewheels are excellent. Shimano also makes cassette hubs that combine the hub and freewheel body into one unit.

SunTour is another notable Japanese manufacturer of bicycle components. The SunTour Pro-Compe and

combination you desire. SunTour and Maillard Helicomatic cog boards are common in many bike shops.

If you decide to build a custom combination freewheel, you will need to determine what high and low gear you need and how you want to space the in-between gears. Read chapter 16 on gearing starting on page 262 for advice on how to determine the proper combination for your riding style and circumstance. Then consult your bicycle dealer about which freewheels can be built into that combination.

### Freewheel Threads

Most freewheels attach to wheel hubs by threading onto them. Thus, it is most important to get a compatible match between the two. Freewheels and hubs are available with three thread patterns: French, English, and Italian. French-thread freewheels are unique and compatible only with French-thread hubs. English and Italian threads, on the other hand, are very similar and one can be put on the other in what is called a Class B fit. A Class B fit is one that works but damages the threads slightly because they are not precisely the same. By contrast, in a Class A fit, threads mesh perfectly.

If you do decide to combine English and Italian components in a Class B fit, you will have to stay with that combination as long as you keep either of the components. Once threads have been damaged in a Class B fit, there is no going back to a Class A fit. Trying to do so will only damage your threads further and may lead to thread failure.

Most hubs and freewheels available in the United States are English-threaded. To get Italian or French threads you would probably have to special order them. To determine the threading of your freewheel, look first at the identity of the manufacturer. Ninety-nine percent of all Japanese hubs and freewheels are English-threaded. Italian hubs are almost always either Italian or English in threading. The threading on freewheels made elsewhere should be checked.

You can check the threading in two ways. On some freewheels the thread type is marked on the back side of the freewheel body. You will, of course, have to remove the freewheel to look for this. Some manufacturers label the freewheel by country—France, England, or Italy. Others mark the dimensions of the threads—34.7mm × 1.0mm for France, 1.370″ × 24 tpi for England and 35mm × 24 tpi for Italy. If the freewheel is simply marked "metric," this means it is French-threaded.

The other way to check the threading is to measure the threads using a thread gauge. Thread gauges are usually available through stores that sell tools. If you can't find any markings and you don't have a thread gauge, take your freewheel into the shop where you plan to buy the new freewheel or hub and have them check it for you.

## Cleaning and Lubricating the Freewheel

Most of the time when you clean a freewheel you clean only the outside. This is because the outside is the part that gets the dirtiest. Bear in mind that you do not have to remove the freewheel from the wheel in order to clean it, so don't hesitate to tackle this job. Once your freewheel is clean, you can lubricate it with a medium-weight oil. Sturmey-Archer gear oil or 30-weight motor oil will work fine.

There is very little need to overhaul a freewheel body, because the moving components work only when they are not under a load. If the freewheel body produces a grinding sound, as if it has sand or dirt in it, all that is usually required is to flush the body with oil to remove the dirt.

Some bicycle shops will flush the freewheel with solvent to remove any grit and then use a special grease fitting to inject grease into the bearing and ratcheting mechanism. This grease will quiet the freewheel and make it difficult for dirt to penetrate. However, such extreme steps aren't really necessary.

To clean a freewheel, first lift the chain off the cogs and remove the rear wheel from the bike. Take a rag and wipe the dirt from the surface of the cogs. Use the edge of the rag to clean between the cogs, then use your finger and the rag to clean in the troughs of the teeth.

Lubricate the freewheel by squirting medium-weight oil into the opening between the inner and outer freewheel bodies. To find this opening rotate the freewheel cogs counterclockwise with the wheel sitting horizontal on a table or the floor. The outer body will rotate while the inner body will remain stationary. It should thus be easy for you to see the separation between the two. That is the opening where you want to apply the oil. You should rotate the outer body while applying the oil so that it will work its way into the internal parts of the freewheel.

After applying the oil, wrap the rag between the freewheel and the spokes to catch the excess that will drain out. If after you have done this the freewheel still makes grinding sounds while freewheeling, repeat the lubrication process. This time, however, you may wish to first use a light oil and solvent mixture like WD-40 to try to carry out the dirt. Then lubricate the body with medium-weight oil, as before. If you use a stronger solvent, like kerosene, you may have to lubricate your freewheel several times before all the parts get coated with oil again.

## Removing the Freewheel

To remove your freewheel you will have to have a freewheel removal tool. It is next to impossible to remove a freewheel without one. These tools fit into special notches on the freewheel and allow it to be removed.

Almost every type of freewheel requires a different tool, one especially made for it. You can damage your freewheel trying to take it off with the wrong tool, so it is very important that you get the correct one. You should be able to purchase the needed tool at your local bicycle shop. But take your freewheel and wheel along to make certain you get a proper match between tool and component. In addition to the freewheel tool you will need a large adjustable wrench or a bench-mounted vise to fit the freewheel tool's wrench flats.

Before you can remove your freewheel you need to remove the rear wheel from your bike. Once the wheel is off, completely remove the axle nut or the quick-release skewer nut from the freewheel side of the wheel. Fit the freewheel removing tool into the slots made for it in the freewheel body, then tighten the axle nut or the quick-release skewer nut down over it to hold it securely in place. You will be using a lot of force to remove the freewheel. If the freewheel tool slips it could break the freewheel removal notches or the tool itself, so make sure it is properly seated and firmly fastened to the freewheel before you apply pressure to it.

Set the wheel upright on the floor, the freewheel side pointing away from you. Fit a large adjustable wrench on the flats of the freewheel tool so that as you bend over the wheel you can either push down hard with your right hand or pull up hard with your left hand to break the freewheel loose from the hub. If you prefer to use a bench-mounted vise, bring the wheel down horizontally over the vise and lock the freewheel tool in its jaws.

If you use the wrench, you must hold the wheel stationary while applying force to the freewheel tool. If you use the vise, the tool will be held stationary, so you must turn the wheel to apply leverage on the tool. In either case, you must twist the wrench or the wheel in a counterclockwise direction to unscrew the freewheel from the hub. Because of the constant tightening action that results from pedaling, it may take a lot of force to break the freewheel free. If your freewheel proves quite stubborn, you may have to get a bigger wrench or slip a length of pipe over the handle of your wrench to get extra leverage.

Once the freewheel begins to unscrew, you need to loosen or remove the axle nut or quick-release skewer before continuing to turn the freewheel removing tool. At this point, you may be able to unthread the freewheel by simply turn-

Photo 6-2: An axle nut or quick-release skewer nut can be used to hold the freewheel removal tool inside the freewheel. Just remember to loosen the nut as needed to allow the freewheel to thread off the hub.

ing the removal tool with your fingers. If that is the case, you can take the entire quick-release assembly off the wheel and set it aside. But if you still need the leverage of a wrench or vise to unthread the freewheel, it is best to keep the tool fastened in place while you turn it so that it cannot slip out of its grooves. In this case you will have to continually unthread the fastening nut as you spin the freewheel off the hub. You can do this by holding the axle or quick-release skewer still on the left side of the hub while you spin the freewheel, the removal tool, and the fastening nut counterclockwise on the right side of the hub. Whenever the nut becomes too tight against the tool, loosen it a bit by twisting the axle or skewer from the other side of the hub.

## Installing a Freewheel

No tools are required to install a freewheel. But be sure the threading on your freewheel and hub match before attempting to put the freewheel on. Also, you should thoroughly clean the threads on both the freewheel and the hub, then lubricate them with a medium-weight grease, before trying to put them together.

Hold the freewheel in one hand and steady the wheel in the other. Bring the freewheel together against the hub and turn it counterclockwise at first. This unscrewing action will align the fine threads of the freewheel and hub to prevent cross-threading. Once you feel the threads drop into alignment, reverse direction to begin threading the freewheel onto the hub.

Spin the freewheel on carefully for the first few turns. If you meet any resistance you have probably cross-threaded it. Stop, remove the freewheel, and try again. Once the freewheel has been threaded down three or four full turns you can safely assume that you have got it right and can continue until it is threaded all the way on. There is no need to get the freewheel tight, since your pedaling action when you resume riding your bike will finish tightening it.

## Replacing a Cog

There are two reasons to replace a freewheel cog. One is to get a different gear ratio. To accomplish this you change the cog to one with more or less teeth. The other reason is simply because the old cog is worn out.

Cogs wear due to the friction of the chain against their teeth. If a cog is worn out you can tell when you ride in a gear that uses it. When you put a lot of pressure on the pedals, such as when accelerating or going up a hill, the chain will skip over the defective teeth of that cog. You can easily feel and hear this when it happens. The smaller the cog size the quicker it will wear out because it has fewer teeth to share the load.

Replacing a cog is not particularly difficult, but you do need the appropriate equipment. To start with, you will need two cog removal tools. These are often called chain whips because they consist of a steel handle with a piece of chain attached so the combination looks like a whip. It is possible to get by with only one chain whip if you use a holder called a freewheel vise to immobilize the freewheel body. But actually, the job can best be done by using a freewheel vise along with a pair of chain whips.

The freewheel vise has special prongs made to clamp on to the largest cog of your freewheel. This small vise must then be held immobile between the jaws of a bench-mounted vise while you use the chain whips to apply force to the cogs.

If you don't plan on changing your cogs very often, it might be a good idea to let a bicycle shop remove the cogs for you, since that will probably cost less than the price of the tools needed to do the work. Also, before you attempt to replace a cog, check with your local bicycle shop to see if spare cogs of the type you need are available.

### Cog Removal Procedure

Assuming you have the tools and the cogs are available you can proceed with removing your old cogs. If you are using a freewheel vise, lock the freewheel in it. Remove the smallest cog by wrapping the removal tool chain around it and using the handle to turn the cog counterclockwise.

If you are using two chain whips, one will be used to hold the freewheel steady and the other to remove the cog. By setting the tools on the cogs in such a way that you are able to squeeze their handles together, you can get good leverage while avoiding skinned knuckles. But, be careful when using chain whips. If you don't keep the force you are exerting in line with the cog, you can warp the cog and ruin it.

Look closely at these tools. Each has two sections of chain: a short section attached to the handle at both ends and a long section with one end free. When you fit the tool on a cog, keep the gap between the two pieces of chain as small as possible. This will minimize your chances of twisting the handle out of line and warping a cog.

Depending on the brand and how many speeds your freewheel has, you will usually have to remove between one and five threaded cogs. The remaining cogs are notched and slide onto the freewheel body. As you remove each of the cogs lay them out in the order and orientation they came off. This will assure getting the cogs back on properly. Before you put the cogs back on the body, check the order against the manufacturer's chart, if it is available. Make sure the threads are clean and lubricated with a light oil, not grease.

As you install the cogs make sure that none of them are put on backward. It's easiest to make a mistake with the slide-on cogs. The side of the tooth that is sloped (chamfered) usually faces the spokes. The threaded cogs should be tightened with a chain whip as they are installed so that a threaded cog is snug against the cog below it. The cogs will tighten fully when you ride.

The first time this freewheel is used you should start out riding on the largest cog, pedal a few feet then shift to the next cog and pedal a few feet. Do this until you have tightened all the cogs.

## Special Maintenance Situations

Shimano cassette hubs combine the inner workings of the freewheel and the hub into one unit. In this system, the freewheel and hub are not easily separated since the freewheel cannot be "replaced." You can, however, remove the

*Photo 6-3: A Maillard Helicomatic freewheel has splines for quick installation and removal. A special tool (lower right) is needed for the threaded lockring.*

cogs with the techniques just described. Should you ever need to overhaul or service the freewheel or hub, you will need special tools and the service bulletins that come with them, available from Shimano.

The Maillard Helicomatic freewheels require a special hub. Due to the special helical splines, the freewheel body is held in place with a small lockring. A special tool, available from bicycle dealers who handle Peugeot, Trek, or Motobecane bikes, easily removes the lockring. Once that is off, the freewheel can be lifted straight off the threads.

Generally speaking, all types of freewheels are very dependable. Basic maintenance requires only that you wipe away any surface dirt and drop a little oil into the bearings periodically. Most people replace freewheels not because they are broken, but because they want a new set of gear ratios or have so many worn cogs that it would cost no more or even cost less to buy the whole unit than to replace the defective cogs. Otherwise, freewheels seldom need replacement. So if you provide your freewheel with proper care, you can expect it to provide you with thousands of trouble-free miles.

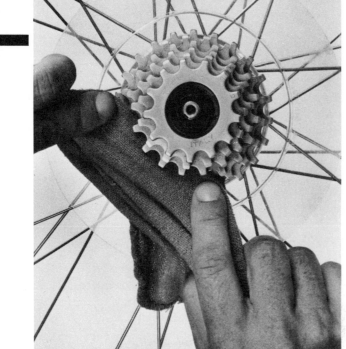

**F**reewheel maintenance consists basically of cleaning and lubrication. We recommend that this be done at least once a month. If you ride in a heavy rainstorm, you should clean and lubricate both your chain and freewheel afterward.

A thorough job of cleaning your freewheel can best be done with the wheel off the bike. Lift your chain off the cogs, release the axle and remove the wheel. Lay the wheel down on a bench top or other flat surface to free both your hands for cleaning.

Take a rag and wipe the grease and road grime off the surface of the cogs. You may want to moisten the rag with solvent or spray some solvent directly on the cogs to help loosen grime. After cleaning the outer surface of the first cog, hold the rag with both hands. Pull it taut and slide it down between successive cogs, cleaning both sides of each one. (Photo 1)

In addition to cleaning the sides of the cogs, make sure you clean the troughs between adjacent teeth. If you have difficulty getting the cogs clean with a rag alone, use an old toothbrush or some other stiff brush to loosen the foreign matter, then use the rag to wipe it away. (Photo 2)

Make a special effort to clean the teeth of the cogs as well as you can. When the chain pulls against those teeth, any gritty matter there serves as an abrasive, causing both the chain and the freewheel cogs to wear at a faster rate than would otherwise be the case. Cleaning your chain and cogs not only will help prolong their life, it will improve the quality of your shifting as well.

Now that the cogs are clean, turn your

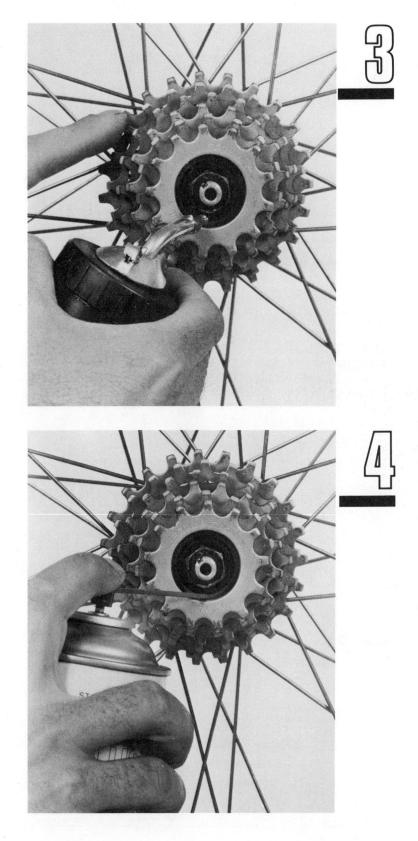

attention to the inner parts of the freewheel. Spin the freewheel around a few times. If you hear only the familiar sound of the ratcheting mechanism, you can proceed with lubrication. However, if you hear grinding sounds, as if your freewheel has little particles of sand inside, you should try to clean out this grit.

Freewheel bodies can be dismantled, but it is a painstaking job and really not necessary for cleaning out their insides. The foreign matter can simply be flushed out by drizzling oil or some type of solvent through the mechanism.

Spin the freewheel to help you locate the line between the outer and inner bodies, the part that moves and the part that stays still. Then drizzle bicycle oil or medium-weight motor oil into the mechanism, spinning the freewheel to help the oil work its way around. (Photo 3) Put a rag underneath to catch any excess that drains through.

If your freewheel still feels or sounds gritty, try flushing out the foreign matter with the help of a penetrating oil and solvent mixture such as WD-40. Rotate the freewheel while you spray the solvent mixture into it. (Photo 4) Wipe away any excess, then lubricate the freewheel once again with the oil used before.

Some people use more potent solvents, such as kerosene, to clean freewheels. However, after using such a substance, you may have to oil your freewheel several times before the lubricant is adequately replaced. A penetrating oil should be able to do the job satisfactorily. ▲

# FREEWHEELS
## removal and replacement

There are several reasons why you may sometimes wish to remove the freewheel from the rear wheel of your bike. You may have discovered the convenience of setting up separate freewheels with distinct cog combinations for use on different terrain and different riding situations. Or perhaps you have an old freewheel you want to switch to a new hub or vice versa. Then again, you may decide to take the freewheel off your bike to make cleaning it easier or to replace one or more of its cogs.

Whatever the reason, before you attempt to remove your freewheel make sure you have a removal tool made to fit your particular brand of freewheel. Almost is not good enough when it comes to matching a freewheel and its removal tool. A sloppy fit is an invitation to disaster. Botch the job and you may never get that freewheel off the hub.

Begin your freewheel removal by taking the rear wheel off the bike. Thread the axle nut or quick-release skewer nut completely off the freewheel side of the axle. Slip the removal tool over the axle and into the body of the freewheel. (Photo 1) Make sure you have good contact between the prongs or splines on the tool and the grooves of the freewheel body. Then hold the tool securely in place by threading the axle nut or skewer nut down over it. (Photo 2)

Set the wheel upright on the floor with the freewheel facing away from you. Lean over the wheel and fit a large adjustable wrench on the wrench flats of the removal tool. (Photo 3)

You will be turning the freewheel in a counterclockwise direction to loosen and remove it. Taking that into account, fit your wrench on the tool in whatever position will give you the most leverage, since it may

take considerable force to break the free-wheel loose from the hub. If you wish to use your right hand, set the wrench on the right side of the hub so you can push down on it. Reverse the position for left-hand work.

Now grasp the wrench in one hand and steady the wheel with the other. Take a deep breath and push down hard (pull up hard if the wrench is on the left side of the hub) to break the freewheel loose.

An alternative to using a wrench for freewheel removal is to lock the wrench flats of the removal tool in the jaws of a bench vise. Grab the wheel and twist it in a counterclockwise direction to loosen the freewheel. (Photo 4)

Once the freewheel begins to move, stop and loosen the nut holding the tool in place to give the freewheel room to thread its way out of the hub. You may be able to dispense with the wrench at this point. If so, remove the axle nut and turn the removal tool by hand to spin the freewheel the rest of the way out.

If you still need the wrench, hold the axle or quick-release skewer still with your other hand. Then try to get the freewheel and the axle nut to unthread at the same rate until you reach the point where you can remove the nut and finish the job by hand.

Mounting a freewheel on a hub is easier than removing one. First make sure both sets of threads are clean, then lubricate both with a thin coat of medium-weight grease. (Photo 5)

Thread the freewheel carefully on the hub beginning in a counterclockwise direction to align the two sets of threads. Then reverse direction and screw the freewheel on as far as you can by hand. (Photo 6) Riding the bike will take care of any further tightening that might be needed. ▲

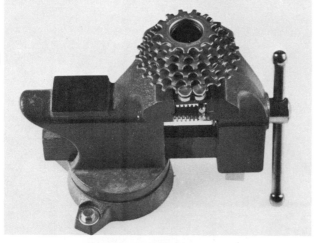

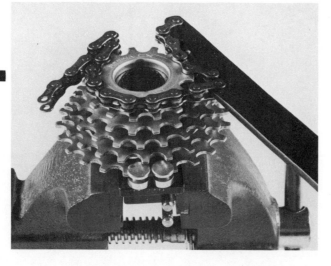

**C**ogs occasionally wear out, especially the smaller ones with fewer teeth to share the load placed on them. Sometimes, though, a perfectly good cog is removed to make room for a cog of a different size. Cog removal is not particularly difficult and can prolong the life and expand the usefulness of a particular freewheel.

As is true with many other bicycle repair jobs, having the right tools is the key to successful cog removal. The right tools in this case consist of a freewheel vise and at least one, but preferably two, chain whips.

A chain whip consists of a metal bar and two lengths of chain, one long and one short. Both ends of the short piece of chain are attached to the bar. One end of the long piece of chain is attached to the bar, while the other end remains loose so it can be wrapped around a cog. (Photo 1)

A freewheel vise consists of two small pieces of angle iron that slide back and forth on parallel metal rods. Each piece of angle is topped by a pair of metal studs sized to fit between adjacent teeth of a freewheel cog. Once closed around a cog, this little vise is locked between the jaws of a bench vise to prevent the cog from moving. (Photo 2)

To remove the small, outside cog of a freewheel, immobilize the freewheel in the freewheel vise. Then fit the chain whip on the right side of the cog, wrapping the loose length of chain underneath and around the cog in a clockwise direction. Push on the handle of the tool to twist the cog in a counterclockwise direction to loosen it. (Photo 3)

It is possible to use a second chain whip in place of a freewheel vise to immobilize the freewheel while loosening one of its cogs. In this case you have to place the second chain

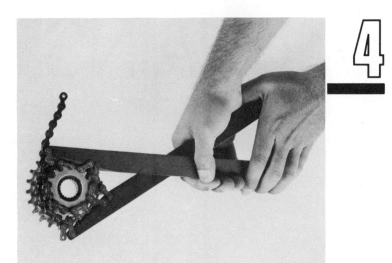

**4**

whip on the opposite side of the freewheel from the first and wrap it in the opposite direction. Try to set them up in such a way that the handles of the tools crisscross. Then by squeezing the ends of the two tools together you can get the leverage needed to break one cog free. (Photo 4)

When you attempt to remove a cog with a pair of chain whips, it is important to keep the tools fairly close together. This means you should allow no more than one cog to separate the two cogs against which pressure is being applied. The farther apart the tools are, the harder it is to channel their force in the right directions. If you twist a tool sideways you may damage some cog teeth.

The most reliable method of all is to immobilize the freewheel in a freewheel vise and use two chain whips. This gives you maximum control and leverage for the job.

As you begin removing cogs, pay attention to how they come off. (Photo 5) You may find separate spacers between some cogs. Other cogs may have a built-in spacer protruding from one side. Attention to how the freewheel comes apart will aid later reassembly.

When in doubt, look closely at the cog teeth. The chamfered or sloped side usually faces the spokes. Check that orientation before removing the cogs so you will know the proper way to put the new ones on.

Most likely you will discover that some cogs have no threads, but are held in place by adjacent cogs. When replacing a cog that is threaded, hand-tighten it first. (Photo 6) Snug it up further with a chain whip, if you'd like, but depend on riding the bike to make all cogs properly tight. ▲

**5**

**6**

# 7 CHAINS

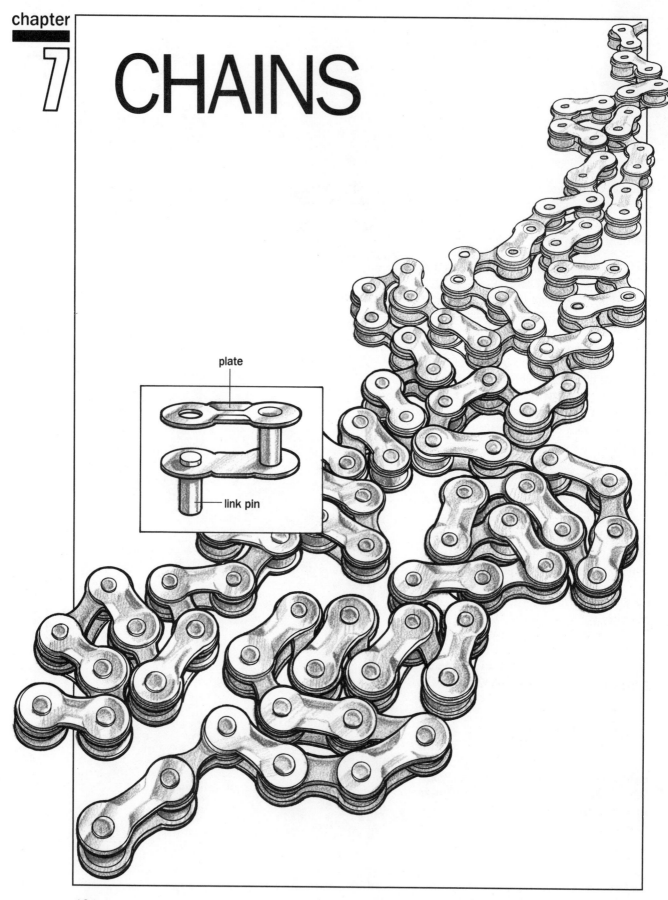

plate

link pin

It's easy to take your bicycle's chain for granted. Almost every bike has one and the way the chain works appears so simple that it is hardly interesting. Besides, who wants to have anything to do with a piece of hardware that's often the dirtiest thing on a bike, a part that calls attention to itself mostly by the marks it leaves on a clean pair of slacks or a bare leg?

You should, if you are a regular rider. No one likes the results of contact with a dirty chain. But the grease it transfers to your hand or leg is not its only drawback; it can also rob you of some of your pedaling power. Furthermore, on derailleur-equipped bikes a dirty chain can impair shifting performance and accelerate wear on derailleurs, freewheel cogs, and cranksets.

For these reasons, you should pay attention to your bike's chain and develop the habit of frequently cleaning and lubricating it. But before you begin working on your chain, you should know what kind of chain you're dealing with.

## Chain Identification

There are two common sizes of bicycle chain: 1/8-inch width, which is used on most BMX bikes and all 1-speed and 3-speed bikes; and 3/32-inch width (also known as derailleur chain), which is used on all 10-, 12-, 15-, and 18-speed derailleur bikes. The width referred to is the thickness of a compatible gear tooth. The span between the two inner plates of a chain link must, by necessity, be slightly wider than the teeth that will fit into the space.

If you can't identify the chain size of your bike from its type of drive train, measure the thickness of one of your bike's gear teeth. It should be either 3/32 inch or 1/8 inch. The task of determining your chain size is finished if your bike uses 1/8-inch chain; however, there's one more step to go if your bike's equipped with 3/32, or derailleur, chain.

Corresponding to the two types of freewheels, there are standard, or "normal," width derailleur chains, and narrow, or "ultra," width derailleur chains. If you're replacing a derailleur chain, it's important to correctly identify its type. A mistake here will, at the very least, diminish your bike's ability to shift smoothly. At the worst, it may no longer shift at all!

## Standard Width

With practice you may be able to distinguish standard, or "normal," width chains by their slightly greater width. If not, look first at the edges of the inner plates. Most standard derailleur chains have straight-edged plates. In addition, standard-width chain pins protrude about 1/32 inch beyond the sides of the outer plates.

One important exception to the first rule is Shimano's Uniglide design; its inner plates have a bulge toward the outside bent into them. Because of this design, the chain has even larger gear tooth "holes" than a standard-width chain, which results in excellent shifting. The bent links make this an easy chain to identify.

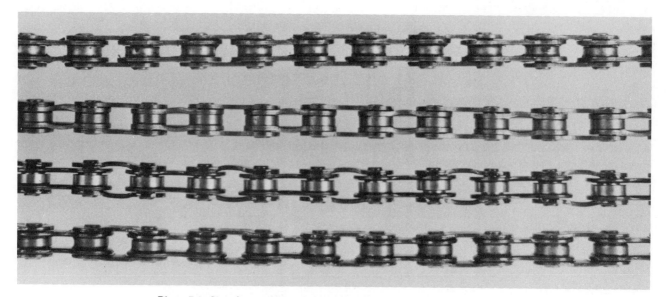

*Photo 7-1: Close inspection reveals subtle differences between different bicycle chains. Some have bulges or flared edges on plates for more positive shifting. This is most commonly found in narrow-width models.*

### Narrow Width

The inner links of most narrow, or "ultra," width chains have slight bulges on their edges. This is to help counteract the slightly smaller opening in the narrow chain that the gear teeth must fit into. That narrower opening makes shifting less positive. So, even though a narrow-width chain will work with a standard-width freewheel, don't try it! That combination just doesn't shift as well as a properly matched chain and freewheel.

Another visual tip-off to narrow chains is their flush chain pins. The ends of these pins barely protrude beyond the surface of the chain's outer links. The extra side clearance the flush pins provide allows the narrow chain to settle down onto the teeth of an "ultra" freewheel's cogs without interference from each cog's neighbors. If you ever try a standard-width chain on a narrow freewheel, you'll see firsthand how neces-sary that clearance is: the standard-width chain won't be able to engage any of the cogs!

## When to Service Your Chain

There are three reasons to service your chain: dirt buildup, poor shifting, and component changes.

Dirt can have several harmful effects. Mixed with the oil often found on bike chains, it can permanently stain clothing. The same mixture also greatly accelerates chain, sprocket, and derailleur pulley wear. Finally, dirt trapped between chain links and pins can degrade your bike's shifting ability by reducing the chain's flexibility.

Do you ever find yourself over-shifting your rear derailleur almost to the next cog to complete rear shifts and reducing pedal pressure to finish front shifts? These problems can be caused by a chain that has too much lateral, or sideways, flexibility. Although it's often called chain "stretch," the problem is not caused by actual lengthening of the chain's steel links, but rather by wear on the chain pins and bushings. As the chain wears, or "stretches," the distance between its chain pins increases. This condition won't cause problems as long as the sprockets on which the chain works wear at the same rate.

Unfortunately, chains usually wear faster than sprockets. When that happens, the chain links may no longer be able to settle down snugly over the sprocket teeth and you may experience chain skip. It's even more likely to occur when you replace an old chain but not its matching freewheel. Chain skip can also occur on relatively unworn equipment if you keep putting wheels with different freewheels into service with the same chain. For example, if you're using an Italian chain/freewheel combination on your bike and you buy another set of wheels, put an Italian freewheel on the second rear wheel, too.

If your bike begins to skip in a gear, check first to see if your chain is excessively dirty or has a tight link. That's a joint in the chain that doesn't bend easily and, consequently, doesn't run through the rear derailleur or settle onto the cogs easily. To find a tight link, watch your rear derailleur's jockey cage closely while you turn the crankset slowly backward. A tight link won't lie snugly on the pulleys.

If neither of those causes is present, and your bike skips in only one gear, replace the offending freewheel cog. If it skips in more than one gear, weigh the cost of replacing the individual cogs against the cost of a new freewheel.

The freewheel as a unit is frequently cheaper than a set of replacement cogs. If your bike skips in all gears and your chain is old, you may need a new chain instead of a new freewheel.

Even if your bike isn't skipping in any gear, it's worth checking your chain periodically to make sure that you're not causing excessive wear on your freewheel or crankset by riding with a "stretched" chain. To check your chain, lean your bike against a wall or some other object that will hold it upright and immobile. Tension the chain by pressing lightly on the right pedal while you hold a 12-inch ruler up to the top half of your chain. On a new chain, 12 full links measure exactly 12 inches long. When the same number of links measures $12\frac{1}{8}$ inches, replace the chain.

The final reason for working on your chain is to achieve correct chain length after component changes. The changes that may affect chain length include the replacement of your freewheel with one that has a different range of cogs, the installation of a wider range or triple chainring crankset, and a change in rear derailleurs.

A general rule for chain length is that there should be enough chain to permit shifting onto the largest freewheel cog while also on the largest chainring. This will prevent you from damaging your derailleurs in the event you unintentionally shift into this normally unused combination. With some triple cranksets that have a "granny" or small inner chainring, this may mean that the derailleur will double over onto itself when your chain is on the smallest chainring and any of the outer, or smaller, freewheel cogs. However, it's considered acceptable practice to use the granny chainring only with the three largest inner freewheel cogs. In those positions the rear derailleur shouldn't double over onto itself.

Modifying your chain length provides you with the opportunity to use those seemingly useless scraps of chain you had left over from your last chain installation. Don't throw away any short lengths of new or usable chain until you have a substantial collection. You never know when you're going to need to lengthen a chain or replace a tight, damaged, or broken link. Smart touring cyclists carry a few links and a chain tool along on their journeys—if you have a chain mishap far from help, you usually have to repair only one or two links, not an entire chain.

## "Breaking" Chain

If your bike has ⅛-inch chain, that chain can be disconnected, or "broken," at its special master link. Use a small screwdriver or a pair of needle-nose pliers to pry off the spring clip, then pull off the outer link on that side of the chain. Next, slide either end of the chain off one of the exposed pins of the master link. Reverse the procedure to put an ⅛-inch chain together.

There is a new type of master link that needs no tool to be taken apart. You simply bend the chain sideways at this link to spread the pins a little further apart. In that position the inner plate of the link can be slipped off the ends of the pins, allowing the chain to be broken. You may have to loosen the rear wheel of the bike to get the slack you need to give the chain lateral flex. Otherwise, it is a very simple and quick procedure. The plate is replaced in the same manner in which it is taken off.

The master links found on single-speed coaster-brake bikes and 3-speed bikes are slightly fatter than the rest of the links in the chains. That helps you spot them when you want to take them apart. This size difference would create problems if found on a ³⁄₃₂-inch, or derailleur, chain. It would lead to chain snags on the front derailleur cage and the rear derailleur pulley. That's why master links have traditionally not been used on these chains.

Therefore, if your bike has ³⁄₃₂-inch chain, you will probably need what is commonly referred to as a "chain tool" in order to break and reassemble it. Buy an inexpensive, screw-type chain tool for at-home maintenance. It isn't as fast as the plier-type tool most shops use, but it's lightweight and less costly. Never go on an extended tour without one of these tools. If your bike has a Shimano Uniglide chain, make sure you get a chain tool that's compatible with the shape of its links.

Any chain tool works by pressing a chain pin almost all the way out of a link. The object is to have the inside end (i.e., the end nearest the bike) of the pin protrude a little on the inside of the outer plate of the link (i.e., the plate nearest you when you face the chain). If you've done it right, you'll have to grab the chain on either side of the link you're breaking and bend it a little to wedge the link apart. It's worth the aggravation to get it right; later, that little bit of pin will help hold the two ends of the chain together while you get the chain tool aligned to press the pin back in.

If you're using a screw-type chain tool, take the time to unscrew the tool and periodically check on your progress before you've gone too far and pressed the pin all the way out of its link. Once the pin is out, that link is no longer ser-

*Photo 7-2: The Rivoli chain tool is an inexpensive device for breaking a chain, which also provides a method for loosening a stiff link, though that can be done simply by flexing the link with the fingers.*

viceable and should be removed by breaking the chain at the second pin from the one you just overdid. Press it out the way you would have liked to have done the first one and replace the damaged link from your supply of extra links!

You will note that our description assumes that you will break the chain by pressing the chain pin out toward you, rather than the other way around. This may seem a bit awkward, but if you do it this way, when you're ready for the more difficult task of rejoining the chain ends, you'll be working on the pin from your side of the chain instead of the hard-to-reach back side.

Chain tools do their job all right if used carefully. Still, the job of breaking a derailleur chain is a lot easier if it has a master link. Two types, the Super Link II and the Shimano Link Lock, have been developed specifically for derailleur

applications. Both of these masters work exceptionally well. If you have to break your chain frequently, you might consider installing one of them.

The Super Link II uses a thin metal clip permanently attached to one link pin to hold the two halves of the link together. This locking clip can be unfastened with the aid of a coin or a small screwdriver. The Shimano Link Lock is opened by placing its inner and outer links at a 90-degree angle to one another. This allows a special link pin to be removed, separating the links.

## Cleaning and Lubricating Chains

After you remove your chain from your bike, immerse it in a solvent, such as a commercial degreasing/cleaning

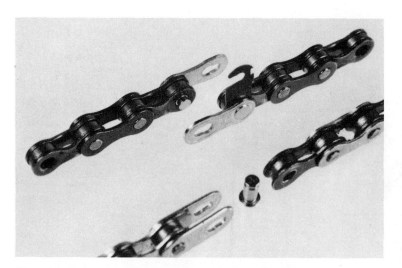

*Photo 7-3: Two master links made for derailleur chains are Shimano's Link Lock (bottom), which uses a loose pin and an oversized plate to lock its two sections together, and R.L.L. Ltd.'s Super Link II (top), which uses a thin clip to hold its two parts together. The latter comes in two models: one for standard-width, the other for narrow-width chains.*

fluid or kerosene. Pour enough solvent into the container to cover the chain. If it's particularly dirty, let the chain soak a while to float off the worst of the dirt. Then, if you have an extra container, carefully pour off the upper, cleaner layers of solvent and leave the grit from your chain behind. You don't want to force that grit into the inner bearing areas of your chain while you finish cleaning the chain with a small brush.

When you're done cleaning with the solvent and brush, dry the chain thoroughly with an old rag and hang it somewhere to dry. Don't try to lubricate the chain until all the cleaning solvent has evaporated.

Most people prefer to lubricate their chain while it's on their bike. If that is true with you, your next step is to reassemble your chain on your bike. If you're cleaning and lubing several chains at once or simply prefer to do it off the bike, hang each chain from a finishing nail or some kind of coat hanger hook so you can work on them easily.

There are many specialized chain lubricants available that consist of a light lubricant in a volatile carrier and that are usually applied from an aerosol can. Because they end up dry to the touch, these lubricants attract and hold a lot less road dirt on the chain than lubricants like motor oil that remain moist. Applying them over a relatively new chain and wiping the chain off before the solvent dries will reduce dirt pickup on the new, and undoubtedly heavily lubricated, chain while maintaining good lubricating properties.

You can also use the same type of spray lubricants to help minimize the number of times you have to remove your chain for cleaning. Spray a wet coat of lubricant on the chain and wipe away the excess and whatever dirt you can. From time to time, you will still need to thoroughly clean and relubricate your chain or replace it. But this type of treatment can help you stretch out the time between major cleanings.

If you've thoroughly cleaned your chain, spray lubricants may not suffice. If your chain squeaks, apply a light coat of bicycle oil or an oil-based chain lubricant to the chain. Wipe it as clean as possible and then maintain the chain with your spray lubricant until you give it another thorough cleaning.

Whatever you do, don't use 3-in-1 oil: it's vegetable based, which means it will gum up your chain, and it doesn't protect against wear as well as a lubricant that is mineral-oil based.

## Reassembling a Chain

Run the end of the chain without the pin sticking out (remember, the pin should protrude toward your side of the bike) through the rear derailleur cage, over the freewheel, through the front derailleur cage but not over the chainring teeth, around the bottom bracket, and back to the other end of the chain. If you do place the chain over the chainring at this point, there will be tension in the chain and you may find it difficult to keep the two ends of the chain together while you attempt to rejoin them.

Wedge the inner link end of the chain into the outer link end—the little bit of pin protruding inside the outer link should hold the two ends together. Use your chain tool to press the pin back through the links until the pin protrudes equally from each side of the outer link. At this point the newly rejoined link will be tight. There are two ways to free it.

First, if your chain tool has an alternate position for holding the chain, unscrew the tool enough to move the chain into the other position. There the chain is held in place by its inner link instead of its outer one. That means that if you press on the pin just a little more, the outer link will be free to move away from the inner link, freeing the chain.

The second, cruder method involves grabbing the chain firmly on either side of the tight link and bending it sideways, back and forth a few times. If the link doesn't free up, bend the chain again a little harder. Don't overdo it or you may permanently bend the chain.

Once your chain is back on your bike, take the time to wipe it off occasionally and lubricate it when it starts to look "dry." Regular preventive maintenance will reduce the number of times you have to go to the trouble of a major cleanup. It will also help you maintain good shifting and minimize the number of chain stripes you end up wearing. Once you discover how nice it is to have a clean, smooth-running chain, you will never take this valuable part of your bike for granted again.

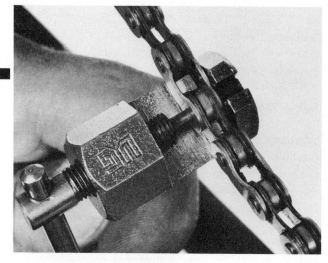

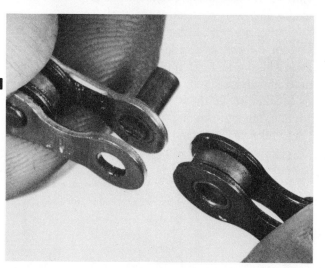

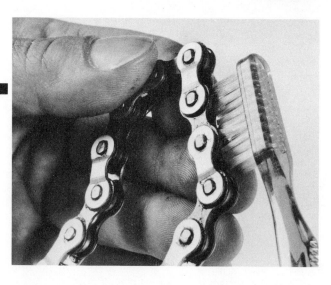

The chain is a hardworking component of the drive train, a part whose smooth functioning is critical to the overall efficient operation of the bicycle. Yet the chain may also hold the honor of being the one component on a bicycle that gets dirtier than all the rest. It should come as no surprise then that the primary maintenance needed to keep a chain operating well for a long time is to give it frequent cleaning and lubrication. It is especially important to wipe down the chain and spray it with a lubricant after it has been subjected to puddles of muddy water or a drenching rain.

To really clean a chain thoroughly, you need to remove it from the bike. Since most chains found on derailleur bikes are not equipped with master links, the customary method of removal involves the use of a special tool to break one of its links. Bike shops use a tool with pliers-type handles, but less expensive tools are available that work quite well.

To break a chain, you may find it helpful to first slip it off of the front chainrings to remove tension from the chain. Some people like to keep tension on the chain to break it—the choice is up to you. Wind the center rod of the chain tool back far enough for a link of chain to slip into the slot provided for it, then screw the rod forward against the rivet. (Photo 1) Make sure the rod and rivet are properly aligned, then continue to wind the rod forward to push out the rivet.

When the rivet appears to be most of the way out of the link, remove the tool and see if the link can be broken. If not, replace the tool and drive the rivet farther out. But be careful. Stop when the rivet end against

which you are pushing is still visible on the inside of the outer plate. (Photo 2)

A rivet that is pushed all the way out of a chain link can be put back in. But the process is so difficult that it is simpler to move the tool to the next rivet and work on it, completely removing and discarding the first link.

After breaking the chain, pull it off the front and rear sprockets and soak it in a can of solvent. Once the grease and grime have begun to loosen, use a brush to clean inside the bearing areas. (Photo 3)

Wipe the chain off with a clean rag and hang it up until all the solvent has evaporated, then reassemble it on the bike. Line up the parts of the broken link and use the chain tool to force the rivet back in. If the rejoined link is stiff, flex it back and forth sideways to get it to loosen up.

Now take your oil can or aerosol spray can with a thin nozzle and direct some lubricant into the bearing areas of each link. (Photo 4) When the entire chain has been lubricated, wipe off the excess with a clean rag. Oil left on the surface of the chain will only attract more dirt.

Chains on juvenile bikes and 3-speed bikes have master links that make removal fairly simple. One type of master link has a clip that must be pried loose with a screwdriver. A newer type has a plate held between two special grooved rivets. To remove it, you simply bend the chain sideways to move the tips of those two rivets closer together. (Photo 5) Once the plate is out of the grooves, it can be slipped off by hand. (Photo 6) The link then comes apart easily. It is fastened back together just as easily. ▲

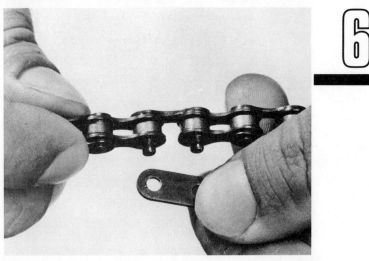

# 8 GEAR SHIFT LEVERS

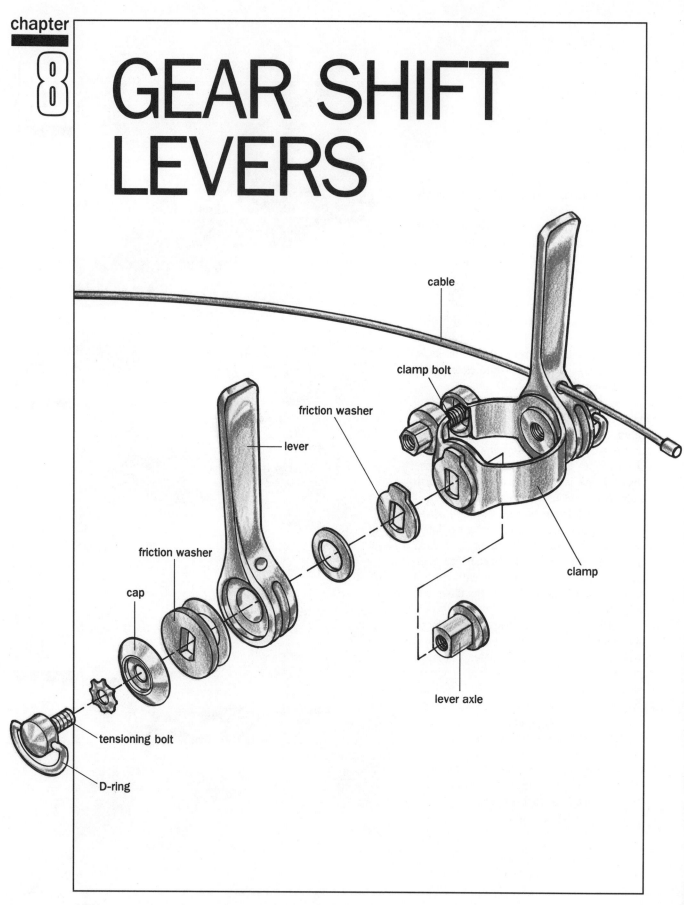

cable

clamp bolt

friction washer

lever

friction washer

clamp

cap

lever axle

tensioning bolt

D-ring

Shift levers are your link to the derailleurs and the gearing of your bicycle. On a standard 10-speed bicycle the shift levers can be mounted in three different locations: the down tube, the stem, or the handlebar ends. All-terrain bicycles mount the shift levers on the tops of the handlebars, near enough to the hand grips to allow gears to be shifted with the thumbs while the hands remain on the bars. That's why these levers are called "thumb shifters." Three-speed bicycles also use a type of thumb shifter, one that has three distinct positions rather than being infinitely variable like the shifters found on ATBs.

Despite differences in size, shape, and location, all shift levers have much in common. On a 3-speed bike, the single shift lever is connected by cable to a gear system housed inside the rear hub. Bikes of five speeds or more have one or two shift levers, each connected by cable to a derailleur. Moving these shift levers back and forth tensions or relaxes the cables, moving the derailleurs so that they can shift the chain from one cog or chainwheel to another to produce the various gears of the bike.

Since derailleurs are spring-loaded, they will always move quickly to the most relaxed position unless restrained by the shift levers. Thus, shift levers on derailleur bikes are equipped with friction washers to enable them to resist the tension of the springs and hold the derailleurs in whatever gear you have selected. A derailleur shift lever achieves this tension resistance through the use of friction washers and, in some cases, by means of a special ratcheting system.

## Choosing the Best Location for Shift Levers

Anytime there is a choice on where to put something on a bike there will always be differing opinions on why you should or should not select a particular location. This is certainly the case with shift levers.

The stem is the popular choice for locating shifters on most 10-speed bicycles that cost less than $250. The reason people want their levers on the stem is that they perceive stem-mounted levers to be easier to use than down-tube–mounted levers. While it is true that stem-mounted levers are easier to reach, they are actually a bit more difficult to use than those mounted on the down tube. Why? Because you must be sitting fairly upright and actually have to twist your body to pull on a stem-mounted lever. When you sit upright you raise your center of gravity, making yourself less stable; and when you twist your upper body, this contributes further to your state of instability. Any two-wheeled vehicle is inherently unstable; there is no need to add to the problem when it can be avoided. Also, stem-mounting produces a sharp bend in the cable as it runs from the shifter to the down tube. This bend makes shifts a little less precise than they would otherwise be.

The down tube is the most popular choice for the lever position on dropped handlebar bikes. When you go to shift you reach down, lowering your center of gravity and thereby actually increasing your stability. Also, the cable runs are very direct and make very positive shifts. Moreover, many down tube shift levers are designed to mount on brazed-on bosses. These fittings are actually part of the frame and can't slip or break like regular band clamps. The bosses make the frame look very clean.

Bar end shifters have the longest cable runs of the three popular positions and have the slowest shifting of the three choices. But since you never have to take either hand off the handlebars to shift, this type of shifter has less effect on your steering than the others. Bar end shifters are very popular among touring and tandem riders, since the weight of these bicycles can make them difficult to control with only one hand.

The bar top thumb shifters used on all-terrain bicycles have the same long cable drawback as bar end shifters, but the need to keep your hands on the handlebars continuously when riding an unpaved dirt path is all too obvious.

## Basic Shifter Designs

There are two basic designs of shift levers, the friction type and the ratcheting type. The friction-type lever employs several friction washers to prevent the derailleur from moving in response to the pressure from the spring in the derailleur body. The ratcheting shift lever resembles the friction type in its dependence on friction to hold the shift lever from moving in reaction to the spring. But it has an added feature, a

*Photo 8-1: Ratcheting shifters (top) contain parts similar to those found in friction washer shifters (bottom), along with ratcheting devices that help equalize the effort needed to shift up as well as down.*

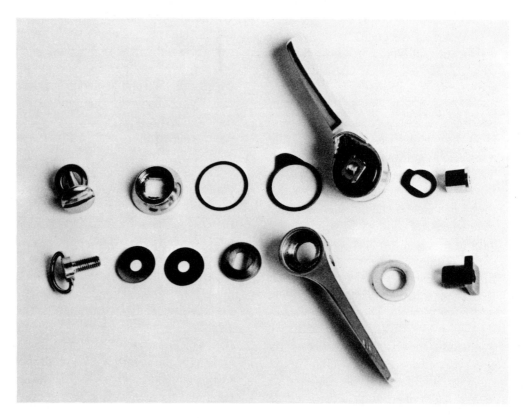

built-in ratcheting device that allows you to move the lever backward, shifting into lower gear without having to overcome the resistance of the friction washers. The idea behind this design is to equalize the force needed to move the lever in either direction.

Technically speaking, the ratcheting system is an advance over the simple friction system. However, both types of levers are available in different levels of quality, so we cannot simply say one type is always better than the other. A top-quality friction washer lever works quite well and is to be preferred over an average or low-quality ratcheting lever.

## Factors Affecting Lever Performance

The most important factors that affect lever performance are the length of the lever and the diameter of the wrap-up barrel. The longer the lever or the smaller the wrap-up barrel the more leverage you get, but also the longer the arc through which the end of the lever must move. The shorter the lever or the larger the diameter of the wrap-up barrel the less leverage, and thus also the shorter the length of the throw. However, the force required to move the lever a given distance increases along with the diameter of the barrel or the shortening of the lever.

Most shift levers are designed to work with derailleurs manufactured by the same company. They are designed to be used as a set, the front derailleur, the rear derailleur, and the two shift levers. You should try to maintain these sets. If you change to a different type of lever, it will affect, for better or worse, the way your derailleurs shift.

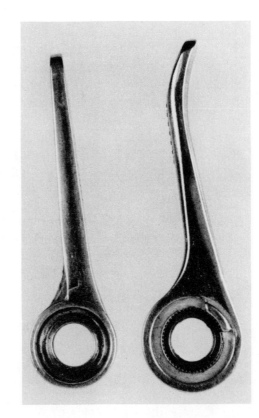

Photo 8-2: Shift levers differ not only in length, but also in the size of their cable wrap-up barrels. Therefore, it is wise to use levers designed to work in tandem with your particular derailleurs.

Shift levers do not ordinarily require much maintenance. The most common problem people have with them is allowing them to loosen and then losing parts. If your levers do not work well, chances are they are mismatched to your derailleurs or they are simply poor in quality. No amount of servicing will remedy these problems. Replacement is the only solution.

## Removing Shift Levers from a Bike

Most shift levers are either held on the stem or down tube of the bike by means of removable clamps or they are fastened to brazed-on bosses on the down tube. The removal method is similar for all these levers. First release the shift cables from the front and rear derailleurs by loosening the cable anchor bolts on both. If the levers are clamped on the bike, loosen and remove the clamp nut and bolt. Gently bend the clamp wide enough to clear the down tube or the stem and remove it.

Using a screwdriver—or your fingers if the tensioning bolt has a D-ring for you to grip—loosen the tensioning bolt. The tensioning bolt is the part that holds the lever in place on the clamp. Gently wiggle the shift lever and pull outward, until it and the washers on both sides of the lever come off the fitting, or the braze-on boss, depending on the way it is mounted. Make either mental or written notes on the order of the parts so you will be able to put the lever back together later.

### Handlebar End Shifters

Release the shift cables from the front and rear derailleurs by loosening the cable anchor bolts on both. On one side of the shift lever body (i.e., the part sticking out from the end of the bar) there is a screwdriver slot in the end of a bolt. Insert a screwdriver and unscrew the bolt. Once the bolt is free pull the shift lever away from the body. Remove the lever by pulling the cable all the way out of the housing.

Behind the lever, inside the body, you will see a fitting for an Allen wrench. Insert a wrench of the proper size and turn it counterclockwise. After one or two turns the expander should be loose enough for you to pull the lever body out of the handlebars.

### Thumb Shifters

Three-speed thumb shifters are very simple to work with. If they don't work, replace them; there are no user-serviceable parts inside. The cable can be replaced by releasing it at the hub, freeing its upper end from the catch in the lever, and pulling it out. You may have to use a small screwdriver to lift a catch plate on the lever in order to do this.

ATB thumb shifters are similar to regular down tube shift levers. There are many kinds and the exact construction varies from manufacturer to manufacturer. The lever is held on by a tension bolt. You must remove this bolt to release the cable and remove the lever. Once the lever is off, the clamp can be removed or repositioned. Some thumb shifters do not require that the lever be removed in order to adjust the shifter's position.

## Servicing Shift Levers

Take the lever apart and clean all its parts with a safe solvent. Use alcohol on any parts made of plastic. Alcohol may be adequate for the metal parts as well. Allow all parts to dry before reassembling the lever.

When you reassemble the shift lever, only the metal-to-metal surfaces get any lubrication. The nylon washers used in shift levers are normally self-lubricating, and grease or oil will make them too slippery. Remember, the main purpose of these washers is to generate friction, so you don't want them to be too slick.

If the reason you are working on your shift lever is because it slips all the time, you may need to replace its washers. Check with your local bike shop to see if washers for your particular lever are available.

If you can't find new washers, there are a few things you can do to make the old ones work better. To start with, you can turn the washer upside down and see if it works better that way. You can also rough up the surface of the washer with sandpaper to eliminate some of its slickness. Finally, you can fit a regular flat washer over the old washer.

# Installing
## Clamp-On Levers

If you are replacing an old lever, reassemble the lever parts on the clamp in the same order they were removed. Now gently bend the clamp wide enough to slide it around the down tube or the stem.

Insert and tighten the clamp nut and bolt on the stem or the down tube. Position a stem-mounted shifter assembly so that the tops of the levers are just a bit higher than the top of the stem. Position down tube shifters so that they are located at the point where your hand naturally falls when you are sitting on the bicycle. Some frames will have a little stop to prevent the shifter from slipping down the frame. If you see one of these stops, set your shifter against it.

Reattach the shift cables to the front and rear derailleurs by pulling the cable taut and tightening the cable anchor bolts on both. If you are installing new derailleur cables, shift the derailleurs several times, then recheck the cable tension. These first few shifts may cause the new cable to stretch, requiring you to loosen the anchor again, take up the slack, and retighten it.

# Installing
## Braze-On Levers

Gently slide the shift lever and the associated washers back on the bosses in the same order as they were removed. Using a screwdriver or your hand as appropriate, retighten the tensioning bolt.

Reroute the shift cables to the front and rear derailleurs and tighten the cable anchor bolts on both. If you are installing new derailleur cables, shift the derailleurs several times to recheck the cable tension. If the cable stretches, loosen the anchor bolt, take up the slack, and retighten it.

# Installing
## Handlebar End Shifters

If you are installing handlebar end shifters for the first time, you will also have to install the cable housing. There are three ways to route the cable housing.

**1.** Externally with a major loop. The cable housings run from the bar end shifter along the bottom of the bar until the bar turns up toward the brake lever. Here the cable stops following the bar and loops out and around to the cable stop on the down tube.

**2.** Externally with no loop. The cable housings run from the bar end shifter along the bottom of the bar and turn up toward the brake lever. They follow the shape of the bar, staying on the bottom side, until they exit from under the tape about 1½ to 2 inches from the stem and loop down to the clamp on the down tube.

**3.** Internally. Some people prefer to run the gear cables inside the handlebars so they do not feel them when they grip the bars. Before the cables can be routed in this way, the bars have to be drilled to allow each cable housing to enter the bar a couple of inches from where the housing butts against the shifter and exit 1 or 1½ inches from the stem.

Before you pick the third method, there are a couple of things to take into account. First, if you weigh more than 160 pounds or your handlebar does not have a reinforcing sleeve over the center section, the unit simply should not be drilled. The drilling will weaken it too much. Second, the holes need to be drilled at a place and at an angle that will minimize bending of the cable housing. The holes will also need to be smoothed up after the drilling. In short, this is one of those jobs that's best left to a professional. When properly done, the internal routing of cables looks nice and functions well. However, because of the difficulties and drawbacks posed by the technique, it is not often done anymore.

All three routes for the gear cables require that the handlebar tape be wrapped after the cable has been run. When running the cable externally the cable housing can be held in place with a piece or two of electrical tape to make it easy to wrap the handlebars.

Some people like to cut a short section off the end of the bar to compensate for the extra length that is added by the shifter body. If you decide to do this, make the piece removed the same length as that added by the body of the shifter, so you will end up with bars of the same overall length as before.

When you are ready to install the shifter, insert the shifter body into the end of the handlebar and tighten the expander. (The expander is located inside the body.) You will see an Allen key fitting. Insert the proper Allen key and turn it clockwise. After one or two turns

the expander should be tight. Make sure that the body is oriented so the lever moves vertically rather than off at some odd angle.

If the cable housing has not already been installed, install it now so that the opening of the housing lines up with the hole in the housing stop on the body of the shifter.

When both the shifter body and the cable housing are attached to the bar, run the cable through the shift lever, then through the hole in the body and on through the cable housing. Fit the lever in place on the shifter and insert the lever pivot bolt through one side of the shifter body, through the center of the shift lever, and on through the other side of the shifter. Thread the nut onto the end of the pivot bolt and tighten.

Route the cables to the front and rear derailleurs. Run the cable ends through the anchor bolts, pull them taut, and tighten the nuts to hold them secure.

If you are installing new derailleur cables, shift the derailleurs several times to give them their initial stretch, then check the cable tension. If the cables stretched, loosen the anchor nuts, pull them taut again, and reanchor them.

## Final Words of Advice

If you have trouble shifting because a lever is too easy or too hard to move, the problem can usually be solved simply by adjusting the tensioning bolt. Those nuts fitted with a D-ring can easily be adjusted while you are riding your bike. If that doesn't solve the problem, try taking the lever apart, cleaning, and reassembling it. Only when these approaches fail should you consider buying a new set of levers.

Modern shift levers come in various shapes and designs. The handles on some are rough, while others are polished very smooth. Some have an aerodynamic look, others are plain and ordinary. But despite the many levels of quality and price to be found among shifters on the market today, most shift levers are quite reliable, especially when matched with the derailleurs for which they were designed. With proper adjustment and occasional cleaning, your shifters should last a very long time.

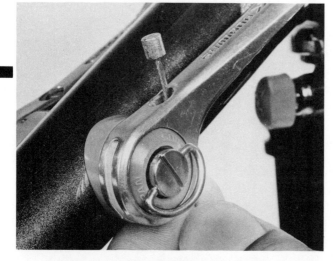

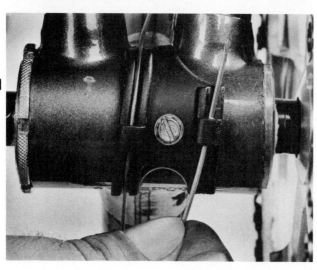

A gear shift lever on a derailleur bike is an assembly of several separable parts. Unfortunately, it is not always easy to determine how a dismantled lever assembly goes together simply by looking at all the parts. For this reason, it is very important to pay close attention to the arrangement of parts while you disassemble a lever, so you will be able to put them back together correctly later.

Fortunately, when you buy a new set of levers they will already be assembled. Braze-on–type levers will come attached either to braze-on bosses or to plastic facsimiles. You will have to unbolt the lever assembly from the substitute boss in order to attach it to the boss brazed to the bicycle frame, but you can hold the internal parts of the lever together during this process to simplify the installation.

Fit the lever unit on its braze-on boss, making certain all parts go on in the correct order. Thread the tensioning bolt into the boss to hold the unit in place. (Photo 1) The head of this bolt will either be slotted to accept a screwdriver, recessed to receive an Allen key, or fitted with a D-ring for hand tightening. The proper tightness of this bolt can be set only after the gear cables are in place.

Before reinstalling an old gear cable, wipe it clean. Give the cable, new or old, a thin coating of grease before threading it through the lever. Cables are generally unhoused for most of the length of their runs, and the grease helps protect them from the elements. It also helps reduce friction in those short sections of cable housing, which may be used near one or both derailleurs.

To install the cable, push the lever as far forward as it will go and thread the cable down through it from above. Pull the cable

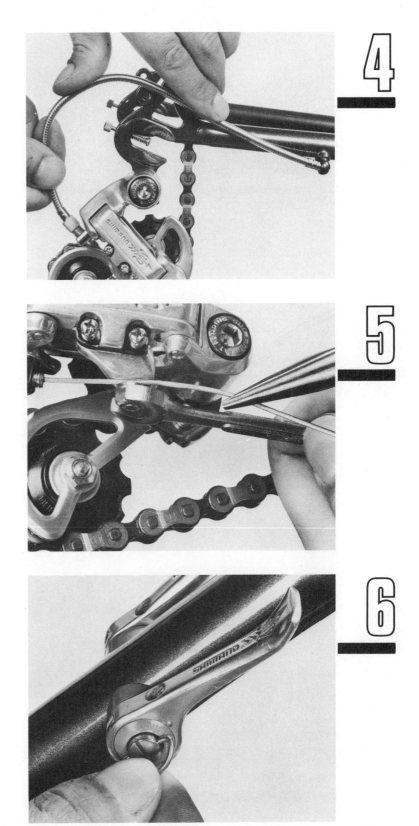

all the way through until the fitting on its end is seated in the lever. (Photo 2) Then run the cable down toward the bottom bracket.

Some bicycles are equipped with cable guides that are either brazed or clamped on the down tube just above the bottom bracket area. These guides direct open cable over the top of the bottom bracket on their way to the two derailleurs. On other bicycles, the cable guides are located on the underside of the bottom bracket. (Photo 3)

Install the cables. If a section of housing is to be used, set it in place and run the cable through it. (Photo 4) Pull the end of each cable through the anchor bolt at the derailleur that it will operate. Hold the end of the cable with a pair of pliers to keep it taut while you tighten the anchor bolt with a wrench. (Photo 5)

When new cables have been installed, move each shift lever back and forth a few times to prestretch the cables, then recheck the adjustment. If a lever must travel a ways before activating the derailleur to which it is attached, loosen the anchor bolt and make the cable more taut, then retighten the bolt. Leave about 2 inches of cable beyond the anchor bolt. Trim away the rest with a sharp pair of cable cutters.

With the cables in place, the final step is to check the tension on the lever. Check the front and rear derailleur in turn, running through all the gears. This can be done on a repair stand, but can more adequately be done while riding. If the lever is hard to pull down, there is too much tension on it. If it is easy to pull down, but wants to upshift on its own, it needs more tension. Adjust the tension by loosening or tightening the tensioning bolt as needed. If the bolt is fitted with a D-ring you can make the needed adjustment while riding the bike. (Photo 6) ▲

**1**

**2**

**3**

The handlebar tip location of bar end shifters creates special problems for the cables that connect the levers to the derailleurs. The cables must be long and flexible enough to allow side-to-side movement of the handlebars, but rigid enough to effectively operate the derailleurs. This is why the cables must be routed through housing until they reach the down tube, after which they can travel unhoused along the bicycle frame. But the housing cannot loop directly from the levers to the down tube without flexing too much when under tension. This is why the initial run of housing is usually bound to the handlebars with handlebar tape. Keeping the housing relatively rigid makes shifting gears crisper than it would otherwise be.

Begin the installation of the shifters by completely cleaning off the old tape from the handlebars. Position the cable housing beneath the bars with each section beginning flush with one tip of the bars. Decide whether you want the cable to leave the bar near the first bend or follow the bar until it almost reaches the stem, then fasten it in place temporarily with two or three pieces of electrical tape, or some other thin but sticky tape. (Photo 1)

When you have the cable housing positioned the way you want it, wrap each side of the bars with regular handlebar tape, beginning at the top near the stem and working your way around and down. (Photo 2) Tuck the final bit of tape into the end of the bar where it will be held by the shifter body.

Insert the body of the shifter into the end of the handlebar, turned so that when the lever is attached it will move in a vertical line. Also, make sure the cable hole in the lower part of the shifter body is properly aligned with the end of the cable housing.

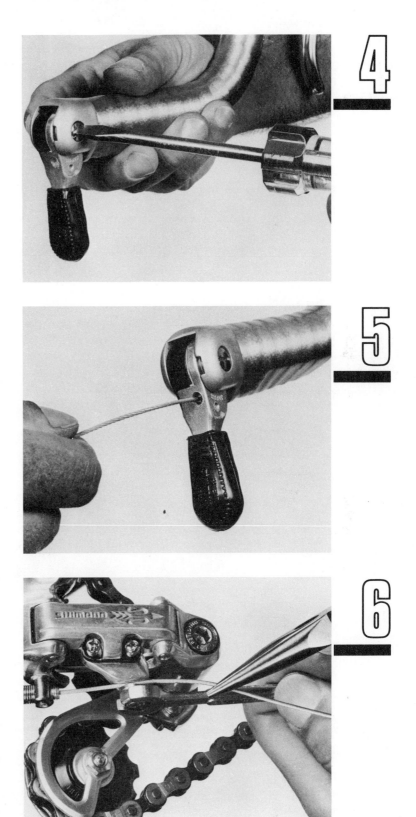

Fit an Allen wrench of the appropriate size into the bolt located inside the shifter body. Turn the bolt clockwise to tighten the expander wedge. Make sure the wedge is snug enough to prevent the shifter from twisting from side to side or slipping out of the end of the bar. (Photo 3)

Hold the lever in position between the sides of the shifter body while inserting the tensioning bolt through both. Tighten the bolt to hold the lever in place. (Photo 4)

Give the cable a thin coating of grease to help protect it from rust and to minimize friction within the housing. Push the lever down and run the end of the cable through it into the housing. (Photo 5) Work the cable all the way through the housing and route it to the derailleur for which it is intended.

Push the cable through the anchor bolt and grab hold of the end with a pair of pliers. Pull the cable taut enough to seat the fitting on the upper end inside the lever, then tighten the anchor bolt. (Photo 6)

Now check out the tension on the cable. If the bicycle is mounted on a repair stand, spin the crankarms with one hand while shifting through each gear with the other hand. For an even better test, take the bike out for a ride around the block.

Work through the entire gear sequence a few times. If this causes the cable to stretch, get out the tools again. Loosen the anchor bolt, take up the cable slack, then tighten the bolt once more. Allow a couple of inches of cable to extend beyond the anchor bolt and cut away the rest with a sharp pair of cable cutters.

Adjust the tension on the lever as well. If the lever is too hard to move up and down, loosen the tensioning bolt slightly. On the other hand, if it is so loose that it shifts under load on its own, add a little tension to it. ▲

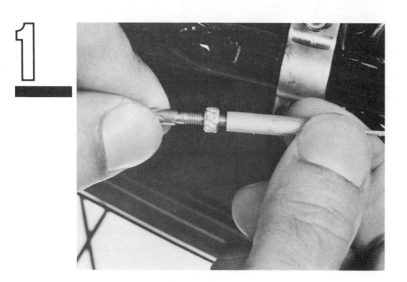

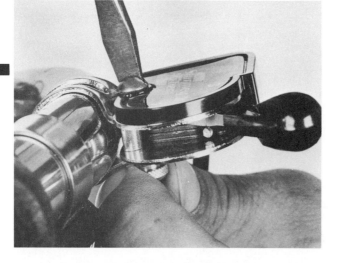

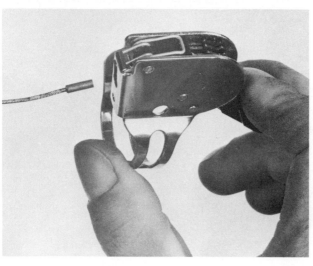

The thumb shifter on a 3-speed bicycle is generally fastened by a removable clamp to the right side of the handlebars. The shifter is connected by cable to a set of gears that are located inside the rear hub of the bicycle. When a thumb shifter of this type goes bad, it simply must be replaced. It cannot be dismantled for repair or replacement of parts.

Begin the removal of a 3-speed shifter by loosening the cable at the hub. This is done by unscrewing the fitting on the end of the cable from the fitting connected to the short length of chain that emerges from the rear hub. (Photo 1)

Now use a screwdriver to loosen the clamp that holds the shifter on the handlebars. (Photo 2) Take out the bolt, spread the clamp apart, and remove it and the shifter from the handlebars.

Free the fitting found on the upper end of the cable from the lever and slip the cable out of the shifter. There may be a catch plate in the way that must be lifted before you can disconnect the cable. Or, the entire body of the shifter may be enclosed in a plastic cover that must be slipped off before the cable can be freed. (Photo 3)

Fit the end of the cable inside the new shifter and fasten it to the handlebars, reversing the steps of the removal procedure.

Thumb shifters found on all-terrain bikes and the new ATB hybrid, the city bike, are mounted on handlebars in much the same way as 3-speed shifters. Like the 3-speed shifter, the ATB shifter is clamped to the handlebars in a location where it can quickly and easily be reached by the rider's thumb. But here the similarities between the

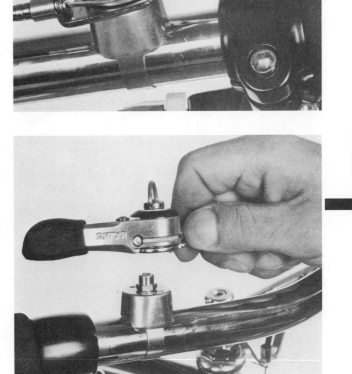

two types of shifter end, since in its manner of operation, the ATB shifter resembles the conventional stem or down-tube–mounted shifter found on skinny-tired derailleur bikes.

Like down tube shifters, ATB thumb shifters come in pairs, one for each derailleur. And they are infinitely variable in position rather than made to click into a few set positions as is true with 3-speeds. Also, like their down tube cousins, these thumb shifters use friction washers and tensioning bolts to regulate the level of friction.

One way in which ATB shifters differ from most shifters found on 10-speed bikes is that they use ratcheting mechanisms in addition to friction washers to equalize the force needed to move the lever in either direction.

To move an ATB shifter to a different location on the handlebar, turn the D-ring on the shifter body counterclockwise to unscrew the tensioning bolt. (Photo 4) When the bolt is free, lift the lever along with the bolt and washers off the shifter base. (Photo 5) Fit a wrench on the nut at the top of the base to loosen the clamp. (Photo 6) Then slide the clamp along the bar to the desired position and retighten it. Set the lever and its inner parts back on the base and retighten the tensioning bolt.

To completely remove a lever for replacement, loosen the cable anchor bolt to free the lower end of the cable and pull the cable out of the lever and the cable housing. Then follow the above procedure to remove the lever and its clamped-on base from the handlebar. ▲

# 9

# FRONT DERAILLEURS

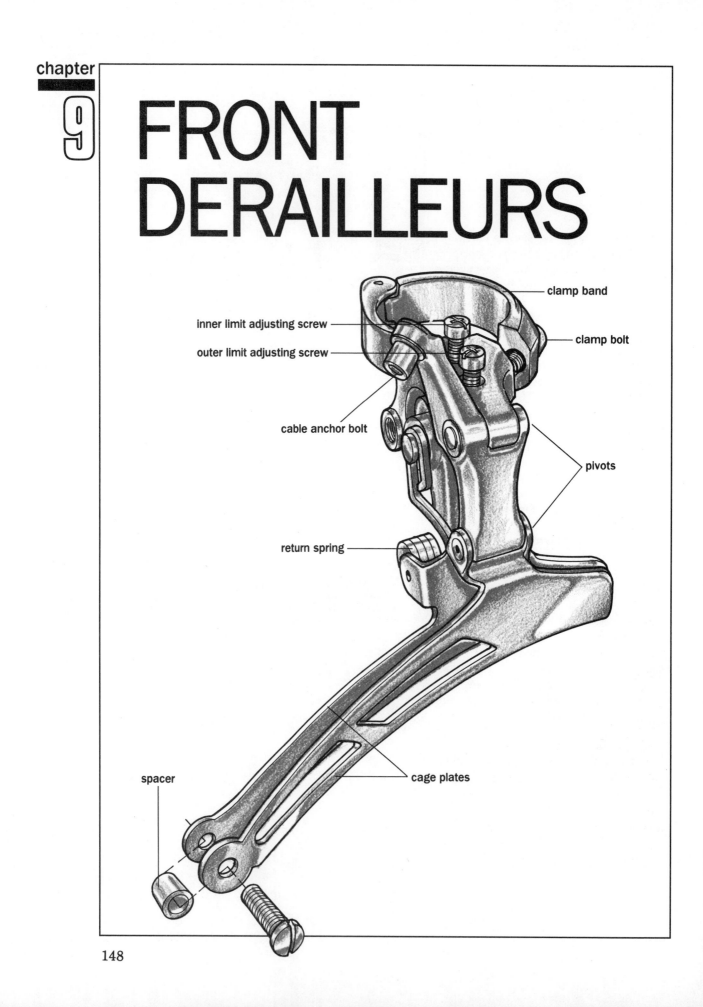

clamp band

inner limit adjusting screw

clamp bolt

outer limit adjusting screw

cable anchor bolt

pivots

return spring

spacer

cage plates

## How They Work

The front derailleur is a very simple component, but the task assigned to it is an engineering nightmare in actual execution. That task is to move the chain from one chainring to another, effectively doubling or tripling the number of gears on your bicycle.

The front derailleur must accomplish its task of moving the chain from one front sprocket to another while the chain is under tension, because it operates on the top or loaded part of the chain rather than the slack lower run like the rear derailleur.

In most cases the derailleur moves back and forth between two chainrings, or what is known as a double chainwheel set. As more and more people have sought a wider gear selection, three chainrings, or triple chainwheel sets, have increased in popularity. Triple chainwheels require a front derailleur that can move over a wider range than is necessary for a double chainwheel set. For this reason derailleurs that are perfectly acceptable for doubles may not work well on triples.

Due to the subtle touch required to initiate a quick, clean, and positive shift, the front derailleur and its operation intimidate many novice riders. This is often due to a misunderstanding of the derailleur's operating principles. Understanding these principles will help you shift smoothly and should also provide you with the knowledge needed to service the front derailleur.

Many front derailleurs are designed only to push the chain from side to side, rather than to both push and lift it. The speed at which they do this, the speed of the shift, is determined by several design factors: the height of the cage plates (the cage plates are the two horizontal plates that push the chain back and forth), the width or distance between the cage plates, the rigidity of the entire derailleur body, and the size and shape of the shift lever. The distance between the derailleur and the chainwheel teeth and the type of chain used will also affect the speed of the shift. For purposes of this discussion we will let the chain be a constant.

The width of the cage plate is important since this determines how much of the chain is pushed. The wider the cage plate, the more area there is to push against the chain. However, the derailleur designer is limited in how wide the inner cage plate can be. The outer cage plate must be positioned to clear the outer chainring by only 1 or 2 millimeters. So, if the inner cage plate is too wide, its bottom edge may strike the top of the inner chainring as you try to shift to the outer ring. Front derailleurs used on cranksets with half-step gearing, which usually only have a four to five tooth difference between chainrings, must have inner cage plates of normal width to avoid this problem. By contrast, front derailleurs designed for use on ATBs or other bikes with chainring steps of eight or more teeth often have very wide inner cage plates.

Earlier we noted that a wide cage plate has more area to push against the chain. But we could turn this around and

*Photo 9-1: Front derailleurs designed for wide-range gearing have wide inner cage plates, which can hang up on the middle chainring teeth if that chainring is almost as large as the outer one.*

say that the wider the plate the greater the area the chain has to push against. This means that as the derailleur cage gets wider its body must get stiffer to resist twisting because of the chain's extra leverage. The base and the arms of the derailleur must resist flexing or twisting during the shift. The stiffer the base of the derailleur the faster the unit will shift.

The distance between the cage plates also plays a role in the speed of the shift. The closer the cage plates straddle the chain the more control you will have on the chain and the speed of the shifts. The drawback to this is that the narrower the cage the more you will have to adjust it as you shift the rear derailleur, since as you shift in the rear, the angle of the chain changes, which can cause it to rub on the tail of the front derailleur.

The final factor affecting derailleur performance, one that many people ig-

nore, is the shape of the shift lever. The length of the lever and the diameter of its wrap-up barrel are the critical qualities in this case. The longer the lever or the smaller its cable wrap-up barrel the more leverage it provides, that is, the less energy it takes to push down. Conversely, the shorter the lever or the larger the diameter of its wrap-up barrel the less leverage it provides.

However, greater leverage has its price. The end of a long lever must move through a longer arc than that of a short lever in order to accomplish the same task. In the same way, a lever that wraps up a small amount of gear cable as it rotates must rotate farther than one that rapidly wraps up cable in order to accomplish the same shift. The shorter lever or the lever with a larger wrap-up barrel takes more energy to move, but the length of its throw is decreased, increasing the speed of the shift.

Most front derailleurs are designed to work as one part of a larger system that includes the rear derailleur and the shift levers. Generally, for best performance you should stick to a set of levers and derailleurs that were manufactured to be used together. If you change to a different lever for your front derailleur, it will affect, for better or worse, the way the front derailleur shifts.

Some newer front derailleurs are equipped with a cage designed not only to push the chain sideways but to lift it as well. This lifting capacity improves the speed of the shifts from small to large chainrings.

## Selecting a Front Derailleur

When selecting a front derailleur you must first consider the capacity you need. Most derailleurs specify the range in teeth, 10 teeth, 14 teeth, or whatever, which it can handle. This number refers to the difference in size between the small and large chainring. To find the range of your chainrings subtract the number of teeth on the small ring from the number of teeth on the large ring.

Racing derailleurs usually have ranges from 10 to 16 teeth. Sport derailleurs can often handle differences of 20 teeth, whereas wide-range touring units can go as high as 26 teeth.

These numbers provided by derailleur manufacturers are usually conservative, and if you make a small compromise you can often exceed them. The specified range is based on the calculation that if the chain length is correct and the correct rear derailleur is used the chain will not drag on the front derailleur cage when you shift to the small cog/small chainring combination. When a chain drags it does so across the lowest point of the derailleur, which is the spacer that connects the tail ends of the two cage plates.

Actually, you should not ride in the small/small combination even if your chain does not drag, since the extreme angle that this gear creates accelerates chain wear. By not shifting into this combination you can use a slightly smaller inner chainring than would otherwise be possible without experiencing chain drag. On triple chainwheel sets the tiny inner chainwheel is often usable only with the two or three innermost cogs on the freewheel for this reason.

Front derailleurs designed for racing usually have narrower cage plates than the touring units. Racing derailleurs will shift faster because of their narrow cages, but need more correction as you shift in the rear. That is to say,

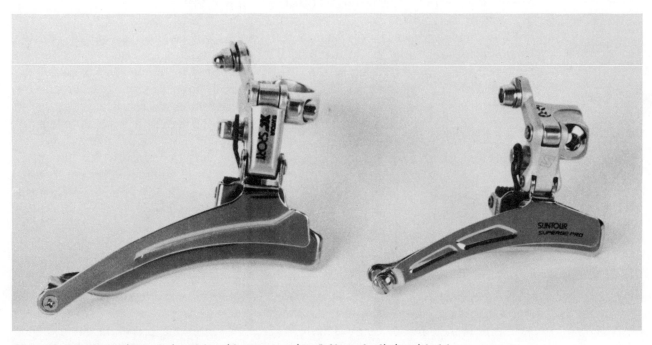

*Photo 9-2: A front derailleur designed for wide-range gearing (left) can be distinguished from a narrow- or mid-range model (right) by its long cage and wide inner cage plate.*

the front derailleur will have to be moved slightly in or out as the chain moves in and out on the rear to avoid the chain rubbing on the cage plates.

When you are selecting a new front derailleur, look at the routing required for its shift cable. Some derailleurs require an open cable routed through cable guides. Others are designed to work with cable enclosed in one or more sections of cable housing that fit between housing stops, including a stop built into the derailleur. If your bike is equipped for open cable but you have chosen a front derailleur that requires an enclosed cable, you may have to put on a cable guide clamp to make everything work. You may also have to replace the shift cable since the new routing may be longer than the old one. If you are concerned about this, check with the dealer from whom you are buying the derailleur.

Many frames today have braze-on front derailleurs. This means that there is no band around the seat tube to hold the derailleur. Instead a special fitting is permanently attached to the seat tube. If you have a braze-on fitting be sure that the derailleur you want is available in a braze-on model. Otherwise, you will have to have the braze-on fitting removed by a frame builder before you can install a clamp-on front derailleur. Removal of the braze-on, in turn, will require that your frame be repainted.

## Removing a Front Derailleur

A front derailleur is easy to remove from a bike. Start by pushing the shift lever in the direction that will make the cable go completely slack. Then use a wrench to loosen the anchor bolt that fastens the cable to the derailleur and pull the cable free. Loosen and remove the nut and bolt that hold the cage plate spacer in the tail of the derailleur so the chain can slip through. Then loosen the derailleur clamp bolt and remove the derailleur from the frame.

## Installing and Adjusting a New Front Derailleur

Remove the nut and bolt that hold the cage plate spacer and remove the spacer to allow the chain to enter the cage. Loosen and remove the clamp bolt from the new derailleur and fit the clamp around the seat tube in approximately the same position as the old unit. Install and tighten the clamp bolt just enough to keep the clamp from sliding down the tube. Fit the chain between the cage plates, then replace the spacer and bolt it into position.

Now the derailleur must be set at the right height. First, make sure the cable is not anchored, because tension on one of the lifting arms could pull the derailleur out of place. Also, be sure the derailleur clamp bolt is loose enough to allow the derailleur to be moved up and down or sideways on the seat tube.

Slip the chain off the inner chainwheel onto the bottom bracket shell to get it out of the way. Then pull the derailleur cage out against its spring until the cage is over the outer chainring. Adjust the height of the derailleur clamp so the cage clears the teeth of the outer chainwheel by 2 millimeters when it moves across it, then tighten the derailleur clamp bolt slightly.

After the proper height has been set, the derailleur still must be properly aligned. Replace the chain on the inner chainwheel of a double chainwheel set or the middle chainwheel of a triple, then shift it onto the middle cog of the rear cluster. This should make the chain parallel with the bike. Now align the front derailleur cage so that the inner cage plate is parallel to the chain. When that is done, tighten the clamp bolt fully. The derailleur is in its proper position on the bike.

The next step in the process is to adjust the cable length. Push the front derailleur shift lever forward (or for bar shifters, the direction that makes the cable most slack). Fit the end of the cable through the cable anchor bolt and pull the cable taut. Hold the end of the cable with pliers in one hand while tightening the anchor bolt with a wrench in the other. Leave about an inch of cable extending beyond the anchor bolt and cut away any extra with sharp cable cutters. If the cable is new, move the lever back and forth a few times to get some of the initial stretch out of it, then take up any slack at the anchor bolt.

You can now turn your attention to setting the inner and outer throw of the derailleur. The aim of this adjustment is to enable the front derailleur to shift easily onto both the inner and outer chainwheels without overshooting either and dumping the chain.

Shift the chain to the largest rear cog and the small chainwheel. Adjust the inner stop screw (usually the innermost or uppermost of the two adjusting screws on the body) so that the inner cage plate clears the chain by about 2 millimeters. You may need to fine-tune this adjustment later. When riding the bike, if the chain rubs when you stand and pedal hard, readjust the inner stop screw so that the derailleur cage moves a little closer to the seat tube.

Once the inner throw is set, shift to the smallest rear cog and the large chainwheel. Adjust the outer stop screw (usually the outer or lower of the two adjusting screws on the body) so that the outer cage plate clears the chain by about 2 millimeters. Fine-tune the adjustment the same way as before. But take note: In no case should the derailleur strike the crankarm as you pedal.

## Adjustments for Special Problems

If your derailleur is sluggish or shifts too far and the situation cannot be corrected with the adjusting screws, it often helps to custom-tailor the shape of the cage.

If the chain tends to overshoot the outer chainwheel, or if the derailleur shifts sluggishly from the large chainring to the small chainring, bend the nose of the outer cage slightly in toward the chain. However, do not bend it so far that the cage rubs the chain.

On the other hand, if the chain won't shift to the large chainwheel, look at the inner cage from the top. The nose of the cage plate should bend slightly in toward the chain. If it does not, then bend it, but not so far that the cage rubs the chain.

Check the cage plates from the front if you are still having problems. If the inner cage plate is not parallel to or slightly toed in toward the outer chainwheel, bend it in until it is.

Finally, make sure your shifting problem is not caused by a poorly adjusted gear cable. If your shift lever moves some distance before putting tension on the cable, there is too much slack in the cable. Push the lever all the way forward and take up the slack at the cable anchor bolt.

## Maintaining the Front Derailleur

A front derailleur has few working parts but it is important to keep the unit clean. The grit that builds up on the derailleur body eventually works its way into the bearing surfaces. Once inside, the grit acts like sandpaper and cuts into the bearing surfaces causing premature wear. This wear translates into play or slop in the mechanism, which causes the derailleur to shift poorly. Remember, stiffness is important for crisp shifting performance.

Clean the grit off the outside and out of the inner workings of the derailleur with the help of a solvent. Wipe the derailleur clean and allow all the solvent to evaporate, then lubricate the bearing surfaces with a light lubricant. Tri-Flow or Super Lube works very well for this. Spray a little of the lubricant in the openings at the ends of the lifting arms, shift the derailleur and spray a little more.

Wipe away any excess or it will quickly attract new dirt.

## Custom Derailleur Modifications

If you are happy with your front derailleur except for the fact that you must adjust it after every one or two shifts of the rear derailleur, you can modify it to make the cage a bit wider. Loosen and remove the bolt holding the spacer in the tail of the derailleur and slip a small washer between the spacer and the inner cage plate. Spreading the cage plates farther apart in this way allows the chain to move through a wider angle without rubbing.

By paying close attention to these simple but important matters—cleanliness, proper lubrication, and adjustment, you will provide your front derailleur with all the help it should need to perform its challenging task of crisply and accurately moving your bicycle's chain from chainwheel to chainwheel. The benefits in good performance will then be yours to enjoy.

A front derailleur that moves sluggishly and is difficult to shift probably has grit and grime in its few moving parts. Most likely a thorough cleaning and lubrication will dramatically improve its performance.

Lubrication of a front derailleur is most easily done with the derailleur on the bike. Leaving the derailleur in place allows you to shift it back and forth while the lubricant is being applied to its pivot areas. However, cleaning is another story. The best way to thoroughly clean a front derailleur is to remove it from the bike and soak it in solvent. Fortunately, removing a front derailleur is a simple process, one that takes only a small amount of time. First, shift the lever forward to take tension off the gear cable, then loosen the cable anchor bolt and disconnect the cable from the derailleur. (Photo 1)

The main thing that now prevents you from removing the derailleur from the bike is the chain that is trapped inside its cage. The chain can be broken with a chain tool, but a simpler solution to the problem is to remove the pin that serves as a spacer between the tail ends of the two derailleur cage plates. Unscrew the bolt that holds the spacer in place, remove the pin, and the chain will be free to slip out of the cage. (Photo 2)

When both the cable and chain are out of the way, the derailleur can be removed from the bike. Locate the bolt that fastens

the derailleur's clamp to the seat tube or the derailleur to a braze-on mount. Loosen and remove that bolt. (Photo 3) If the derailleur is attached to the seat tube by means of a clamp, spread the jaws of the clamp and remove it from the tube. (Photo 4) Soak the derailleur for a while in a small container of solvent to loosen the grit in its bearing areas. While it soaks, give the lower part of your seat tube a cleaning and polishing, especially the area normally covered by the derailleur mounting clamp.

Now use an old toothbrush or other stiff brush to loosen any grit or grease clinging to the derailleur. Rinse the derailleur in the solvent once more, then wipe it clean with a rag. Let the clean derailleur sit a little while to allow time for the solvent to evaporate from its working parts.

Fasten the front derailleur back on the bicycle in the approximate location where it was before. Then use the instructions on page 158 to properly adjust its location. When the derailleur is properly located, re-attach the gear cable to it. Squirt a little light oil or an appropriate spray lubricant into each of the derailleur's pivot points. Shift the derailleur over a little and apply more lubricant. Shift the derailleur back and forth a few times to spread the lubricant around its working parts, then use a clean rag to wipe away any excess. Oil left on outer surfaces will only attract fresh contaminants. ▲

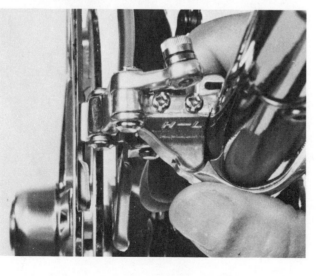

When installing a front derailleur, if the bicycle chain is already on the bike, it is not necessary to break it. Simply remove the spacer pin from the tail of the derailleur cage, drop the cage down around the chain, and replace the pin. (See photo 4 on page 159.) However, if the chain is already broken, there is no need to remove the spacer pin. Just install the derailleur, run one end of the chain through it, and rejoin the ends of the chain. If the derailleur is equipped with a clamp, take out the clamp bolt and spread the jaws of the clamp band. Fit the clamp band around the seat tube of the bike at the approximate height where it should go and replace the bolt.

Tighten the clamp bolt just enough to prevent the clamp from slipping by itself, but not so tight that it cannot be moved by hand. (Photo 1) If the derailleur is a model of the braze-on type, fasten it securely to the braze-on mount, then partially loosen the height-adjusting bolt.

Before reattaching the gear cable, set the derailleur to the right height and angle. Keep the chain out of the way during these adjustments by slipping it off the chainwheel to the inside and letting it rest on the bottom bracket.

Pull the derailleur cage out over the large chainwheel, watching the outer plate of the cage as it passes over the chainwheel teeth. Adjust the derailleur height so that the cage clears the chainwheel teeth by 2 millimeters. (Photo 2)

Let go of the derailleur cage and sight down from above. Make sure the cage is aligned parallel with the chainwheels. (Photo 3) Once both the height and horizontal align-

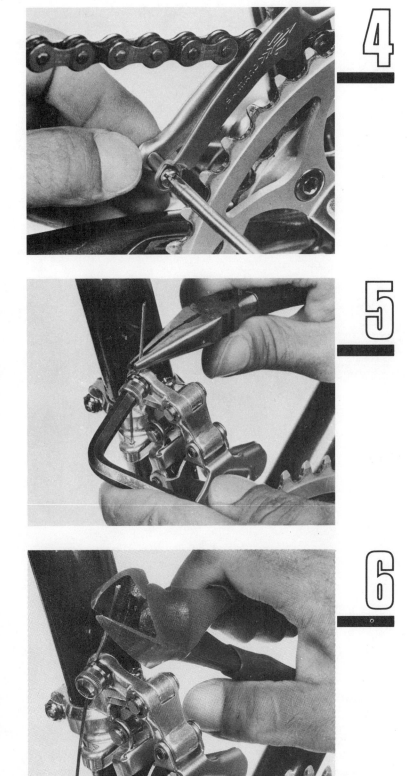

ment are set, tighten the clamp bolt to hold the derailleur in that position.

Push the chain inside the derailleur chain cage and wrap it around the small chainwheel. Fit the spacer pin back into the tail and bolt it into place. (Photo 4)

If you are installing a new gear cable, give it a thin coating of grease, then thread it through the shift lever and the cable housing and route it to the front derailleur.

Be aware that some bikes are set up for the cable to run above the bottom bracket and others below it on the way to the front derailleur. Also, note that some front derailleurs are designed to receive open cable; others have a cable housing stop and are designed to be used with a section of housed cable. If your new derailleur is not already compatible with your bike, get the person who sold you the derailleur to help you adapt it to your bike.

Run the cable through the anchor bolt on the derailleur and pull it taut. Hold the end of the cable with a pair of pliers while you tighten the anchor bolt. (Photo 5) Shift the lever position a few times to prestretch the cable, then loosen the bolt, take up any slack, and retighten.

A new gear cable will almost certainly be longer than necessary. So after installing a new cable, leave approximately 1 inch of wire extending beyond the anchor bolt and use a sharp pair of cable cutters to trim away the rest. (Photo 6)

After installing a front derailleur, check it out to make sure it is properly adjusted before riding the bicycle out on the open road. ▲

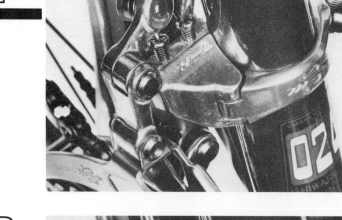

After installing a new derailleur, its range of motion must be set. Periodically, the same adjustment may need to be made to an old derailleur. If you have trouble shifting onto any chainwheel or if a full shift in either direction tends to throw the chain past the intended chainwheel, it is definitely time for an adjustment.

Begin by shifting the chain to the inside onto the small chainwheel and largest freewheel cog. Now locate the adjusting screw for setting the inner stop on the derailleur. Usually, if the screws are positioned horizontally, it is the one on the inside. (Photo 1) If they are positioned vertically, it will probably be the one on top. Set the stop so that the inner plate of the derailleur cage is held 2 millimeters to the inside of the chain.

Now shift the chain to the outside, onto the large chainwheel and the smallest rear cog. Set the other adjusting screw so that the outer plate of the cage is held about 2 millimeters outside the chain. (Photo 2)

These settings should be approximately what is needed to allow you to shift decisively between chainwheels and not be left with the chain rubbing the derailleur cage after the shift. However, this will have to be tested in actual riding situations, especially in hard, out-of-the-saddle pedaling. If there is any tendency of the chain to rub on the inside with the first setting or the outside with the second, these limits will have to be slightly expanded. But don't set them so wide that the chain can be spilled by a rapid shift.

If you are getting sloppy shifting performance with your front derailleur, look closely at its shape. Most manufacturers bend the front ends of the cage plates slightly in toward one another to create a

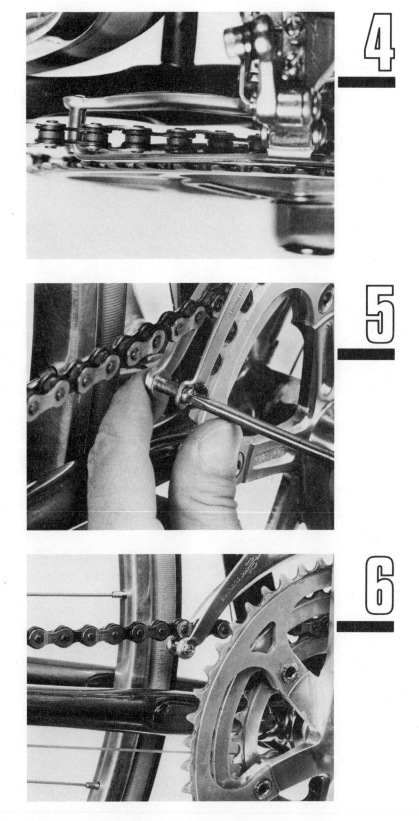

narrow nose for more authoritative shifting. If your derailleur needs its nose narrowed, take a pair of pliers and gently toe the plates in. (Photo 3)

Often, when a shift is made with the rear derailleur, the change of angle causes the chain to rub the tail end of one of the front derailleur cage plates. (Photo 4) This is especially common on a racing-style bike with a narrow derailleur cage. Such rubbing can be immediately corrected by a slight change in the front derailleur lever position and is more of an annoyance than a real problem.

However, if you want to eliminate or reduce chain rub after rear shifts you can widen the back of your derailleur cage a bit. Partially remove the bolt holding the spacer pin in the tail of the cage. Slip a small washer between the pin and the inner cage plate of the cage, then retighten the bolt. (Photo 5)

One final problem that may be encountered with a front derailleur is chain drag on the tail pin in certain gear combinations. For example, shifting the chain onto both a small chainwheel and small rear cog drops it low in the cage, which may cause it to drag. The solution is simple: don't use the chain in this gear combination. Even if no chain drag occurs, such a gear combination puts the chain at an extreme angle and should be avoided.

Chain drag may also result from a mismatch between the front derailleur and the chainrings, such as using a tiny inner chainring with a derailleur designed for a sport touring bike. (Photo 6) The solution here should be obvious: if you intend to use extra-small chainrings, equip your bike with a derailleur designed for them. No mechanical adjustment can compensate for mismatched chainrings and derailleurs. ▲

# 10 REAR DERAILLEURS

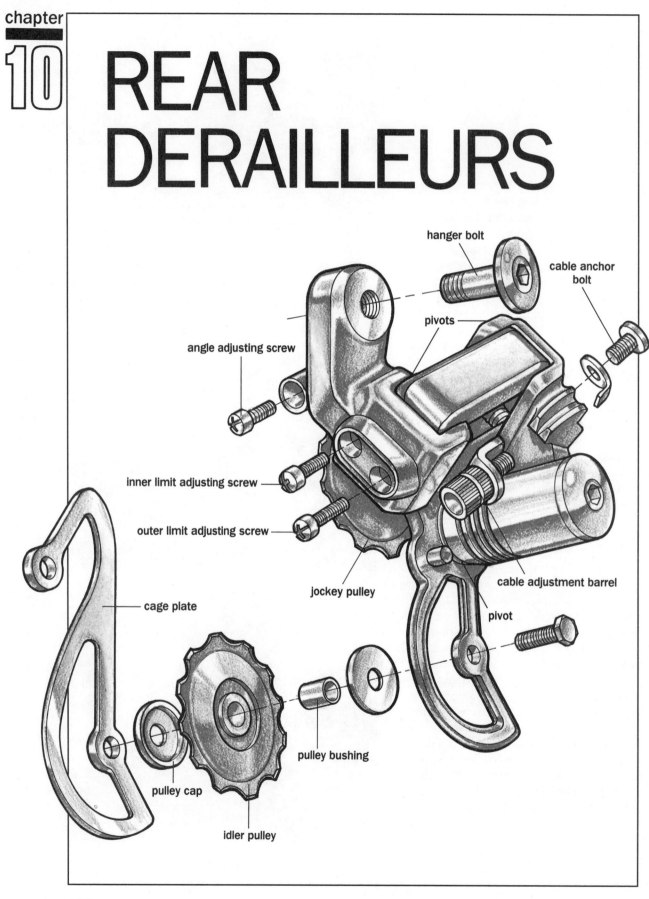

hanger bolt

cable anchor bolt

pivots

angle adjusting screw

inner limit adjusting screw

outer limit adjusting screw

jockey pulley

cable adjustment barrel

pivot

cage plate

pulley bushing

pulley cap

idler pulley

No single bicycle component is more instrumental in making riding an easy and pleasurable experience than the rear derailleur. That's due largely to the fact that it is the one component over which you have control that you use more than any other. Dangerous though it may be, you can manage to get by with poorly adjusted brakes. And if your front derailleur is hard to shift? Well, you can always stick to the smaller chainwheel. But, if you cannot depend upon a range of gears at the rear of your bike, you might as well park it and walk.

If you've ever had the unfortunate experience of riding a bike whose rear derailleur did not provide smooth, fast shifts, you know how frustrating it can be. It's almost enough to make you long for an old-fashioned 3-speed "English" bike with its predictable, though limited, gears. Fortunately, most rear derailleurs manufactured today are more than up to the task of shifting over the five or six cogs typically found on a freewheel, whether it be a racing "corncob" or a wide-range 13-34T (teeth) model.

The task assigned to the rear derailleur is, as its name implies, to "derail" the chain, to push it off of one freewheel cog and onto another. Unlike the front derailleur, which moves against the upper section of the chain, the part under tension from pedaling pressure, the rear derailleur moves beneath the freewheel cogs and pushes the chain from one cog to another at a point where the chain is under very little tension.

What tension there is on the chain during a rear shift is introduced by the derailleur itself, which is equipped with a spring to take up excess chain slack. This is necessary to ensure that the chain remains wrapped around the cogs as it shifts from one to another.

## Kinds of Rear Derailleurs

There are three categories of rear derailleurs: racing, touring, and sport. Racing derailleurs are designed for the special needs of racers, which are to be able to shift quickly and reliably. The rigors of professional racing can take their toll on derailleurs. It is estimated that a professional racer over the course of one year may shift gears on his bike more than 100,000 times, and sometimes prize money can be lost because of a single missed shift. Obviously, a good racing derailleur must be durable, dependable, and very predictable.

Touring cyclists also want durability and would like to have quick shifts but also must have a rear derailleur with the capacity to handle a wide range of gears. When carrying a load over widely varying terrain it is necessary to have a full selection of gears, especially low gears. Otherwise, the cyclist may end up pushing rather than riding the bike up a long hill.

The sport cyclist is a recreational rider, one whose needs fall somewhere between those of the racer and the tourist. Thus, the gears on a sport touring bike are usually of a wider range than those on a racer, yet narrower than those provided for a loaded tourer. Of course, it is not uncommon to see sport cyclists riding racing or touring bikes, with their specialized derailleurs, but such cyclists usually are either unable or do not know how to use the gears on these bikes to their full capacity.

If you want to replace the rear derailleur on your bike with one of better quality, go talk to a knowledgeable salesperson at your local bicycle shop. Bear in mind that even if you were to discover that most of the professional racers in the world use a particular model derailleur, that does not prove that it is the derailleur you need for your bike and your particular riding needs. In fact, a derailleur that is a hot model for racing will almost certainly turn out to be a poor choice for touring or commuting.

It is very important when selecting a new rear derailleur to remember that most models are designed to be used as part of a set, which includes a particular front derailleur and a particular type of shift levers. If you buy a new derailleur and try to use it with your old levers and front derailleur, it is hard to predict in advance how well it will work. You might be lucky and hit a happy combination, but there is no guarantee that will be the case. Generally, you are better off purchasing and using these components in the sets designed to function together.

Small as it is, even the shift lever can be critical to the proper functioning of your rear derailleur. Insignificant as they may look, levers are an integral part of the shifting system and differ in design. The greatest differences among levers are found in their respective lengths and the diameter of their cable wrap-up barrels. Here again, the particular needs of different types of riding are taken into account in the design.

As we said before, high on the need list of a racing cyclist is a derailleur that shifts quickly. Since a racing freewheel is typically fitted with cogs with very small steps in size from one to the next, the racing rear derailleur does not have to be able to push and lift the chain a long distance. It just needs to move it quickly. Similarly, the lever that activates this process does not need to be particularly long, because the longer the lever the more distance its tip must travel to complete the shift. The racer wants a lever that can be moved quickly over a very short distance to accomplish the shift. Such a lever will have a relatively large diameter barrel made to wrap up a lot of cable fast, or be fairly short, or both.

By contrast, the touring cyclist may frequently be confronted with a situation when a shift must be made into a considerably lower gear. A longer lever or one with a small wrap-up barrel will provide him with extra leverage to accomplish that type of shift. The racer is willing to sacrifice leverage for speed. He does not need a lot of leverage anyway. The tourist can do without the racer's lightning fast shifts in exchange for the certainty that when a shift must be made under load, it can be accomplished. He does not want to be caught fumbling with his shifter with a heavily loaded bike on a steep ascent.

These are the type of factors that manufacturers must take into account when they design sets of levers and derailleurs. You have to decide what your primary needs are and buy the system that best fulfills them.

## How Rear Derailleurs Work

Rear derailleurs perform two jobs, they move the chain from cog to cog and they maintain the chain tension as the amount of chain wrap on the freewheel cogs changes. Almost all presently available derailleurs can handle the chain tension, within the limits of the unit, without complaint. The really noticeable differences among various models of derailleurs lie in the area of shifting performance.

Actually, tremendous improvements in rear derailleur systems have occurred over the past two decades so that many moderately priced bikes sold today come with derailleurs that perform better than some systems used by racers in the 1960s. Overall, differences in performance in the current models are not as dramatic as in the earlier period. Before, the range in quality was excellent to awful; these days it is excellent to acceptable.

Apart from some design differences, which we will shortly mention, all rear derailleurs work pretty much in the same way: they move back and forth beneath the freewheel, shifting the chain from one cog to another. The body of the derailleur has a parallelogram form and is equipped with a spring to move it in one direction and a cable to pull it in the opposite direction. The spring is constantly pushing against the derailleur, so that when tension is completely off the cable, the derailleur moves the chain out to the smallest freewheel cog. The gear cable and shift lever must be able to overcome the resistance of the spring to pull the derailleur back in over the larger cogs.

Attached to the derailleur body is a structure called the derailleur cage. The derailleur cage is the part that encloses the chain and actually moves it from cog to cog. The cage consists of two vertical plates (cage plates) and two small rollers. The chain follows an S-path around the rollers and is positioned by them. The upper roller is called the jockey pulley and it guides the chain from one cog to the next. The lower roller is called the idler pulley and it keeps the chain tension constant. When the chain moves from one cog to a larger or smaller one, the derailleur cage pivots and moves the idler pulley forward or back to take up slack or feed out extra chain as necessary.

There are two basic derailleur body designs, the single pivot and the double pivot. The single pivot is found on many older units. In this design the derailleur body sits at a fixed angle in relation to the freewheel. The body of the derailleur stays at this predetermined angle throughout all the shifts. Only the cage changes its angle as it pivots forward and back to feed out chain or take up slack. Single pivot designs have been very popular in racing because it is easier to change a rear wheel equipped with a derailleur of this type than one of double pivot design.

A double pivot derailleur has a pivoting chain cage like the other type. But it also has a spring in the upper end of the derailleur body that causes the derailleur body to move forward as the derailleur is shifted to the smallest cogs. This forward rotation allows more of the chain to wrap around the freewheel cog for a more positive engagement between chain and cog teeth. This swinging action also allows the derailleur to move back and down lower when shifting the chain onto larger cogs. Thus a derailleur of this design has the capacity to handle a much wider range of freewheel cogs than one with only a single pivot.

The cage of the derailleur also affects the performance of the derailleur. The length of the cage contributes to the derailleur's ability to wrap up extra chain. The longer the cage the greater the capacity of the derailleur. That is why rear derailleurs made for wide-range gearing systems typically have double pivots and long chain cages.

Racing derailleurs usually have narrower cage plates than touring units. Racing derailleurs will shift faster but do not have the chain wrap capacity of touring derailleurs.

## Selecting a New Rear Derailleur

When selecting a rear derailleur you must first consider the capacity you need. Most derailleurs specify the range in teeth, 20 teeth, 30 teeth, or whatever, that they are designed to handle. This number refers to the difference between the small and large chainring plus the difference between the largest and smallest freewheel cog. To find the range of your chainrings subtract the number of teeth on the small ring from the number of teeth on the large ring. For the freewheel subtract the number of teeth on the smallest cog from the number of teeth on the largest cog. Add the two numbers together to find the number you need to know to select the proper rear derailleur.

Racing derailleurs usually have ranges from 20 to 26 teeth. Sport derailleurs can often handle differences of 32 teeth and wide-range touring units can go as wide as 40 teeth.

The specified number is usually a conservative estimate on the manufacturer's part. It is based on the possibility that you might try to use all possible gear combinations. But it is never advisable to ride with your chain simultaneously on the smallest chainring and

*Photo 10-1: Rear derailleurs made for racing (right) have short chain cages, while those made for the wide-range gearing of touring and all-terrain bikes (left) have long chain cages for greater chain wrap-up.*

the smallest freewheel cog. If you avoid this gear combination, as you should, you can probably exceed the stated range a little bit. On a triple chainwheel set the tiny third chainwheel is often usable only with the two or three innermost cogs on the freewheel for this reason.

Before purchasing a new rear derailleur, take note of the type of cable routing that it is designed to use. As we noted in the previous chapter, some derailleurs are made to function with completely unhoused shift cables, while others employ at least a short section of cable housing near the derailleur. If your bike is set up to use an open cable, but the derailleur you wish to purchase requires a section of housing, ask the component dealer for assistance in adapting the new system to your bike. If that adaptation proves difficult, then you better reconsider your choice of a new rear derailleur.

### Derailleur Mounting

Rear derailleurs mount on the bike frame in one of two ways, either with a bolt-on hanger or an integral hanger. The bolt-on hanger is the least expensive and is found on most bikes that sell for less than $300. The bolt-on hanger is held in place with a small alignment bolt and the axle of the bicycle.

The integral dropout hanger is found on most medium- to high-priced bicycles. In this case the derailleur hanger is actually an extension of the dropout. An integral hanger is usually stiffer than a bolt-on hanger, which makes for better shifting.

With bolt-on hangers you should use the hanger supplied by the manufacturer. If you are changing derailleurs and you have an integral hanger on your bicycle, check the instructions supplied with your new derailleur to see if it will work with this particular hanger. The name of the manufacturer of an integral hanger is usually stamped in the dropout. Some common names are Shimano, Campagnolo, SunTour, Gipiemme, and Tange.

Once properly adjusted, a rear derailleur that is correctly matched to a freewheel should shift well and be quite dependable. Derailleurs made these days rarely stop working because they have gone out of adjustment. The problems they develop usually arise from crashes, dirt, and misalignment. To work properly a rear derailleur must be kept clean, well lubricated, correctly aligned, and adjusted.

## Rear Derailleur Maintenance

If your rear derailleur fails to perform as well as you think it should, check first to see if it has a special problem. Bend down behind the bike and take a close look at the derailleur to see if perhaps it may have been bent. The pulley cage ought to be parallel to the centerline of the bike. If the cage tilts in toward the wheel, either the cage, the derailleur body, or the hanger (possibly even the dropout tab to which the hanger is attached) may be bent. Check all three.

Bent hangers are easy to fix with an adjustable wrench. Unbolt the derailleur and remove it from the hanger. Leaving the wheel in place, use the jaws of the adjustable wrench to straighten the hanger. If the derailleur uses an Allen wrench mounting bolt, you can leave the derailleur mounted on the hanger. Sim-

*Photo 10-2: A bent derailleur hanger can often be straightened by fitting a tool into the derailleur body and using it for leverage.*

ply insert the Allen wrench into the head of the bolt and use the derailleur itself as a lever for bending the hanger back into line.

Bent cages can be straightened with your hands. However, the derailleur body should be supported so that it does not get twisted out of shape while the cage is being bent into shape. Work carefully; you don't want to overbend the cage. Bent derailleur bodies are the most troublesome. They are difficult to straighten. That's a job best left to a mechanic in your local bicycle shop.

## Cleaning

A rear derailleur has few working parts but it is important to keep the unit clean. The grit that builds up on the outside of the derailleur body also works its way into the bearing surfaces. Once inside, the grit acts like sandpaper and cuts into the bearing surfaces causing premature wear. This wear can be seen as play or slop in the mechanism, which means poor shifting. Remember, with derailleurs stiffness is important for good performance.

A dirty rear derailleur should be cleaned before lubricating. When a bike is being ridden on a regular basis, it's a smart idea to give the chain and both derailleurs a thorough cleaning and lubrication at least once a month. To do the job properly these parts must be removed from the bike.

Begin the removal of your rear derailleur by loosening the cable clamp bolt and pulling the cable free. Then remove the chain. Here you have a choice. You can follow the traditional method of chain removal and use a chain tool to break a link. This has the advantage of being one step that makes the chain completely removable from the bike. But you can also leave the chain intact and remove the rear derailleur idler pulley. Then if you want to take the chain completely off the bike you will have to also remove the spacer from the tail of the front derailleur cage.

Once the chain and cable are out of the way, unbolt the rear derailleur from its hanger and remove the derailleur from the bike. Soak it briefly in a solvent, using a brush to clean the grit out of its working parts, then wipe it clean with a rag. Allow the solvent to dry completely before proceeding.

## Lubrication

Fasten the derailleur back on the hanger. Apply a spray lubricant, such as Tri-Flow or Super Lube, to the derailleur pivots, cage pivot(s), and the pulleys. Push the derailleur body back and forth on its spring, move any pivoting parts, and spin the pulleys after applying lubricant to help it spread to all moving parts. Once you are satisfied all bearings have been lubricated, wipe off any excess oil with a clean rag before it has a chance to attract dirt.

If you disassembled one or more of the pulleys, coat its bushing with grease before assembling. Also, put the chain back on before fastening the idler pulley if you took it off to free the chain. You should also grease the derailleur cable, especially the section that passes through the cable housing.

## Cable and Chain Adjustments

When installing a new derailleur you must first make sure the chain is the right size for your particular combination of derailleur, chainring, and freewheel. Push the shift lever all the way forward. Make sure the chain is on the smallest freewheel cog and not preventing the derailleur from springing all the way out. Loosen the cable clamp bolt at the derailleur and thread the end of the cable through. Pull the cable to remove slack; pull it taut, but not tight. While holding the cable taut with a pair of pliers, tighten the clamp bolt to secure it.

Now shift onto the largest rear cog and the large front chainwheel. The derailleur cage should be pulled forward almost as far as it is capable of traveling. Once you have done this, shift to the small cog/small chainwheel combination to see if there is any slack in the chain. If the derailleur is not near its limit in the first combination, but the chain is loose in the second, shorten the chain by removing links. Judge how many to remove by how much slack you find in the chain.

Conversely, if the chain binds because it is not long enough to fit in the large/large combination, add chain links.

You may find that you have to make a compromise between having plenty of chain for the large/large combination and avoiding excessive slack in the small cog/small chainwheel position (or the small cog/middle chainwheel on a triple chainwheel crankset).

If you have insufficient chain for the first combination and accidentally try to shift into it, you risk pulling hard on your derailleur and bending it. On the other hand, if you have too much slack in the second combination and happen to shift into it, you risk having your derailleur bend back over on itself in an attempt to take up the slack. This could cause the chain to rub against itself and be damaged. The best way to avoid these problems is to provide enough chain for the first combination and use a rear derailleur capable of handling the slack when you shift into the second combination. Switching to a rear derailleur with a wider range will also give you the freedom to switch back and forth between wheels with different freewheel cog combinations, should you desire to do so.

## Rear Derailleur Adjustments

Since the location of the wheel can affect the derailleur's performance, the place to begin your derailleur adjustment is by considering the position of your wheel in the frame. Usually, best results are obtained when the axle is centered in the dropout slots. But if you have a Simplex-type derailleur with a spring-loaded upper derailleur pivot, try moving the axle a little forward of center to improve shifting.

Once the wheel is properly positioned, set the range of motion for the derailleur. Start with the inner throw. Shift into low gear (large rear cog, small front chainwheel). Adjust the low gear adjusting screw, usually the upper or farthest to the rear of the two adjusting screws, so that the pulleys are centered beneath the sprocket. The adjustment is correct when chain noise is at a minimum and the chain shifts onto the cog without hesitating.

Now set the outer throw. Shift into high gear (small cog/large chainwheel). Adjust the high gear adjusting screw so that the pulleys are centered on the small cog and the chain shifts quickly onto the cog. If the chain doesn't shift onto the small cog easily, loosen the adjusting screw to let the derailleur move a little farther out.

Finally, if you have a SunTour derailleur with an angle adjustment screw, set the derailleur parallel to or tilted up slightly toward the chainstay.

## Installing a New Rear Derailleur

Most of what is involved in the installation of a new rear derailleur is identical to what must be done when installing and adjusting an old one after removing it for cleaning. However, some of the adjustments discussed are even more critical with a new derailleur than with an old one. The old chain length and range of motion may be adequate when the old derailleur is remounted, but will almost certainly need changing for a new model.

Chances are the new derailleur will have a cage of a different length than the old one. If so, it will be able to wrap up a different amount of chain and will thus change your ideal chain length. (You may also have to alter the length of the chain if you change the size of your freewheel cogs.) And since the body of the new derailleur may be different than that of the old one, the shift cable and cable housing may have to be lengthened or shortened to get a smooth bend where the cable goes from the chainstay stop to the rear derailleur.

## Modifications and Accessories

There are very few modifications that can be made on rear derailleurs. Some companies make special lightweight aluminum pivot bolts that replace the steel ones found in some of the more popular racing derailleurs. This does lower the weight slightly, but it also makes the derailleur a little more flexible.

Several companies—for example, Bullseye, SunTour and Tacx—offer sealed-bearing derailleur pulleys. These pulleys offer low rolling resistance and are sealed so you don't have to service them.

SunTour offers a special oversized derailleur pulley. If you install it in the upper pulley location it helps the derailleur shift faster because the pulley is closer to the freewheel cog and can better guide the chain. If you mount it in the position of the lower pulley it increases the wrap-up capacity of the derailleur.

Most rear derailleurs don't require a spoke protector. However there is always the danger that if your bicycle falls on its right side your derailleur could get caught in the spokes. Also, if the derailleur hanger gets bent inward, your derailleur could shift past the large cog. If the derailleur passes the large cog and gets caught in the spokes it will probably ruin the derailleur and could damage the wheel and the frame. This danger is minimized by a spoke protector.

Touring bicycles and all-terrain bicycles are more likely than other types of bikes to experience bending of a derailleur because of the conditions to which they are subjected. Spoke protectors are therefore recommended for these bikes. A plastic protector will not rust and makes less noise than a metal one. However, it will eventually crack and have to be replaced. To install a spoke protector, remove the freewheel, slide the protector over the hub threads and up against the spokes, then replace the freewheel.

The rear derailleur is a marvelous invention, one which has helped make the bicycle into an incredibly efficient and enjoyable vehicle to operate. Install a derailleur model designed to fit your bike and its other components; keep it clean, well-adjusted, and properly lubricated; and you will be rewarded by many miles of smooth shifting performance.

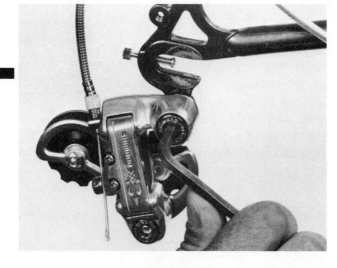

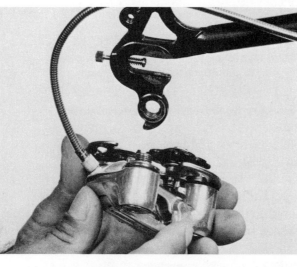

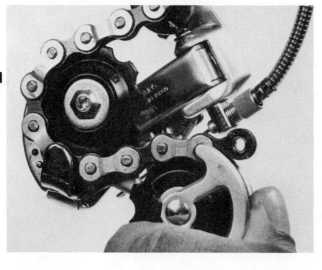

The rear derailleur is positioned beneath the freewheel and is fastened by bolt to a hanger, which is suspended beneath the right rear dropout. (Photo 1) The dropouts are the slotted metal pieces located at the junction of the seatstays and chainstays. Their function is to hold the axle of the rear wheel.

The derailleur hanger on an inexpensive bicycle is usually a separate piece held on the right rear dropout by means of the wheel axle and the axle nuts. A small bolt is used to properly align a removable hanger of this type with the bicycle frame. The hanger on a bike of higher quality is usually integrated into the right rear dropout itself. (Photo 2)

An integral hanger contributes to better shifting by being stiffer than a bolt-on hanger. However, when a change in rear derailleurs is made, you must make sure the new model will fit the hanger. With a bolt-on hanger you can simply purchase the hanger that matches the new derailleur.

Before removing a rear derailleur for cleaning or replacement, you must free it from both the gear cable and the chain. Removing the gear cable is simple. Just loosen the bolt that fastens it to the body of the derailleur and slip it out.

Freeing the chain from the derailleur is a more complicated operation, which can be done in one of two ways. You can use a chain tool to break a link in the chain, then pull one end of the chain free from the derailleur cage. Your other option is to leave the chain intact and free it from the derailleur by removing one of the derailleur pulleys, preferably the idler pulley. This is the one far-

thest from the freewheel and the easiest one to remove and replace.

If you choose the first method, do not try to pull the end of the chain with the rivet protruding from the broken link through the derailleur. The rivet will hang up on the cage. Pull the other end through. (Photo 3)

The alternative method is to take a wrench and loosen the bolt holding the idler pulley on the derailleur. (Photo 4) Remove the idler pulley, then the chain can be lifted off the jockey pulley and out of the way. The derailleur can then be unbolted from the hanger and cleaned or replaced.

When installing a rear derailleur, follow the same procedure in reverse. Bolt it back on the hanger, then replace the chain and gear cable. Before tightening the cable, however, put the wheel back on the bike and make sure the chain is positioned on the smallest freewheel cog so the derailleur is free to move to its outer limit.

Push the shift lever forward to give the gear cable all the available slack, then thread the cable through the anchor on the derailleur body. Hold the cable taut with a pair of pliers while tightening the anchor bolt with a wrench. (Photo 5)

After installing a new rear derailleur, you must check its range of motion and adjust it properly. Even if you are only re-mounting your old derailleur after a cleaning, it is a good idea to check the adjustment. But before fine-tuning the derailleur, make sure the wheel is properly positioned on the frame. Normally, the wheel axle is centered within the dropouts. Many bicycles come with adjustable screws to stop the axle when it is in the proper position. (Photo 6) ▲

**1**

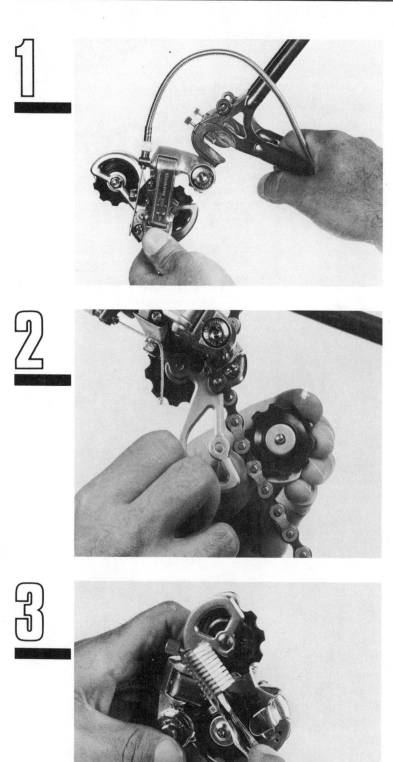

**2**

**3**

The various components of a bicycle's gearing system are subjected to a lot of stresses and strains, which are made worse by the accumulation of road grime. The lubricants used to help keep moving parts working smoothly can also have the opposite effect by attracting dirt that clogs up and accelerates wear in those parts. This is why the chain, chainwheels, freewheel cogs, and both derailleurs need frequent cleaning and lubrication.

One way you can tell when a rear derailleur is in need of a cleaning is by pushing it in with your hand. (Photo 1) If it is difficult to move in and sluggish about springing back out, then you should assume that it has grit in its pivots and needs to be cleaned.

To give a rear derailleur a truly thorough cleaning it is necessary to take it off the bike. While you are at it, remove the wheel and clean the freewheel cogs. Also thoroughly clean the chain and the chainwheel teeth. All these components interact in such a way that grit that accumulates on one is quickly passed on to the others.

You can remove the chain from the bike without breaking a link if you remove the spacer pin in the tail of the front derailleur and the idler pulley from the rear derailleur chain cage. (Photo 2) One advantage of this is that it enables you to more easily clean the pulley and chain cage. In fact, you may want to remove the jockey pulley as well. This will make the cleaning and lubrication process easier and more thorough.

Loosen the gear cable and unbolt the derailleur from the bike. Soak the metal parts in a safe solvent to loosen the grime.

Use soap and water or a mild solvent on the plastic surfaces of the pulleys.

Take the derailleur out of the solvent and scrub it with a small brush, such as an old toothbrush. (Photo 3) Rinse the residue off in the solvent and wipe the derailleur clean with a rag. Let it air dry for awhile so the solvent can evaporate.

Fasten the derailleur back on the dropout hanger. Before replacing the pulleys, coat their bushings with a light coat of grease. (Photo 4) Replace the chain before putting the idler pulley back on.

Before hooking the gear cable back to the derailleur, wipe down the section of cable that runs through housing and give it a new coating of grease. Then thread the cable through the anchor on the derailleur and hold it taut while tightening the bolt.

Fit a can of spray lubricant with a thin nozzle and squirt a little lubricant into each point where the derailleur pivots. (Photo 5) Use the shift lever to move the derailleur back and forth. This will help spread the lubricant over all bearing surfaces and help you tell when enough lubricant has been used.

After you have applied plenty of lubricant and worked it into the inner surfaces of the derailleur, wipe away any excess clinging to the outer surfaces, since it will only serve as an unneeded trap for fresh grit. (Photo 6)

Once the cleaning and lubrication is complete, replace the rear wheel and adjust the derailleur following the instructions on page 176. ▲

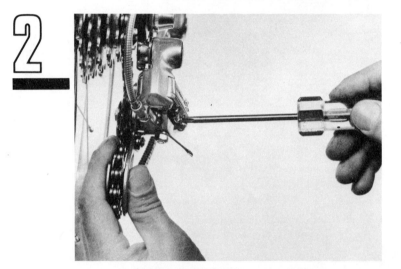

**1**

**2**

**3**

$\mathsf{S}$tart the adjustment of your rear derailleur by setting its inner throw. Shift the chain onto the largest cog in the back and the small chainwheel in the front. Fit a screwdriver into the inner limit adjusting screw. It will probably be the upper one or the one nearest the rear. (Photo 1) Turn it until the derailleur pulleys line up directly under the cog carrying the chain.

Now shift the chain to the smallest freewheel cog and the large chainwheel. Turn the other adjusting screw until the pulleys line up beneath the small cog. (Photo 2)

With your bike still mounted on the repair stand, spin the cranks around and run through the gears you will be using on each chainwheel. Pay special attention to how well the chain shifts onto the rear cogs in the gears used to set the limits.

If there is any hesitation in these shifts or a lot of clatter in the rear after the shifts, try fine-tuning the adjustments until the shifts become smoother and quieter. If you have no repair stand, take the bike out for a spin to check the adjustment.

SunTour rear derailleurs have a third adjusting screw that controls the angle of the derailleur body. Turn the screw to set the derailleur parallel to or tilted slightly up toward the chainstay. (Photo 3)

After installing a new rear derailleur or changing chainwheels or freewheel cogs, the length of your chain may have to be altered in order for the derailleur to shift properly.

Check for maximum chain wrap by moving the chain onto the large chainwheel and the largest rear cog. This is a gear that you do not need and should avoid using because of the extreme chain angle, but it is a good position for checking chain length.

If you cannot get into this gear without

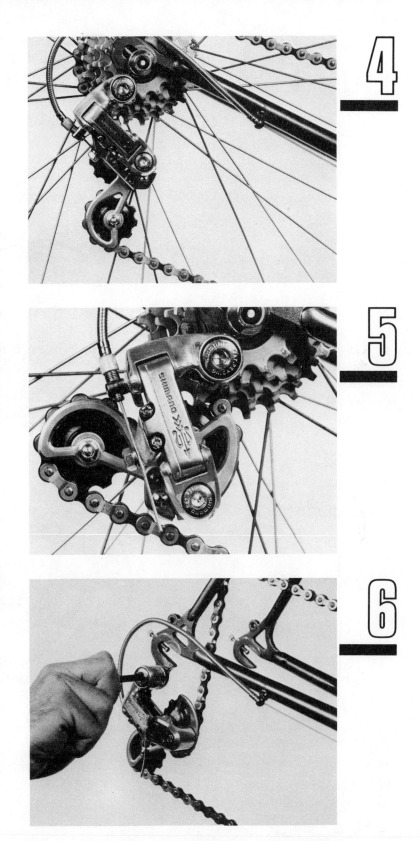

bending the derailleur past its limit, your chain is too short and you need to add some links so that an accidental shift into the gear will not cause damage. On the other hand, if you are able to easily get into this gear and can still push the derailleur cage forward and produce substantial slack, your chain is longer than necessary and can be shortened by a link or two. (Photo 4)

Now shift the chain onto the small chainwheel and the smallest rear cog so that you have minimum chain wrap. This gear is also best avoided because of excess wear on the chain at the angle it creates. If this combination creates a lot of slack in the chain, the derailleur may spring back so far that the chain hits itself, snags, then damages the derailleur. The derailleur shown in photo 5 has a built-in stop that prevents this from happening. (Photo 5) This chain is longer than necessary and should be shortened at least one link.

If your derailleur is stretched near its limit in the large combination, but slack in the small combination, it does not have adequate capacity to handle your gearing range. You should either narrow the range or switch to a derailleur with a longer chain cage capable of wrapping up and feeding out more chain.

When a bike falls over or gets hit on its right side, the rear derailleur can be damaged. Fortunately, the most likely damage is the easiest to correct, a bend in the hanger. If your derailleur fastening bolt has an Allen head, insert a wrench into it and use the derailleur to lever the hanger back into line. (Photo 6) If the chain cage gets bent, try to straighten it by hand. Get the help of a bike shop when dealing with damage of a more serious nature. ▲

# 11 HEADSETS

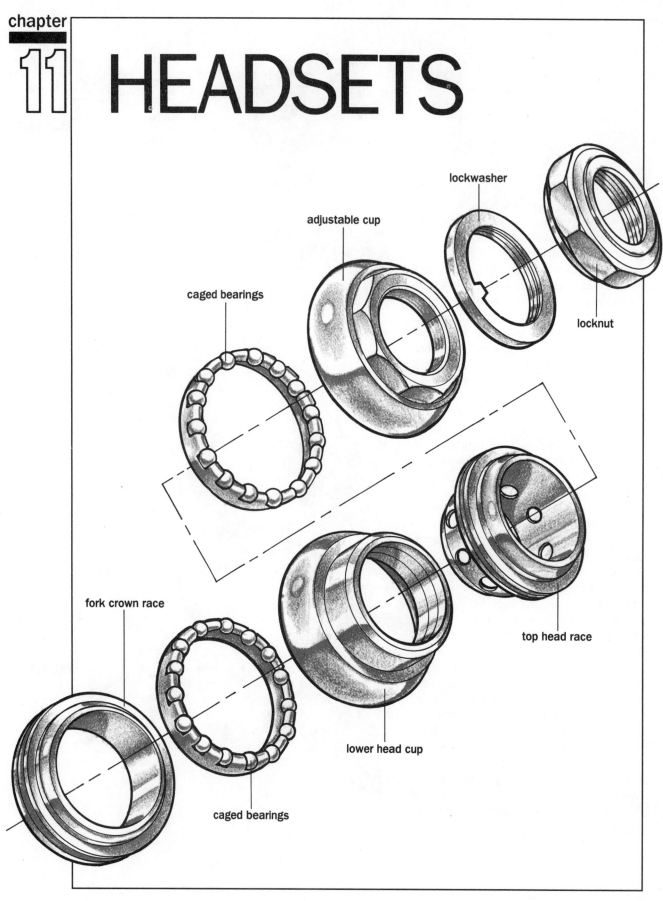

lockwasher

adjustable cup

caged bearings

locknut

top head race

fork crown race

lower head cup

caged bearings

The headset is one of those components most cyclists never think about, not so long as it is functioning properly. It is a component generally treated with benign neglect. Usually, some problem has to develop in this part of your bicycle before it attracts any attention. Then it suddenly becomes the object of grave concern.

Why do people tend to ignore the headsets on their bikes? Mainly because a headset is small, simple, and inconspicuous. It's not bright and shiny like a crankset, and it does not perform intricate movements like derailleurs and brakes. You don't touch it with your feet or hands while you ride. Normally, you don't even hear or feel it working. It simply does its job in stoic silence and does it so well that it is easy to take it for granted. Unfortunately, you do so at your own peril, since a malfunctioning headset may make your bike unmanageable and can cause you to crash.

A properly working headset allows you to control the direction of your bicycle and helps you maintain balance when you hit a rut in the road or glide through a corner. Moreover, it can be generally said that the higher the quality of the headset the more control you have over the bicycle. An inexpensive bicycle purchased at a discount store will most likely be equipped with a headset adequate for making wide turns into a driveway. But the same headset will almost certainly not provide the level of control needed by a professional racer to safely negotiate the corners while descending a steep mountain pass.

So now you know the headset is an important part of your bike, but what exactly is it? Simply stated, it is the component that connects your bike's frame to its front fork. The headset supports the fork in the frame in such a way that the relative alignment of both is maintained, by preventing back-and-forth and side-to-side movement, while allowing the fork to rotate in relation to the frame. The fork rotates on the axis of the steering column, allowing you to control the direction of your bicycle as you ride. While fulfilling its basic function, the headset is forced to withstand the massive pressures that are encountered when the fork transmits road shocks into the frame.

The headset must do all this without adversely affecting the handling of the bicycle. Certainly the headset is not the only component that influences the handling of your bike, but it is a critical one. A poorly installed, adjusted, or maintained headset can make even the finest bicycle difficult to handle. Some symptoms of a neglected headset are movement of the handlebars or rattles and clunks coming from the fork when going over rough pavement. Another indicator of problems is the inability of your bicycle to travel in a straight line when your hands are off the bars. Still another is the handlebars being able to turn, but seeming to have notches that hold the steering column of the fork at various points through its rotation inside the head tube. If the headset makes grinding noises when you rotate the handlebars from side to side, it's time for cleaning and repacking with grease.

## Types of Headsets

The most common kind of headset uses a cup-and-cone arrangement. Two sets of cups and cones, one between the fork and head tube and one on top of the head tube, work together to hold the fork and allow it to turn in relation to the frame. The upper cone and lower cup are attached to the head tube of the frame. The lower cone and upper cup are attached to the steering column of the fork. A set of bearings—either loose or caged—separate each cup and cone, allowing the steering column to twist within the head tube. (Each set of cup, cone, and bearings is referred to as a "stack.") This is the conventional headset, the type most commonly encountered.

In recent years, a number of sealed-bearing headsets have appeared, both as standard equipment on new bikes and as replacement units for older bikes. Also, there are now a number of exotic designs on the market that try a variety of concepts, such as interlocking Teflon sleeves or single-axis roller bearings, in an attempt to improve a headset's ability to do its job. It's unlikely that you will ever stumble upon these exotic variations since they often are plagued by more problems than they solve.

Generally, if you are in the market for a new headset, the conventional cup-and-cone models are your best choice because they are simple in design, easy to maintain, and easy to service. Many of the new "sealed" headsets aren't truly sealed. They are shielded by the addition of a rubber o-ring in the opening between the cup and cone. Some headsets use a labyrinth to act as a shield: the dirt must work its way around the metal barriers before it can get into the bearings. Both techniques of shielding work quite well and have no detrimental effects on a headset's performance, nor do they make servicing any more difficult.

If you wish to shield your headset, you can do so by covering the opening between the cup and race of the upper and lower stack with a piece of rubber. You can cut a section of inner tube, about 1 to 1½ inches long, to form the shield. It is usually necessary for the headset to be disassembled before you can install this rubber doughnut over the lower stack. Only the handlebars need be removed to install such a shield over the upper stack. Usually, people cover only the lower part of the headset (the part between the fork and the frame), since it receives the most dirt and crud from the road.

Some cup-and-cone headsets are now using tapered roller bearings rather than ball bearings. If you dismantle your headset and find a bunch of what appears to be small cylinders rather than balls, these are tapered roller bearings. The load-bearing points of contact are larger on roller bearings than on ball bearings, and this can extend the life of the roller bearing units by spreading the load over a wider area. The only problem with this can be trying to find replacement bearings when replacement day comes.

If you have a headset that uses precision cartridge bearings, commonly called "sealed bearings," it is not user-serviceable and you will have to talk to your local bike shop about your options. Usually, your only option is to replace the unit with a more conventional system. Sealed-bearing systems often require a hammer and punch for installation and removal—not a very tidy method by any standards.

If you are considering replacing your present headset and are thinking of changing to a different brand or model, we recommend that you choose one of the many conventional ball bearing headsets, with or without an o-ring shield. The reliability of these units is hard to beat. If you aren't interested in upgrading to a "better" headset, try to get the same brand and model that your bike originally had. This way you won't have to worry about whether it will fit your bike.

Headsets come in a variety of price ranges. They can run from less than $10 to more than $70. With headsets, as with most bicycle components, you generally get what you pay for. The more you pay the better the quality. More expensive headsets generally perform better and last longer than cheaper ones. The more expensive headsets also look nicer. But, before you spend a lot of money on a new headset, give some thought to the overall worth of the bike. There is not a lot of sense in spending a bundle of money on a top-quality headset for a second-rate bike that you may junk in a couple of years anyway. As a rule of thumb, we recommend that when you purchase a new headset, you spend no more than twice the cost of the original headset that came with the bike.

If you want to upgrade your headset, ask the salesperson at the bicycle shop to consult *Sutherland's Handbook for Bicycle Mechanics* to see if the new headset will fit the existing openings. The openings may be too large for the new headset. If so, you will have to select another model. If the openings are too small you are in luck, since you can always have the bicycle shop make them larger to fit the new unit.

Before you install a professional-grade headset in your bike, have the head tube and the fork prepared with headset reaming and cutting tools made by Campagnolo. This will ensure proper fit and alignment, excellent performance, and long life.

If you transport your bicycle on the roof of your car a lot you may be blowing the grease out of your headset bearings. The 55-mph wind can get through the openings between cups and races and blow the grease out onto the frame. This not only makes a mess but removes the corrosion protection and lubrication from your bearings. Using the headset shield mentioned above will stop this from happening. If you don't have the facility to install such a shield, at least wrap a piece of plastic around the head tube when transporting the bike on your car.

## Basic Parts of the Headset System

Like the crankset and the wheel hubs, the headset on a bicycle is not simply one component, but a series of separate parts that function together as one system. Despite variations in design, all headset systems employ a similar combination of parts. Working from the top down, the typical headset is made up of the following parts, which are shown in the exploded-view illustration found at the beginning of this chapter:

1. a locknut
2. a lockwasher
3. an adjustable cup
4. bearings
5. the top head race
6. the lower head cup
7. bearings
8. the fork crown race

Some headsets also have a reflector bracket or a centerpull brake cable hanger that fits around the fork steering column between the locknut and the lockwasher.

# Headset Adjustment

If your headset seems either loose or tight, you can usually remedy the problem with a simple adjustment. It may take several tries to get the adjustment right, so don't get discouraged if it is not perfect after the first attempt.

The only tools that you will need to do a headset adjustment are wrenches large enough to fit the flats on the locknut and the adjustable cup. Headset wrenches available from your local bicycle shop make the job easy, but they are not absolutely essential. A large adjustable wrench works just fine for the locknut. You can use a pair of adjustable pliers to hold the adjusting cup if it is steel, but wrap a rag around the part to protect the cup's finish. Some adjusting cups have serrated edges to make it easy for you to turn them by hand.

If the exposed parts of your headset are made of aluminum alloy, we recommend that you purchase the proper wrenches to fit the wrench flats on the locknut and adjusting cup. Otherwise you will probably damage these parts when you attempt to tighten and loosen them.

One special type of headset is the Shimano EX. This headset requires a special wrench that you can purchase at your local bicycle shop. A Shimano EX headset can be adjusted with regular headset wrenches, but the area of contact is limited and you may damage the headset in the process.

When making a headset adjustment, leave the stem in place. Many

people also like to leave the front wheel on the bike to act as a handle to hold the forks still while the locknut is being turned. However, leaving the wheel in place makes it more difficult to tell if the headset is too tight. An alternative is to remove the wheel and use the handle of a hammer or some similar tool to hold the forks steady while you apply force to the locknut. It's a good idea to pad the hammer handle with a rag to keep from chipping the paint on the bike frame.

To make a headset adjustment, loosen the locknut by turning it counterclockwise. Then, if the headset seems too tight, loosen the adjusting cup by turning it counterclockwise about an eighth of a turn. By contrast, if the headset seems too loose, tighten the adjusting cup by turning it clockwise. Turn the adjustable cup all the way down until it contacts the bearings, then back off the adjustment between one-eighth and one-quarter turn. Now, while holding the adjusting cup in position, tighten the locknut by turning it clockwise.

## Checking the Adjustment

To see if your headset needs adjusting, or to check an adjustment you have made, grasp the front wheel of the bike with one hand and the handlebars with the other. Alternately push and pull the two toward and away from each other. Do the push-pull check with the forks turned to several different positions. If there is any looseness at any position of the fork, once again loosen the locknut and turn the adjustable cup clockwise. Tighten the locknut and repeat the push-pull test. You can also check the headset by picking up the front of the bike and dropping the front wheel to the

*Photo 11-1: A special wrench is needed to tighten and loosen the locknut on the Shimano EX headset, which has its own unique shape.*

ground while holding the stem. If you hear or feel anything rattle, the headset is still loose.

Make a second check of the headset by lifting the front of the bike and turning the handlebars to see if the bearings bind, causing resistance, at any point in the rotation. If the headset binds, loosen the adjustment a bit, turning the adjustable cup counterclockwise.

Again, don't be discouraged if it takes a couple of tries to get the adjust-

ment where there is neither binding nor play in the headset. If you simply cannot get it adjusted so it's just right—that is, not tight and not loose—always adjust it so that it is a little tight.

If your headset is made of reinforced nylon (these headsets appear on many French bicycles) you will probably have to adjust it so that it feels tight. Once the headset is loaded down with your weight it will loosen up a bit, eliminating the overtightened state.

### Double Locknut

Some headsets have two locknuts. (Normally, you will find these only on bikes imported from Japan.) The extra locknut helps in the initial assembly of the bike but does not provide any substantial benefit to the rider. The second locknut usually resembles a threaded washer with two or three notches in it. If you work on a headset with two locknuts, you must loosen both before attempting to adjust your headset. To loosen the second locknut, it is often necessary to use a hammer and punch. Retighten the top locknut when all the other steps are completed.

If you wish to eliminate this second locknut, simplifying any future adjustments, you can do so by replacing it with extra headset lockwashers to take up the space it occupies. You can get these extra washers from your bicycle shop.

## Headset Overhaul

As part of a regular service program, the headset should be overhauled every one to two years. There is no quick way to overhaul a headset; but after you have done it a couple of times, you will find that it is not that difficult. For this job, you will need the same tools you used in the headset adjustment. The only additional tools necessary will be those required to loosen the stem (usually, a 6mm Allen wrench will do the job) and a wrench of the proper size to loosen the brake cable.

You will also need some medium-weight grease and new bearings. Unless the bike shop is familiar with your model of headset you will have to disassemble it before the size and number of bearings required can be determined.

Why do you need new bearings? Because with use, ball bearings cease to be completely round. Even though they may still look round to your eye, their shape will have changed enough that it will be impossible to reorient them in exactly the same way when you put them back into their races. You will discover that a headset rebuilt with old bearings will come loose after the first adjustment. It can take as many as five adjustments until all the bearings have realigned themselves. So avoid the hassle and install new bearings. They aren't that expensive.

Before you begin the process of rebuilding your headset, it is a good idea to spread an old sheet below your bike to catch any stray bearings that might fall on the floor. Also, if it's at all possible, hang the bike so the front wheel is suspended off the floor. All you need to do is tie a rope to a rafter in the garage or basement and tie it to the top tube of the bicycle. Of course, if you have a home repair stand, that's even better.

Once the bike is on the stand or roped to the rafter, remove the front wheel. Then disconnect the front brake cable from the brake caliper. Loosen the stem by turning the stem binder bolt counterclockwise. Turn the binder bolt two or three full turns and then hit it on the head with a hammer. If the stem hasn't been loosened in a long time, it may take more than one blow to make the stem binder wedge inside the steerer tube drop free. However, it's best not to strike the binder bolt directly unless you use a padded hammer. Otherwise, place a small block of wood over the bolt before hitting it.

Once loose, lift the handlebar and stem unit out of the steering tube and hang it on the top tube because the rear brake cable and shifting cables will still be attached. If you wish to remove the handlebars completely you will have to detach all cables.

If you plan to remove the fork crown race, take the front brake caliper off the frame by loosening the mounting nut found on the back side of the fork and removing the mounting bolt to which the brake is attached. Otherwise, it can stay where it is.

Remove the headset locknut by turning it counterclockwise. If you have a headset with two locknuts, remove the second locknut as well. Then slip off the lockwasher, the reflector bracket, the brake cable hanger, or anything else you find positioned above the adjustable race.

While holding the front fork from underneath, spin the adjustable cup off by turning it counterclockwise. Be careful! If the bearings are loose (not caged in a special retainer) they might momentarily stick to the adjusting cup as it spins away from the top head race and then fall on the floor. If the bearings are loose, you may want to take the frame off the stand before removing the adjustable cup and tip it over on its side near the floor. Then when you remove the race, the bearings can fall the short distance onto the cloth and be controlled. Even though you will be replacing them, you need to know how many and what size were used in each race.

If possible, turn the frame upside down, or at least on its side, before sliding the fork out of the head tube. If the bike is upside down the remaining bearings will be less likely to drop on the floor since they will be held in the cup-shaped race of the lower head cup. Retrieve and save all the bearings. Try to keep the two sets of bearings separated if they are loose, because many headsets use different numbers of bearings in the upper and lower races. Clean and count the bearings before taking them to a bike shop to purchase the proper size and number of replacements. If you discover any damaged bearings, look for corresponding damage inside the bearing races.

Most conventional headsets use $3/32$-inch ball bearings, but a few use $1/8$-inch bearings. The only way to know for sure is to measure them. Take a couple to the bicycle shop to be sure that you get the right size. Even though the difference between the two sizes may seem insignificant, it's enough to make the headset not work. If you are purchasing loose ball bearings, it is a good idea to buy a few extra since they are very easy to lose.

Clean the adjustable cup, upper head race, lower head cup, and fork crown race. Inspect them for pits and cracks. If they have any pits or cracks, all or part of the headset may have to be replaced. We will say more about headset replacement later.

Once you have the new bearings and all the headset components are clean and in good shape, you are ready to assemble the headset. Apply a heavy coat of grease to the fork crown race, lower head cup, upper head race, and the adjustable cup. Never be afraid of using too much grease, since any extra will just move out of the way once the headset is reassembled.

Grease the steerer tube from the fork crown race all the way up to and including the threads. This will help prevent any corrosion of the tube and its threads as well as making it easy to thread on the adjusting cup. If you are using caged bearings, apply a coat of grease to them as well.

If you are going to use a headset shield, slide the first shield over the

*Photo 11-2: Short sections of old tire tube can be fitted over the ends of the head tube during a headset overhaul, then pulled over the cups later to shield the bearings from wind and road grime.*

lower head cup now. Curl the shield up as high on the frame as possible so that it won't interfere with the adjustment of the headset.

Arrange the appropriate ball bearings inside the lower head cup of the inverted frame. If the bearings are loose, put the same number in as were removed. If they are caged, be sure the cage faces the correct direction. To determine what that is, take a close look at the cage. Metal fingers curl around between balls in a kind of C formation. What we call the "closed" side of the cage is the back side of the circle of little C shapes. This is the side of the cage that should always be set against the cup-shaped bearing surface. Since the

cups are above and the cones below the bearings when the bike is upright, that means the open side of the cage faces down toward the cone and the ground.

The grease should hold loose bearings in place while you replace the fork. However, if you do drop a bearing, clean it off before replacing it so that no dirt gets packed into the headset. Then take the fork and slide it carefully all the way into the frame so that the bearings make full contact with the lower head cup.

Hold the fork in place while you turn the frame right side up and install the bearings on the upper head race. Again, if the bearings are loose, use the same number as were removed and use enough grease to hold them in place.

Then spin the adjustable cup down on the steerer tube until it presses firmly against the upper bearings.

Slide the lockwasher, the reflector bracket, the brake cable hanger, and anything else that came off the steerer tube back on in the same order they were removed. After these are in place, thread on the locknut, but don't tighten it yet.

Put the upper shield in place now, if you plan to use one. Slide it over the locknut and down as far as possible so that it won't interfere with the adjustment.

Install the stem and tighten it down. Thread down the adjustable cup by hand until it contacts the bearings, then back it off between one-eighth and one-quarter turn. While holding the adjusting cup in position, tighten the locknut by turning it clockwise.

Check the headset adjustment in the same manner described earlier. Grab hold of the front wheel and the handlebars and alternately push and pull them in relation to each other. Do the push-pull check with the forks turned to several different positions. You can also check the headset by picking up the front of the bike and dropping the front wheel to the ground while holding the stem, listening for a rattle that indicates looseness. If you discover any play in the headset through either method, loosen the locknut and turn the adjustable cup clockwise a little. Then retighten the locknut and check again.

When all looseness has disappeared from your headset, check to make sure it is not too tight. Lift the front of the bike and turn the handlebars to see if the bearings bind, causing resistance, at any point in the rotation. If the headset binds, this will cause excessive wear on the headset and endanger your steering. So turn the adjustable cup counterclockwise a little and recheck it. Keep checking until you find the point between looseness and tightness in your adjustment.

Once the headset is properly adjusted, install the front wheel and fully tighten the stem. Be sure the stem is aligned with the front wheel. Reattach the brake cable and adjust the front brake. Unfold the headset shields so that they fully cover the openings in the upper and lower headset assemblies.

## Troubleshooting Headset Problems

Let's say that you are very careful and take your time, yet you cannot get the headset to adjust properly. Here are some possible sources of the problem and what to do about them.

**1.** If the adjustment of the bearings is always loose, check to see that the correct number are in the upper and lower races. You may have left some out.

**2.** If the adjustment of the bearings is always tight, also check to see that the correct number are in the upper and lower races. You may have put too many in.

**3.** If the bearings are caged, be sure the cage is properly oriented. If it is upside down it will cause the headset to bind.

**4.** Make certain the stem is installed properly.

**5.** Make sure the bearings are the correct size.

**6.** Check to see if the fork is bent. If it is, it will have to be straightened or replaced. Check with your local bike shop on how to remedy this problem.

**7.** Check to see if the steering column is bent. If it is, either the steerer or the entire fork may have to be replaced. Check with your local shop.

**8.** Be sure that all the washers, reflector brackets, and other parts originally on your steerer tube are back in place. If they are left out you will have to replace them with washers, or the locknut will not be able to tighten properly.

# Fitting a New Headset

If you decide to replace your present headset it is best and usually easiest to replace it with the same model you removed. If you are going to install a different model have your bike shop consult *Sutherland's Handbook for Bicycle Mechanics* to be sure that the new headset will fit your frame. Your frame and fork may have to be modified by a professional mechanic to accept the new headset.

You will need the bicycle shop's help in several other areas as well. To remove the old fork crown race, the lower head cup, or the upper head race, without damaging the frame or fork, special tools are required. Special tools will also be needed to install the new headset parts. It may be necessary to have the head tube and the fork crown race cut to fit the new headset components. Tools for this task are very expensive and require special care and skill to use.

We recommend that you have a bicycle shop remove and fit the fork crown, lower head cup, and the upper head race. Attempting to fit a headset without having the frame properly prepared can not only damage the headset but the frame as well. Once the fork crown, lower head cup, and the upper head race are installed, you can then reassemble your headset following our instructions for a headset overhaul.

## Headset Quick Fix

If your forks seem to fall into notches as they twist from side to side, it is because the bearings have made pits in the races. This is known as brinelling. The only permanent way to fix this is to overhaul the headset and replace the pitted parts. However, if you don't have the necessary new parts to replace the pitted ones, you can still make a temporary repair that will help for a little while.

Remove the front wheel, the front brake, the handlebar, and stem. Then spin the forks around three times and reinstall the parts that you removed. This spinning of the forks should cause the ball bearings to realign themselves at slightly different points on the races. Such realignment will reduce the effect of the pits. Keep in mind that this is only a temporary repair and that you should not delay too long going to a bicycle shop to get the proper parts for a complete repair.

The headset is a wonderful invention created to fulfill some very vital functions. It makes it possible for you to steer your bike rapidly in different directions, to turn sharply, or ride in circles.

It also enables you to make the ongoing steering adjustments needed to keep you upright on two wheels. But while enabling the two sections of your bike frame to function together while moving in relation to each other, the headset must be able to withstand the weight of your body and a considerable amount of road shock. When properly lubricated and adjusted it is able to carry out its assignment so well you are tempted to take it for granted.

Don't give in to the temptation. Check the adjustment of your headset frequently, shield its bearings from the wind when you carry it on top your car, and give it a complete and thorough overhaul at least once a year. Smooth and safe handling will be your reward. It's worth the effort.

When a headset is either too loose or too tight it should be readjusted because either problem can negatively affect the steering of the bike and cause unnecessary damage to headset parts. Severe looseness or tightness in the headset bearings will probably be obvious to you while you are riding the bike. However, there are some simple tests that you can make while off the bike to determine whether or not your headset is in need of adjustment.

To check for looseness in the headset, stand beside your bike. Hold the handlebars with one hand and the front wheel with the other hand. Alternate between pulling the two toward each other and pushing them away from each other. (Photo 1) If you feel any play in the bearings, you know the adjustment is too loose. To be really thorough, this test should be repeated with the front fork turned to several different positions. If you discover looseness when the fork is turned to one position, but not when it is at another position, that is a sign of possible pitting in one of your bearing races. In that case, your headset needs to be overhauled, rather than simply adjusted. (See page 192 on headset overhaul for instructions.)

Another method that can be used to check for a loose headset adjustment is to lift the front wheel a few inches off the ground, then let the bike drop. (Photo 2) If you hear rattles in the headset area, that is a sign your bearings are too loose.

To check for tightness in the headset adjustment, grab hold of the handlebars and flick the front wheel of the bike quickly from side to side. (Photo 3) This is best done with the wheel held slightly off the ground so that the movement is not hampered by contact of the tire with the ground. If you feel any resistance at any point in the rotation of the

steerer tube, your adjustment should be loosened a bit.

Adjusting a headset is not particularly difficult, though it may take you several tries to get it just right. Begin by loosening the locknut, which is positioned at the upper end of the steering column. If you have a special spanner made to fit your locknut, use it. Otherwise you can get by with a large adjustable wrench if you are careful not to round the edges of the locknut's wrench flats. (Photo 4) Turn the locknut counterclockwise to loosen it.

If the headset feels loose, turn the adjustable cup clockwise until you feel it make contact with the bearings, then back it off one-eighth to one-quarter turn and check it again. You should be able to adjust the cup by hand, but you can use a suitable tool if you'd like. (Photo 5) If a reflector bracket or brake hanger is in your way, move it, along with the lockwasher and locknut, up the stem while you adjust the cup.

If you feel any binding in the headset, turn the adjustable cup counterclockwise to loosen it slightly. Start with a one-eighth to one-quarter turn, then check it again.

Continue to work in small increments, adjusting and checking until you feel neither binding nor looseness in the headset. Be patient and try to get the adjustment just right. However, if you simply cannot find the precise point between tightness and looseness, then leave the adjustment slightly on the tight side.

Once you have the adjustable cup positioned where you want it, slide the lockwasher and reflector bracket (if there is one) back down. Hold the adjustable cup in position while threading down and tightening the locknut. (Photo 6) ▲

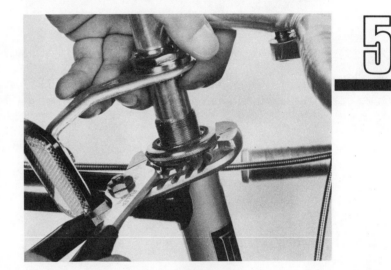

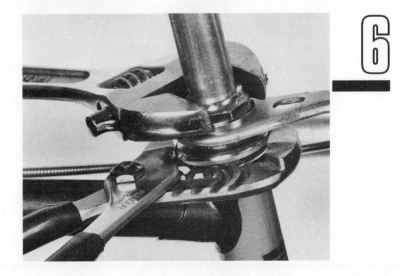

No matter how often a headset receives an adjustment or how smoothly it appears to be operating, periodically it deserves a complete overhaul. This involves taking the headset apart, cleaning and inspecting all its parts, installing new bearings, and repacking all the bearings with fresh grease.

Before taking anything apart, however, see if you can devise some way of suspending the front of your bike off the floor. That will make many steps of the overhaul process much easier. A bike repair stand is ideal, but if you do not have one, you can attach one end of a rope to a beam or rafter and tie the other end around the bike's top tube. The disadvantage of the rope method is that it does not completely immobilize the bike, but at least it is one way to support the frame after you remove the front wheel.

It is also a good idea to spread an old sheet under the bicycle before uncovering any bearings, so that if the balls are loose and fall, they will be trapped in the sheet rather than rolling into some hidden corner. You will not need the old balls for reuse, but you do need to count them and keep track of their number for replacement purposes. Also, you should take some of them with you to the bike shop to make sure you get new ones of the same size.

Taking a headset apart requires the removal of the handlebars and stem from the head tube. That task is complicated by the brake levers and cables. To make it easier, first loosen and remove the brake cable from the front brake calipers. (Photo 1)

Now loosen the handlebar stem by turning the binder bolt counterclockwise two or three turns. (Photo 2) Then set a small block of wood on top of the bolt and give it a sharp blow to dislodge the expander

wedge inside the steerer tube. (Photo 3) A wedge that has not been loosened in a while may take more than one blow to free.

Lift the handlebars and stem out of the steerer tube and hang them on the top tube of the bike. Or, if you prefer, disconnect the cable to the rear brake and shifter cables, if you have them, and set the bars aside while you work.

Loosen the headset locknut by turning it counterclockwise. (Photo 4) Thread it completely off the steerer tube and set it aside. If there is a second locknut, take it off as well. Then lift off the lockwasher, the reflector bracket, the brake hanger or anything else you encounter between the locknut and the adjustable cup. (Photo 5) Just remember the order in which each item comes off so you can replace them in the same way at the completion of the overhaul.

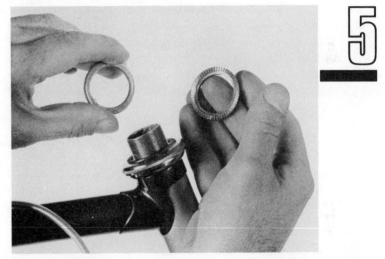

You are now ready to remove the adjustable cup. But while doing this, support the fork with one hand to hold the lower set of bearings inside the fixed cup until you are ready to remove them. (Photo 6)

Be cautious as you remove the adjustable cup. Any bearings clinging to it may drop and roll away. Once the bearings are visible, you may discover that they are caged in a metal retainer. If so, you no longer have to worry about any errant balls getting away from you. However, do not assume that just because the upper set of bearings are caged, the lower set will be also. Be wary of loose balls until you are sure they are all enclosed in retainers.

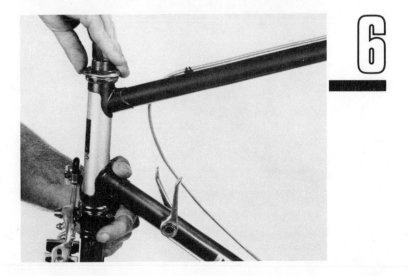

If you find that the bearings beneath the adjustable cup are loose, you may want to momentarily thread the cup back down and lay the bike on its side on the floor. Then when you take the adjustable cup off, the

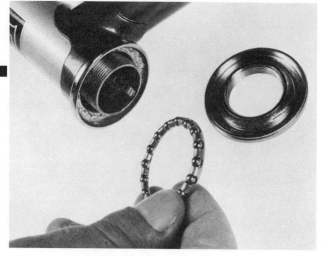

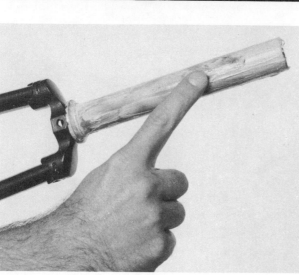

bearings can fall out onto the sheet or rags you have spread on the floor.

Remove the bearings from the top head race and save them for inspection. (Photo 7) Then, if you can, turn the bike upside down to prevent the bearings from falling out of the lower head cup while you lift the fork out of the head tube. (Photo 8) Set the fork aside while you extract the bearings.

Keep the two sets of bearings separate in case they are not identical in size and number. Clean and count each set, then take a sample to the bike shop to buy replacements to match.

Clean all the parts and inspect them for pits and cracks in the bearing areas. Replace any damaged parts. If the fork crown race, the lower head cup, or the upper head race must be removed for replacement, have the work done at a bike shop, which will have the tools and skills needed.

When you are ready to reassemble the headset, coat the steerer tube with plenty of grease, from the fork crown race up and including the threads at the upper end. (Photo 9) This will help prevent corrosion as well as protect working parts from damage and excessive wear.

Also, pack grease into the lower head cup, the adjustable cup, and the upper head race. If you wish, fit a rubber shield over the lower cup and fold it back out of the way until

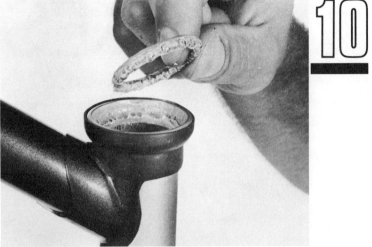

the headset is back together. Then install a set of bearings in the lower cup. (Photo 10)

Drop the fork steerer tube back through the head tube, pushing the fork crown race against the bearings. Turn the bike right side up and install the bearings in the upper race. Then thread on the adjustable cup and turn it down until it makes contact with the bearings. (Photo 11)

There is no point in fine-tuning the adjustment until after the stem is locked back in place. So replace the reflector bracket, brake hanger, lockwasher, and locknut, whatever was taken off. Be sure everything goes back on in the right order, but don't tighten the locknut down yet.

Drop the stem back down into the steerer tube. When it is at the right height and the bars are straight, turn the binder bolt clockwise to tighten the expander wedge. (Photo 12)

Now check the headset adjustment by performing the various tests described on page 190. When you have the cup adjusted where you can feel neither binding nor play between the cup and bearings, hold the cup in place and tighten down the locknut.

Reconnect the brake cable or cables and readjust the brakes. Then replace the front wheel, and your bicycle should be ready to ride again. ▲

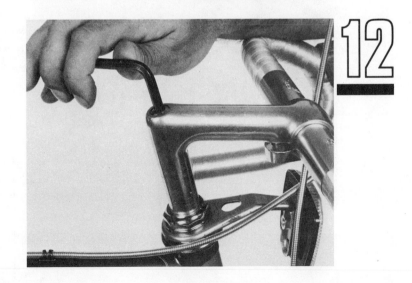

# 12 BRAKES

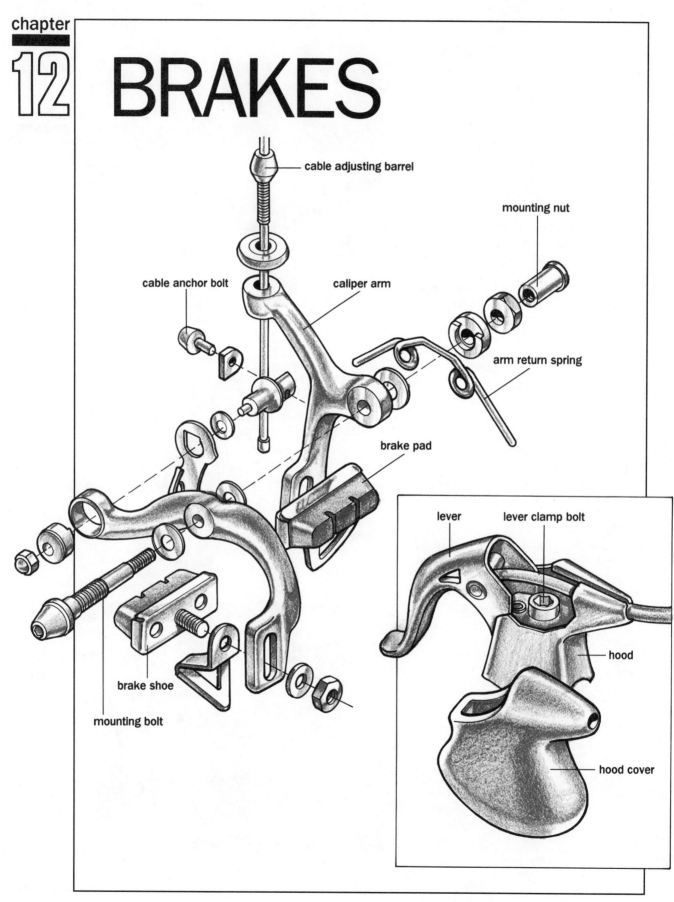

cable adjusting barrel

mounting nut

cable anchor bolt

caliper arm

arm return spring

brake pad

lever

lever clamp bolt

hood

brake shoe

mounting bolt

hood cover

## Hub Brakes

Included in the general category of hub brakes are three types: coaster brakes, disc brakes, and drum brakes. Coaster brakes are commonly found on single-speed juvenile bikes where small hands and young undeveloped coordination would make other types of brakes more of a hazard than help. Since this type of brake is not used on lightweight bikes, we will not describe it further.

Disc brakes and drum brakes are generally found on tandem bikes because of the increased weight and speed potential of these bikes. The advantages offered by disc and drum brakes over rim brakes are mainly that they make use of a greater contact area for braking and have an increased ability to dissipate the heat that is generated when a cyclist attempts to stop in high-speed or high-load situations.

Disc brakes, widely used in the mid-70s, are not being used extensively today. The best-known, and possibly the best-quality, disc brake currently being produced is the one made by Phil Wood. Shimano and Bridgestone formerly manufactured disc brakes, but have now discontinued them.

Hub brakes put stress on a wheel more evenly than rim brakes, which is one mark in their favor. However, recent improvements in the quality of rims and spokes have made this less important a difference than it once was. There are also many disadvantages with hub systems. They require special hub assemblies and hefty stays to resist the torque developed at the hub. They are more complicated to install and service, and also tend to be heavier than rim brakes. For these reasons, rim systems

N ext to wheels, which get you going, brakes, which help you stop, are probably the most important component on the bicycle. Track riders will probably disagree, since their fixed-wheel bikes have no brakes and can only be slowed by backpressure on the pedals. The first two-wheelers didn't have brakes either. But they also did not have drive trains and generally did not travel very fast. Their greatest speeds were achieved on descents, and foot dragging was the accepted slowing technique. (Perhaps this is the origin of the term "brake shoe.")

Early cyclists did not have to deal with traffic lights and congestion on the roads. Similarly, modern track riders need only watch out for each other and can decelerate gradually at the end of a race. At least a track rider does not have to worry about the person in front hitting the brakes suddenly. But cyclists on city streets and country roads often are forced to make rapid stops or slowdowns and could hardly survive without a reliable set of brakes.

## Major Types of Brakes

Today, there are two major classifications of bicycle brakes: hub brakes and rim brakes. Hub brakes work through pressure applied inside a wheel hub, whereas rim brakes work by applying pressure on both sides of the wheel rim.

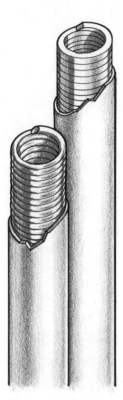

*Illustration 12-1: The uneven inner surface of round-wound cable housing (left) creates the potential for cable snag and excess friction. Flat-wound housing (right) provides a much smoother surface for the cable to contact.*

are most commonly the ones found on bicycles manufactured today.

## Rim Brakes

There are three types of rim brakes in common use today: center-pulls, sidepulls, and cantilevers.

Sidepulls were popular in the early and mid-50s mainly because that was all that was available. Then in the late 50s and early 60s, quality centerpull brakes were introduced by Universal and Weinmann and quickly gained favor. Though seldom found on new bikes sold in the United States today, both these brake systems are still available. One of their major attractions is that after the initial installation and adjustment are complete, these brakes are basically self-centering.

A second attractive feature of centerpull brakes is the greater mechanical advantage they offer over most side-pulls. This is because the pivot points for centerpull caliper arms are not dependent on the distance from the rim to the brake mounting hole as is the case with sidepulls, which pivot on the mounting bolt itself. Centerpulls, by contrast, are provided with a pivot on each side of the brake body, decreasing the distance from the pivot to the brake shoe and thus increasing the mechanical power of the lever.

When it first occurred, this design innovation made possible the use of levers that were smaller and had shallower contours than those previously required for sidepull brakes. This was a distinct advantage for cyclists with small hands, such as younger children and smaller-framed women.

Despite the mechanical advantage of centerpull brakes, by the mid-70s the

trend had reversed and the sidepull was again becoming the brake most favored by riders. Starting with the Campagnolo Record model (still considered the benchmark of all brakesets), sidepulls of greatly improved and refined design began to appear on the market. Many of the attractive features of the popular centerpull systems were now incorporated into the newer sidepulls. Quick-releases, cable adjusters, and better finishes were the order of the day.

A cantilever brake works much like a centerpull brake, but has shorter, stiffer arms that pivot at the forks or stays to which they are attached. The stiffness and fork mounting of cantilevers gives them a great mechanical advantage. This is why they are commonly used on tandem and loaded touring bikes, which carry much greater loads than ordinary lightweight bikes. Cantilevers are also the brakes most often seen on all-terrain bikes, whose fat tires create problems of reach for ordinary caliper brakes.

## Recent Innovations in Brake Components

In recent years, nearly all brake manufacturers have switched over to flat-wound cable housing, first used by Campagnolo, the renowned Italian component firm. The flat-wound housing gives a more solid feel because there is less compression and slippage between the coils when the faces of the coil wires lie flat against each other rather than being round as in the older housings.

Lining cable housing with nylon, now a common practice, also helps produce a brake system that gives a more responsive feel. A further improvement is the coating of cables with Teflon.

When these various recent innovations are combined into one system, most of the friction formerly incurred in the cable portion of a brake system is reduced or eliminated.

## Buying Brakes That Fit Your Frame

Before purchasing a new set of rim brakes, first determine what the dimension is from the frame mounting hole to the center of the rim. There are two general "sizes" in which most brakes are available—short reach 47mm and long reach 52mm. Both have a range of adjustment of approximately 5 to 10mm in each direction. There are other sizes on the market but the two mentioned make up 90 percent of those used on lightweight bikes. So before purchasing, make sure the brakes you want will fit your frame.

# Installing Brakes

The first step in installing a new set of brakes is to fasten the levers to the bars of your bike. Of course, before you can attach new levers, you must remove the old ones, and that means stripping off your handlebar tape. Old bar tape is seldom reusable, so buy a couple rolls of new tape to go along with your new brake system. Even if you are not installing new levers, but only repositioning the old ones, you will need to remove the old tape before the lever clamp can be moved.

Once the tape is out of your way, loosen the brake cable anchor nut and pull the cable free from the brake caliper. Unhook the fitting on the upper end of the cable from the lever and remove

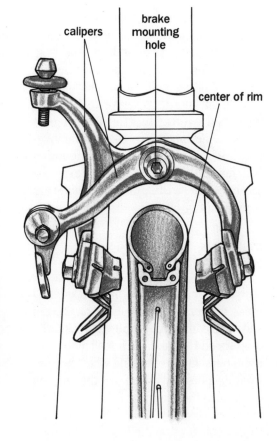

calipers

brake mounting hole

center of rim

*Illustration 12-2: Before buying a new set of brakes, make sure the calipers can be adjusted to fit the distance between the brake mounting hole in the frame and the center of your wheel rim.*

both the cable and the cable housing from the bike. Then squeeze the lever in so that it touches the handlebar. Look inside the lever body and you will see a clamp bolt or nut that is holding the lever to the bar. Find the tool you need to remove that nut: it will probably be either a flat-bladed screwdriver, a thin wall 8mm socket, or an Allen wrench. Loosen the nut, then slide the lever off the handlebar.

The positioning of brake levers varies with the personal riding style of each rider, but a standard used by many veteran riders is to position the lower end of the lever even with the extension of the lower part of the handlebars. You may move them up or down a bit to suit your taste.

Now find the tool that fits the nut on the clamp bolt of your new lever and fasten the lever to your bars. But take care in doing this. Some models of levers have mounting bolts that bear on the lever pivot pin. If you have this type of lever and overtighten the bolt, it may cause some binding in the lever movement. In this case, tighten the mounting bolt just enough to keep the lever assembly from twisting on the handlebars when you tug on it.

## Installing Sidepull Brake Calipers

To remove an old pair of sidepull brake calipers, loosen the nut on the tail end of the mounting bolt and take the calipers off the bike. To install a new set of calipers, first determine which are the front calipers and which are the rear by comparing the length of their respective mounting bolts. The caliper with the longer bolt goes on the front and the one with the shorter bolt goes on the rear. Once you have determined which is which, insert the mounting bolt through

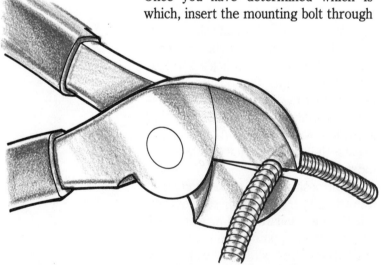

*Illustration 12-3: When trimming cable housing, use a knife to break through the vinyl cover, then work one jaw of a sharp pair of cutters between coils and snip the wire.*

the mounting hole in the frame, thread on the mounting nut and snug it down. Don't worry about getting it really tight until later after you have centered the calipers on the wheel.

## Installing Cables and Cable Housing

The next step is to install the cables. The first decision you have to make is which lever to connect to which brake. The general rule here is to hook up the brakes in such a way that your dominant hand controls the rear brake. Your next decision is how long to make your cables. Many cyclists try to reduce friction in their cables by making the cable runs as short as possible, often trimming several inches off the housing that comes with their bikes.

While there is certainly no need for enormous cable loops over your handlebars, don't go overboard in the other direction either. Unnecessarily long cables are a source of excessive friction, but so are cable runs that are too short, because they produce bends that bind the cable in the housing. So, when you install new cables and housing, cut away the excess, but leave sufficient length for loops large enough to prevent any kinking in the housing or joints when the handlebars are turned sharply to one side or the other. Kinks will cause premature wear and fraying of your cables.

Once the cable runs have been laid out and the lengths determined, the housing must be trimmed. The tools needed for this are a sharp knife, a sharp pair of diagonal cutters, and a small file.

At the point marking the proper length, cut the vinyl covering around the housing with the knife. Position the jaws of the diagonal cutters parallel to the cable coils and exert enough pressure to separate the coils where you want to cut. Once the coils are cleanly separated, cut through the connecting bit of metal. If you are cutting a lined housing, a sharp pair of cutters is essential or the liner will be crushed instead of being cleanly cut.

Look closely at the end of the housing coil wire and you will see that cutting has left it with a very sharp edge. If allowed to remain, this sharp edge may damage your cable at some point. So trim the sharp edge away with the cutters or file it smooth.

If you're installing a new set of brakes, the cable housing will have small metal ferrules mounted on each end or supplied loose in the package. If they are loose, save them to put on the ends of your housing after you cut it to length. These ferrules provide protection for the ends of the housing and help support the housing where it seats in the lever and the calipers. If you don't use the ferrules, the cable will have a tendency to cock to one side and not line up with the lever housing or caliper housing stop, giving a spongy feel and wearing the cable prematurely. When you temporarily take off your cable and housing, try not to lose these ferrules; ask for new ones when you purchase new set of cables.

Before pushing the cable through the cable housing, coat the cable with a lubricant to encourage smooth pulling action and discourage corrosion. If your cable housing is nylon lined, a spray lubricant containing Teflon is adequate for the cable. Otherwise, coat the cable with the same type of grease you use elsewhere on your bicycle.

Remember, before running the cable through the cable housing, install the housing ferrules. Then, thread the cable through the hole in the upper part of the brake lever. Catch the head of the cable in the anchor provided for it inside the lever, making certain the anchor is turned so that the cable head will properly seat itself when the cable is pulled taut.

Once the cable has been routed through the housing, you must fasten it to the calipers and trim away any excess. For this you need some means of holding the calipers against the wheel rim while tightening the cable. There is a tool called the "third hand" made for this purpose. It hooks over both brake shoes and presses them toward each other. If you don't want to invest in this handy tool, you can ask a friend to help you, or create your own third hand by using a shoe string or a toe strap from your bicycle. Still another approach is to slightly tighten the anchor nut on the cable, then hold the calipers together with one hand while jerking the cable taut, then tighten the anchor nut with the other hand. Experiment and you will soon find the method that works best for you.

Before tightening the cable, check to make sure the brake quick-release is shut. Next, screw the cable length adjuster all the way down, then back it off a single turn. Also, check to make sure the cable end is seated properly in the brake lever and the housing ends are seated in their receptacles. If all is in order, pull the cable taut and tighten the anchor nut.

Release the calipers and squeeze the brake lever several times to stretch the cable. If the cable seats and stretches so much that the lever hits the handlebars when you squeeze it hard, squeeze the brake shoes against the rim

Photo 12-1: A third-hand tool can be used to hold brake pads against the wheel rim while a brake cable is being tightened.

again and pull the cable tighter. Anchor the cable at a point that will provide 1/8 to 3/16 inch of clearance between each brake shoe and the rim before you squeeze the lever, and plenty of space between the lever and the bars when you squeeze it hard. Once you have the cable in that position, tighten the anchor bolt enough to prevent any cable slippage when braking hard. Leave 1 to 2 inches of cable protruding from the anchor bolt and use

sharp cable cutters to trim the rest away.

Once you have trimmed the end of the cable, you need to do something to prevent it from fraying. The sharp strands of a frayed bike cable are not kind to human hands. One way to prevent cable fraying is to use premanufactured end protectors. They are available in aluminum or plastic. The aluminum type are slipped over the cable end and then crimped with a pair of wire crimpers. The plastic ones are installed similarly except they don't have to be crimped. They are easier to install, but less permanent.

If you don't have one of the little end caps, you can solder the cable end. To do this, a soldering gun, solder, and flux are needed. You may find it convenient to undo the cable from the calipers. Then wipe off any dirt and lubricant from the end of the cable with alcohol. Next, stick the portion of the cable that is to be soldered into the flux. Apply the hot tip of the soldering gun to the cable—the heated flux will begin to smoke and sizzle as the heat rises. Test the cable with the solder and as soon as the solder starts to melt, work it up and down the cable end. While the solder is still fluid, wipe it with a damp rag to give it a clean finish.

A word of caution: don't solder above the point where the cable is held by the anchor nut. Soldering makes the cable very stiff and the cable must be flexible for the brake to work properly. Also, depending on the nature of your anchor, stiffening the anchor point itself may encourage the anchor to cut through the cable. So it is probably wise to stop just short of the anchor point.

## Installing Centerpull and Cantilever Brakes

Centerpull and cantilever brake systems resemble sidepulls in some ways but differ in others. The method of attaching levers to handlebars is the same, but the way brake cables are connected to the calipers is different. The main cable on a centerpull or cantilever brake attaches to a metal yoke or "pick-up," which in turn is attached to a short transverse or "stirrup" cable. The ends of the stirrup cable are attached to the caliper arms. When you squeeze the lever, the main cable lifts the stirrup cable, which then pulls the caliper arms against the rim of the tire.

The body of a centerpull brake is fastened to the bike frame the same as a sidepull. A mounting bolt and nut lock it to the frame. Cantilevers, by contrast, do not have one body to which two arms are attached. Instead, each side of the brake is independently attached to the frame. Each half of a cantilever brake is bolted to a brazed-on boss equipped with a steel spring that pushes the brake shoe away from the rim after the lever is released.

On a centerpull brake, you will find a cable stop mounted on a hanger that is suspended above the calipers, usually from the top of the headset or the seat tube, depending on whether it is the front or rear brake. Some hangers are integrated into the stem or are brazed to the seatstays. The cable housing will end at the stop while the brake cable will continue to the stirrup cable pick-up.

If the hanger has a quick-release, be sure it is closed before adjusting the cable length. The stirrup cable pick-up will have an anchor with a hole in it. You have to thread the cable through the bolt. Once the brake cable is threaded through the bolt and the stirrup cable is in place in the channel provided for it on the yoke or pick-up, pull the cable taut and tighten the nut on the cable anchor bolt.

You will need to hold the brake shoes against the wheel rim with a third-hand tool or some other means while finishing this cable attachment. As with sidepull brakes, adjust the cable length so that there is ⅛ to 3/16 inch of clearance between each brake shoe and the rim when the levers are released. After you initially tighten the anchor bolt on the cable, squeeze the levers several times to stretch the cable and seat the housing. If necessary, take up the slack at the anchor. Once you have accommodated the initial cable stretch and have anchored the cable in a position where it should remain for a while, trim away the excess cable. Leave only an inch or two sticking through so the loose end of the cable will not foul up the operation of the calipers. Protect the cut cable end from fraying by installing an end protector or by coating it with solder, as described earlier.

## Aligning the Calipers

Before beginning the alignment process, check the wheel by spinning it to see if it's true. If it's not, true the wheel before proceeding. Otherwise, the wheel will either end up dragging on the brake blocks, or the adjustment will have to be on the loose side and may result in a pulsating or jerky braking action. If you have as much as ¼ inch of clearance between either brake pad and the rim at any point during the revolution of the wheel and contact between the two at any other point, your wheel definitely needs trueing.

Once the wheel is running true, check the distance of the brake pads from the rim. The clearance should be equal on both sides. If it is unequal, the calipers need to be centered on the wheel. Loosen the rear mounting nut on

the calipers just enough to allow them to move from side to side. Don't loosen it to the point that the calipers become floppy. Now, squeeze the brake lever to bring the shoes into firm contact with the rim. Keeping the pressure on, snug up the mounting nut enough to keep the calipers from pivoting on the fork crown or brake bridge.

Release the lever and check to see if the calipers are in fact centered. If the arms don't contact the rim evenly or one brake shoe leans against the rim after you release the brake lever, you will have to align the calipers. How this is done depends upon the type of brakes.

There are several ways to center a sidepull. First try loosening the mounting bolt, twisting the caliper, and retightening the mounting nut. If that isn't successful try using the two nuts on the front of the brake that hold on the caliper arms. First lock the two nuts tightly together by turning the inner one counterclockwise and the outer one clockwise. Move one wrench to the rear mounting nut, leaving the other at the front. Twist both wrenches in the same direction to rotate the brake body.

If you need to rotate the brake body in a clockwise direction to center the calipers, keep your wrench on the outer of the two front nuts. If you need to rotate the brake body counterclockwise, keep your wrench on the inner of the two. This way you will not loosen these nuts in relation to each other while making the adjustment.

Some sidepull brakes have a nut with centering flats located behind the calipers, between the calipers and the frame. Placing a cone wrench on this nut allows you to turn the brake to the right or the left and hold it there until you have tightened the nut on the end of the mounting bolt. Once it is tight you can hold the wrenches on these two nuts and turn them together to rock the brake body into the desired position.

Centering a centerpull brake is similar, though simpler, than centering a sidepull because there is only one place to put your wrench. All you need to do is loosen the nut found on the tail end of the mounting bolt with a wrench, twist the body of the calipers (the part the caliper arms attach to) until it is centered, then hold it there while you retighten the nut.

The pads on a cantilever brake should be set equidistant from the rim for even braking action. If the arms do not move against the rim at the same rate, slide the cable pick-up along the stirrup toward the brake shoe that is slowest to reach the rim. To prevent it from sliding back, put a crimp in the stirrup cable next to the pick-up. If that doesn't help you may have to remove the cantilever arm and retension the spring by bending it backward.

Once your brakes are centered, check the cable slack for a final time. If the brake blocks are within $\frac{1}{8}$ inch of the rim, leave the initial adjustment. If not, loosen the cable, take up more of the slack, then reanchor the cable. Then use the cable adjuster to fine-tune the brake so that the pads end up being between $\frac{3}{32}$ and $\frac{1}{8}$ inch from the wheel rim.

As you use the brakes you will discover some gradual stretching of the cable. This can be taken up with the adjuster as it becomes noticeable. If the stretch becomes so great that you use up all the fine-tuning available with the cable adjuster, simply screw it down as you did in the beginning, hold the calipers against the rim, and take up the slack at the cable anchor.

## Solutions to Common Problems

A common problem with new brake installations or newly installed brake shoes is the nerve-wracking squeal that is caused by pad misalignment. To solve this problem, many mechanics simply take a wrench and twist the caliper arm to toe the trailing edge (i.e., the edge closest to the front of the bike) of the shoe toward the rim. This is one way of adjusting shoes, but not the best one. If done forcefully, it can cause the mounting bolt to bend or the caliper arm to crack.

To do this operation correctly you need some medium-grit sandpaper and a flat surface. First, watch how the shoes contact the rim as you gradually apply pressure to the lever. If the leading edge touches the rim first, remove the shoe from the caliper and, with the sandpaper face up on the flat surface, gently draw the leading edge of the brake block across the sandpaper. Repeat this as many times as required, with trial fits on the calipers, until the trailing edge hits the rim first.

Another possible cause of intermittent squealing is residue buildup on the rim. The least abrasive way to remove deposits is to fold some nylon mesh into a pad and then lightly scrub the rim until all residue is gone. Glazing or hardening of brake blocks can also cause squealing. The most permanent way of curing this is to simply replace the shoes.

*(continued on page 208)*

table 12-1    TROUBLESHOOTING BRAKES

| Problem | Possible Cause | Check | Solution |
| --- | --- | --- | --- |
| Dragging brake shoes | Calipers not centered | Space between rim and shoes should be equal on both sides of wheel | Center the calipers as described in text |
| | Wheel not true | Spin wheel and note lateral runout or deformations in rim | True wheel or install new rim |
| | Cable adjusted too tight | Gap between brake pads and rim should be about ⅛″ | Readjust cable length or loosen cable adjuster |
| Noisy brakes | Misaligned shoes | Trailing or front end of brake pads should contact rim first | Sand surface of brake pads as described in text |
| | Brake pads are old, hard, or glazed | Brake pads should feel resilient when pushed with fingernail | Replace brake shoes |
| | Road grime deposits on rim | Visually check rim for grime buildup | Clean rim as described in text |
| Loss of braking power | Grease on rim or brake pads | Visually check rim and brake pads | Clean rim and replace brake shoes |
| | Worn brake pads | Make visual check of wear on pads | Replace brake shoes |
| | Misaligned brake shoes | Pads should contact rim squarely | Realign brake shoes |
| | Deformed rim | Visually check shape of rim | Straighten or replace rim |
| | Foreign matter embedded in brake pads | Inspect brake pads for foreign matter | Remove embedded material or replace brake shoes |

| Symptom | Cause | Check | Remedy |
|---|---|---|---|
| Brake lever bottoms out | Worn brake pads | Inspect pads for wear | Replace brake shoes |
| | Loose or broken brake cable | Check cable run | Readjust or replace cable |
| Binding | Lever and/or cable needs lubrication | Check lever action | Lubricate lever |
| | Tight cable adjustment | There should be a ⅛" gap between pads and rim | Readjust cable length or loosen cable adjuster |
| | Damaged cable and/or housing | Inspect condition of cable and housing | Replace cable and housing |
| | Lever is damaged | Check lever movement | Replace lever |
| | Lever clamp bolt too tight | See if tight clamp bolt obstructs movement of lever pivot pin | Loosen clamp bolt |
| Chattering or vibrating brakes | Warped or dented rim | Check rim for dents and trueness | Straighten or replace rim |
| | Loose brake pivot bolt nut | Check for play in caliper arms | Adjust pivot bolt nut to eliminate play, then tighten locknut against it |
| Binding caliper | Bent caliper arms | Visually check trueness of arms | Straighten or replace calipers |
| | Bent pivot bolt | Disassemble brake body, check trueness of pivot bolt | Replace pivot bolt |
| | Pivot bolt nut too tight | Check for excessive pressure on calipers at the pivot point | Loosen locknut, adjust pivot nut, retighten locknut |

Cables also may suffer the ravages of the elements. Coated cables and those parts of uncoated cables protected by housing may fare fairly well, but exposed sections of cable need special care and protection. Periodically, you should wipe your cables clean with a rag, then coat them with a thin layer of grease. Actually, on any brake system, we would recommend replacing the cables at least once a year. This way you should always have cables in reliably good condition. It is a small price to pay for proper maintenance of this critical part of your bike.

Since brakes slow down a bike because of the friction created between the brake blocks and wheel rim, we don't recommend going overboard with lubrication of the calipers. In fact, we lubricate calipers only when we take them completely off the bike for a thorough cleaning. And, when we do lubricate calipers, it's with a very light coat of lithium grease (or a spray lube that dries without leaving an oily film) at the pivot points—the mounting bolt shank, the mating surfaces of the caliper arms (if there are any), and the return spring anchor points.

This minimal amount of lubrication reduces chances of any grease getting on the brake blocks or rim. Remember, unlike the other points on a bike that rotate or generate friction where the aim is to make parts as slippery as possible, brakes are just the opposite. In this case, we want to maximize the friction that occurs when the brake blocks make contact with the rim.

## Regular Maintenance Procedures

To keep the brake system on your bike working at optimum level, a good habit to get into is to clean the system after each ride. A wipe-down of the tires with a damp rag will keep any dirt on the wheels from setting up hard. And a good once-over with a clean rag will remove surface dirt from the calipers. After completing these wipe-downs, use a clean medium-bristle paintbrush to remove the dirt from the cracks and crevices too small to get into with a rag or fingers. Keep the brush clean by washing it frequently with liquid detergent and warm water. This is especially important when you finish cleaning the bike after a particularly dirty ride. The minimal use of lubricant also helps to keep dirt from being attracted and sticking to the calipers.

Finally, open the quick-releases and inspect the brake shoes for anything imbedded into the soft material. If you spot anything, carefully pick it out with a small screwdriver, being careful not to slip and damage the tire or rim.

## Coping with Brake Breakdowns

Regardless of how much care one takes, the law of averages indicates that one day a breakdown in your braking system will occur at an inopportune time. The one most common and devastating occurrence on a ride, short of a broken lever or caliper, will be the snapping of one of your cables. For that reason, we recommend that when you go out riding, you carry a spare brake cable, along with a spare derailleur cable.

Since bending a cable sharply may cause a permanent kink that will render it useless, about the only place to carry the cables is under the saddle. The way to do this is to coil up the cables to about a 6- to 7-inch diameter, put a piece of tape around the coil to keep it from unwinding, then put it into a small plastic bag. The whole thing should then be tucked under the saddle horizontally and pushed gently toward the nose. Since saddles vary in shape and dimensions, use some good judgment here. You don't want to push the cables into a space so small or narrow that they will be kinked. So, take some care when you fit the cables to the underside of your saddle. Once the cables are in position, take a couple of plastic-coated twist ties and secure each side of the coil to the saddle wires.

But what if you are caught without a spare cable? You may have to function temporarily with only one brake. In such a circumstance, your first inclination may be to favor the rear brake. However, the front brake on a bicycle is actually more valuable than the rear brake because it performs about 65 to 70 percent of the effective slowing provided by an equal application of both brakes. Therefore, if the cable breaks on the front caliper, you would be wise to re-move the cable from the rear brake and install it on the front. This will give you maximum braking power, under the circumstances, until you get to some place where you can replace both cables. However, keep in mind that the use of just the front brake will tend to pitch you forward more than the use of both brakes, so your speed should be kept to a point where it won't override your braking capabilities. If you must brake rather fast, slide your body as far back on the saddle as possible to compensate for the tendency of your bike to want to pitch you headfirst over the handlebars.

The brake system on your bicycle is extremely important and should be treated with care and respect. When other parts of your bike stop working, it usually means some inconvenience, the bike goes slower or makes noise. But if your brakes stop working it may mean you won't make that last big downhill curve, and serious injury could result. Don't play games with your brakes. Keep them working at the optimum level all the time.

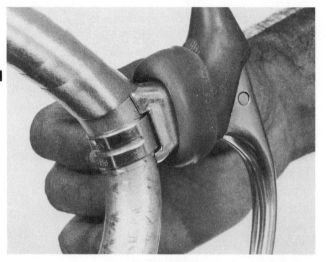

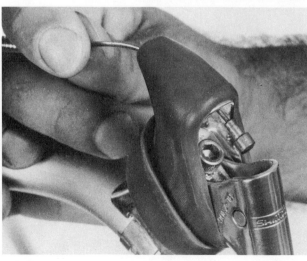

It is not too likely that a pair of brake levers will wear out or break, but there may be occasions when you will need to remove them. Perhaps you wish to keep your old set of brakes, but want to replace the handlebars and have to remove the levers for that reason. Or, you may decide to upgrade your old bicycle by fitting it with a whole new set of brakes. New levers will be part of the package, so the old levers will need to be removed.

On the typical dropped handlebar bike, the levers cannot be removed or relocated without the handlebar tape first being unwound from the lever clamp. (Photo 1) You may as well completely remove the old handlebar tape at this time and replace it with new tape after the levers are back in place.

If your intention is to completely remove a lever from the bike, you should first release the cable attached to it. Loosen the small bolt that anchors the cable to the brake calipers and pull the cable free. (Photo 2) Then unhook the fitting on the upper end of the cable from its seat in the lever. (Photo 3) Now pull the cable all the way out of the lever body and cable housing.

If you wish only to relocate a lever on the handlebars, rather than remove it, you may be able to leave the cable inside the lever body. Just unhook it from the lever and pull it out of the way while you loosen the clamp.

When you are ready to loosen the lever clamp, squeeze the lever against the handlebars and look inside the lever body. You will see a bolt or screw that is used to fasten the clamp to the bar. Find the appropriate tool to remove this fastener. (Photo 4) You will probably need either a Phillips screwdriver, an Allen wrench, or a thin-walled socket.

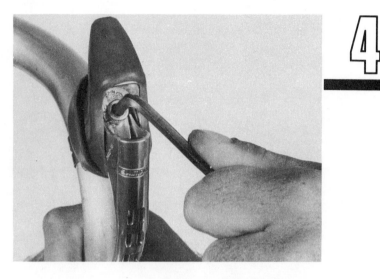

Loosen the clamp fixing bolt enough to allow you to reposition the lever or to slide it around the bend and off the end of the bar. When both levers are off the handlebars, clean the bars of any residue left behind by the old tape.

Many brake sets come with rubber covers that fit around the lever bodies. These covers increase the comfort of riding with the hands resting on the lever hoods. If you are reusing a set of levers that lack these covers or need new ones, you may wish to buy a pair. Fit them over the levers before sliding the levers back on the handlebars. (Photo 5)

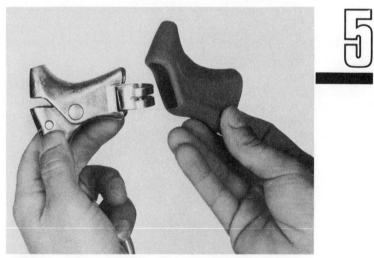

After putting the levers back on the bars, you will need to position them both horizontally and vertically. The levers should be set in locations that feel comfortable and also allow you to get a good grip for solid braking action. Horizontally, the best location is almost certainly directly in front of the bars, rather than off at an angle.

The vertical position for levers is more open to individual preferences. However, a standard used by many experienced cyclists is to set the levers at a height where their tips line up with the lowest part of the bars. A straightedge held beneath the bars will show you exactly where that is. (Photo 6)

When you have the levers where you want them, tighten the clamp bolts. Then check to see if the tightened bolts interfere with the lever action. If they do, try loosening them slightly to see if that eliminates the problem. However, make certain the clamps are tight enough to prevent the levers from twisting on the bars when squeezed hard. Once the levers are properly secured, re-tape the bars, then install and adjust the brake cables. ▲

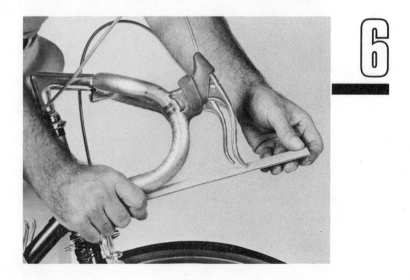

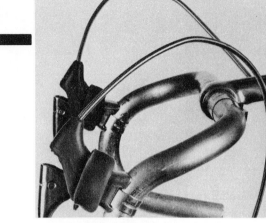

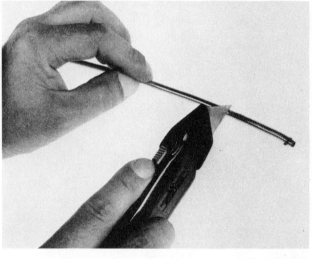

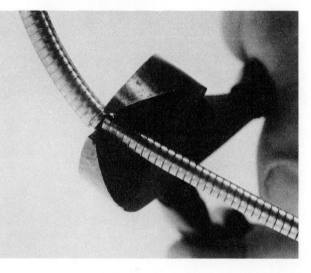

No aspect of bicycle maintenance and repair could appear to be simpler than installing a brake cable. You might think that all you have to do is run a wire through the lever down to the brake calipers and fasten it with a bolt. But actually, it is more involved than that.

At the outset, some important decisions have to be made. First, you must decide which lever to connect to which brake. The recommended rule is to connect the lever controlled by the dominant hand with the rear brake, since it takes more force to operate. However, if your dominant hand is the left, but you are used to operating the rear brake with the right hand, set it up that way to avoid confusion.

Once that decision has been made, you have to determine how long the cable housing should be. Many new bikes come fitted with excessively long housing. This means large cable loops that can be a nuisance to the rider. Cable that is longer than necessary also creates unneeded friction in the braking system. Ideally, the brake cables should arch as low as possible over the bicycle handlebars. (Photo 1)

However, you should avoid going to an extreme when you start to cut back on the length of your brake cable housing. If you make the housing too short, it will bend sharply and kink the cable. Short housing can also obstruct the proper movement of the handlebars. So pick a length sufficient to allow your handlebars to move from side to side through their full range of motion without creating cable kinks. Trim the housing to that length.

Mark the position on the housing where you wish to trim it and cut through the vinyl covering with a sharp knife. (Photo 2) Then

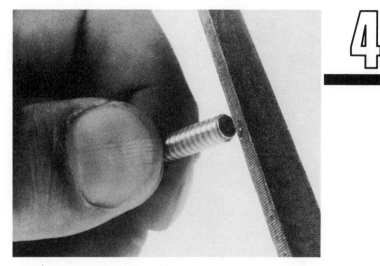

take a sharp pair of cable cutters and work one jaw between coils so that you can make a clean cut through a coil without smashing the housing. (Photo 3)

After trimming the housing, file the cut end smooth to prevent the possibility of it snagging and damaging the cable. (Photo 4)

Now get out one of your new cables. Unless these cables were made specifically for your brake system they probably will have a different fitting attached to each end. Determine which fitting you need by looking at the rotating barrel inside the lever into which it must fit. Then trim away the fitting you do not need. (Photo 5)

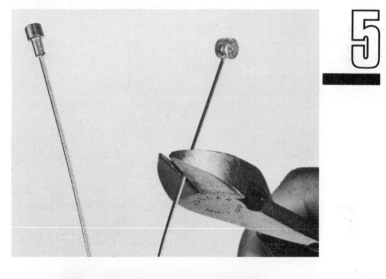

Lubricate the cable before running it through the housing. The medium-weight grease you use elsewhere on the bike will work fine. Just put a little on your fingertips and pull the cable through to coat it lightly. Then squeeze the lever open and thread the cable through the lever body and into the cable housing.

Push the cable on through the housing but do not fasten it to the brake body yet. Leave yourself some slack at the upper end so you can hook the cable fitting onto the lever. Rotate the cylinder as needed and tug on the loose end of the cable to make sure the fitting is properly seated in the lever. (Photo 6)

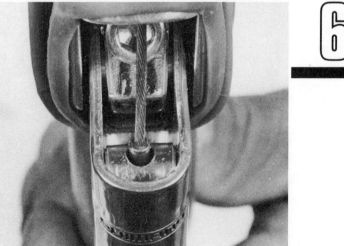

Thread the loose end of the cable through the housing stop and pull on it to seat the housing against the stop. (Photo 7)

If you have sidepull brakes, run the end of the cable through the anchor bolt. If you have centerpull brakes, first make sure the fittings at each end of the short stirrup cable are properly seated in the slots provided for them in the upper ends of the caliper arms. Then run the end of the main cable through

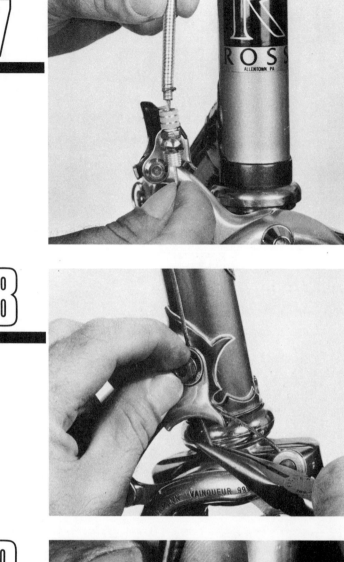

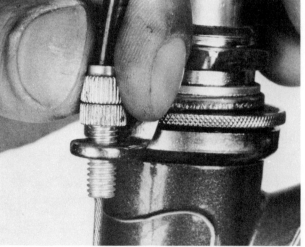

the anchor on the yoke used to lift up the stirrup cable. You may wish to tighten the nut with your finger to prevent the cable from pulling free until you are ready to firmly anchor it. (Photo 8)

Before you securely anchor the cable, check back over the entire braking system. First, find the cable length adjusting barrel. On sidepulls this barrel may be located either at the lever end or the caliper end of the cable housing. A few systems have adjusting barrels in both places. On centerpulls, the adjusting barrel will probably be on the cable housing hanger.

Thread the barrel all the way down, then back it off a couple of turns. (Photo 9) This will leave you plenty of room to take up slack in the cable as it stretches in later use.

If your brake system is equipped with a quick-release lever, make sure it is closed so the calipers can be adjusted to their operating position. (Photo 10)

Now check again to make certain the fitting at the upper end of the cable is properly seated in the lever, then use a toe strap or a third-hand tool to hold the calipers shut against the rim while you pull up the slack in the cable and anchor it firmly. (Photo 11)

Release the calipers and squeeze the lever firmly a few times to see how quickly the cable is going to stretch. If this immediately produces a good deal of slack in the system, fasten the calipers back against the

rim, loosen the anchor bolt, pull the cable tight and reanchor it.

After prestretching the cable in this way, you should be able to handle slack for a while by turning the adjusting barrel so that it moves away from the brake calipers and thus tightens the cable.

When you reach the point where there is very little room left for fine-tuning the cable length by means of the adjusting barrel, thread the barrel almost all the way down again and readjust the cable length at the anchor bolt.

A new brake cable will almost certainly be longer than necessary. So after the installation process is complete, allow an inch or two of cable to extend beyond the anchor bolt and trim away the rest. (Photo 12)

The cut end of a new cable is likely to fray if left unprotected. To prevent fraying, you can cover it with a little aluminum or plastic cap made for this purpose. Another possibility is to coat the cable with solder from the anchor area to its tip.

To solder the cable end, you must release it from the anchor and clean away all grease and dirt with alcohol. Stick the cable tip into flux, then heat it with a soldering gun. When it starts to sizzle hold solder against it. As the solder begins to melt rub it up and down to coat the entire area, then wipe it smooth with a damp rag. ▲

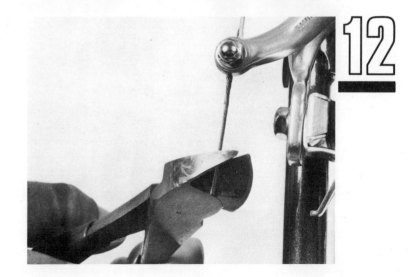

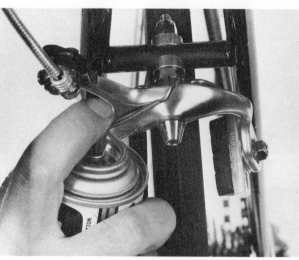

To remove the body of a sidepull brake, first loosen the cable anchor bolt and free the end of the cable. Then loosen and remove the nut on the rear end of the mounting bolt that runs through the brake body. (Photo 1) Thread the nut off the end of the bolt, then pull the brake body away from the frame. (Photo 2)

If you have removed the brake to service it rather than replace it, clean it thoroughly. Use a rag dipped in solvent and a brush to loosen the grease and dirt collected on the surface of the calipers and hiding inside all nooks and crannies.

Unless you are using something mild like alcohol, keep the solvent away from the rubber brake pads. Better yet, remove the brake shoes to clean the pads separately.

Since oils and greases have a tendency to attract dirt, they should be used only where they are needed. On sidepull brakes that means only at the pivot points and the spring anchors on the back of the calipers.

To minimize the possibility of getting lubricant on your brake pads, use grease rather than oil on the spring where it rubs against its anchors. Since it is difficult to work grease into the pivot area without dismantling the brake, you can spray those points with a small amount of one of the fast-drying lubricants that leaves a Teflon film behind. (Photo 3)

To install a brake body, insert the mounting bolt through the hole in the frame and thread on the mounting nut. Tighten the nut fairly tight, but leave it loose enough for the brake to be centered on the wheel by hand. Reconnect the brake cable to the brake calipers and adjust the cable length following the instructions starting on page 212. Then check the caliper alignment.

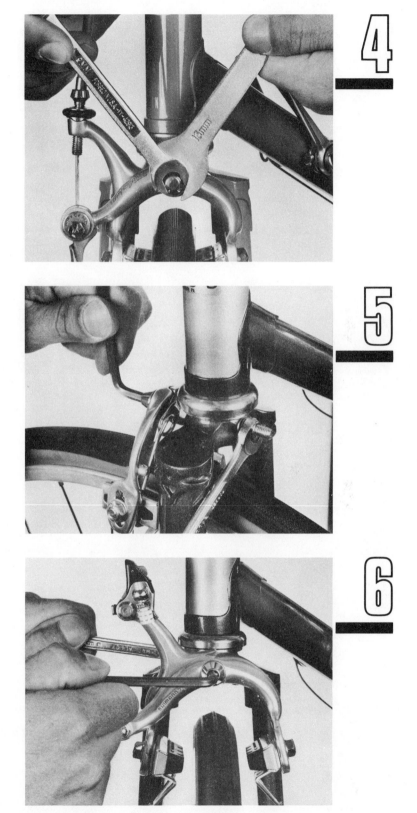

Before you can properly align the calipers you have to make sure the wheel is true and centered in the frame. If the wheel is out of true, no amount of brake adjustment will give you good performance.

Before attempting to center the brakes, check the relationship of the caliper arms to each other. If they are too tight, they will not spring back after you release the lever. If they are too loose, they will vibrate excessively when you press them against the rim of the moving wheel. They should be as tight as they can be and still operate freely.

The tightness of the calipers is controlled by a nut or pair of nuts on the front end of the mounting bolt. Since this part of the bolt functions as the pivot for the calipers, it is often referred to as the pivot bolt. If there are two nuts, the outer nut must be loosened and the pressure on the calipers adjusted with the inner one. Stop tightening the inner nut just before the calipers start to show resistance to pivoting, then lock the two nuts against one another to maintain the adjustment. (Photo 4) If your brakes have only a single nut or bolt head in front, turn that to adjust the caliper tension.

Now rotate the brake body to center the calipers on the wheel. Hold the brake in that position while you snug up the mounting nut. (Photo 5)

Squeeze the brake lever a few times to see if the brake pads are striking the rim at the same time and whether or not the brake remains centered after being used. If not, hold the brake steady again while you snug up the mounting nut a bit more. Then turn both wrenches together to rock the entire brake body in the direction needed to center it. (Photo 6) ▲

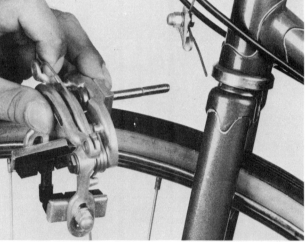

A centerpull brake system makes use of two cables: a long main cable similar to that used in a sidepull system and a short transverse or "stirrup" cable. The two connect with each other by means of a triangular metal yoke. The main cable is bolted to the yoke, which curls around the center of the shorter cable. (Photo 1)

Each end of the stirrup cable hooks onto one of the caliper arms. When the lever is squeezed, the main cable lifts the yoke, pulling up the center of the stirrup cable and thus pulling the calipers against the wheel rim.

To remove a centerpull brake body for cleaning or replacement, release the main cable from the yoke and unhook the yoke from the stirrup cable. Loosen the nut on the rear end of the brake mounting bolt and remove the brake body from the bicycle. (Photo 2)

If you intend to reuse the old brake body, clean it thoroughly. Use a rag dipped in solvent and a small brush to remove the grease and grime from the caliper arms and the areas where the arms pivot on the mounting bolt. Avoid bringing any strong solvent in contact with the brake pads. Clean them with alcohol and fine-grit sandpaper.

After the calipers are clean and dry, lightly lubricate the moving parts. Work a small dab of grease or some spray lube into the area where contact is made between the two arms and into each arm's pivot points. (Photo 3)

To mount a new or renewed centerpull brake body, insert its mounting bolt through the hole in the frame and thread on the

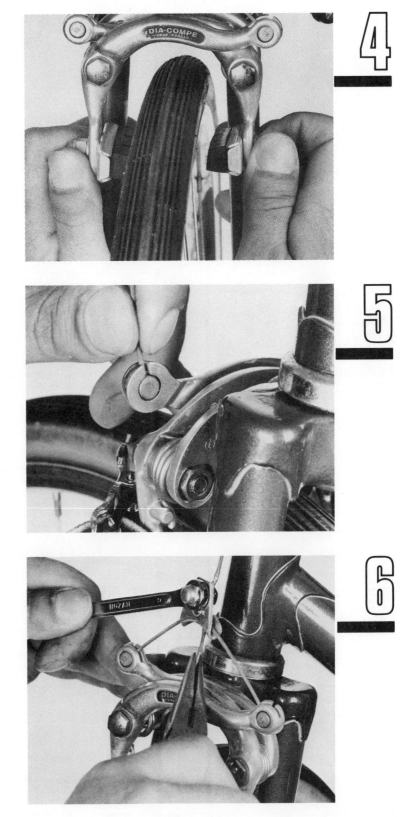

mounting nut. Before tightening the nut, center the brake on the wheel. First make sure the wheel is true and centered between the forks.

Rock the brake body by hand until the pads appear to be equidistant from the sides of the wheel rim. (Photo 4) Then tighten the mounting nut on the mounting bolt to hold the brake in that position.

Make sure the fittings on the ends of the stirrup cable are properly seated in the slots in the caliper arms. (Photo 5) Then hook the yoke under the center of the short cable.

Turn the cable length adjusting barrel down almost all the way to give yourself room for later fine-tuning. Then hold the brake shoes against the wheel with the help of a toe strap or third-hand tool. Pull the end of the main cable taut and hold it with a pair of pliers while you tighten the anchor nut with a wrench. (Photo 6)

Release the calipers and test the brake by squeezing the lever a few times. If you have installed a new cable, it may stretch enough that you need to take up the slack at the anchor nut. Otherwise, fine-tune the length of the cable with the adjusting barrel. Leave only $3/32$ to $1/8$ inch of space between each brake pad and the wheel rim.

When you squeeze the lever, check to see that the brake pads contact the rim at the same time. If they do not, shift the position of the yoke on the stirrup cable in the direction of the slower arm. If that does not solve the problem, try bending the spring to increase the tension on that arm. ▲

The brake shoes are a small but important part of the bicycle braking system. If the shoes are allowed to become loose, the brakes cannot be relied upon. If the shoes are set too high, their pads may rub the side of the tire and damage it. If they are not aligned correctly in relation to the wheel rim, they may chatter and squeal when the two are pressed into contact. And if the pads are excessively worn or glazed over with road grime, their stopping power may be dangerously reduced. Thus, cleaning and adjusting shoes is a critical part of bicycle brake maintenance.

One good habit to develop is to check the condition of the brake pads at the completion of every bike ride, especially rides along routes with a lot of sand and gravel. Open the brake quick-releases and examine the surface of the pads. Remove anything embedded in them.

If you ride your bike regularly, give your wheel rims and brake pads a good cleaning with alcohol at least once a month. For a more complete inspection and cleaning, the shoes must be removed from the bike.

The removal process is quite easy. Find a wrench of the right size and loosen the nut that holds the shoe in position on the caliper. (Photo 1) Take off the nut and the washer and slip the shoe out of the end of the caliper. (Photo 2) Clean away as much road grime as you can with alcohol, then lay a piece of fine-grit sandpaper on a flat surface and rub the surface of the brake pad across it. (Photo 3)

The sandpaper treatment serves two purposes. It removes the built-up road grime from the braking surface of the pad and it also reshapes that surface. This is important in correcting uneven wear, such as when a pad has been positioned too low on the rim.

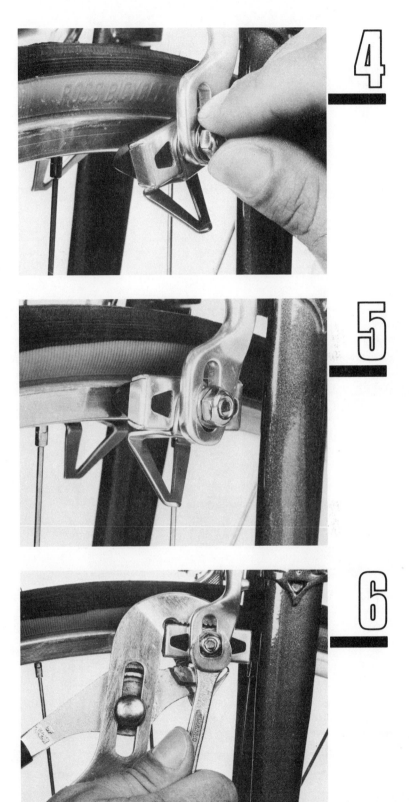

If you have a problem with squealing brakes, it is usually caused by the leading edge of the brake pad striking the rim before the rest of the pad. This starts a process of vibration in the brake shoes, which creates the nerve-racking noise. You can reduce or eliminate this problem by altering the surface of the pad with sandpaper. Change the angle of the pad surface so that the trailing edge touches the rim slightly before the rest of the pad. This should quiet your brakes and give them a more solid feel.

If the pads are badly worn or otherwise deteriorated, they should be replaced. To mount new or reworked shoes, run their posts through the slots on the ends of the calipers. Fit washers on the posts and then thread on the nuts until they are finger tight. (Photo 4)

Adjust the position of the pads so they will strike the center of the wheel rim. Avoid setting them high where they may touch the tire or low where part of the pad surface misses the rim. Also, make sure the shoe is set parallel with the rim. (Photo 5)

To prevent your careful adjustment from being lost, hold the pad firmly with a pair of pliers while you tighten the nut. (Photo 6) Avoid applying so much torque that you strip the threads in the nut, but do not hesitate to make it quite tight. You do not want the brake shoe to loosen because of vibration and fail to work when you need it most. ▲

All-terrain bikes typically are equipped with motorcycle-type handlebars, brake levers, and cantilever brakes. Since ATB handlebars are not wrapped with tape, brake levers can be relocated or replaced fairly quickly. To reposition a lever, locate and loosen the clamp bolt. (Photo 1) Move the lever to the desired place and retighten the clamp.

Brake lever location is a matter of personal preference. However, the usual method of positioning levers is to set them parallel with the front of the bars and make their tips even with the ends of the bars.

The cantilever brakes used on ATBs, tandem bikes, and most loaded touring bikes are mounted differently than sidepull and conventional centerpull brakes. Each front cantilever is fastened by bolt to a metal stud that is brazed on to the front side of one of the front forks. (Photo 2) Cantilevers on the rear are attached to studs brazed on the back sides of the seatstays.

The brake shoes on cantilevers are slightly different from those on caliper brakes. The posts that extend from the backs of the shoes on cantilevers are fairly long and are used to adjust the distance of the shoes from the tire rim.

When installing a new set of cantilevers or readjusting an old set, make sure the wheel is true and centered between the forks of the bike frame. Then set all the brake shoes equidistant from the rim. You will probably need an Allen wrench for the head of the shoe mounting bolt and a box wrench for the nut at its end. (Photo 3)

There are two factors to take into account in determining the proper setting of the shoe. First, the shoe should be turned so that its pad is parallel with the rim. Second, it should be set at a place that will cause it to

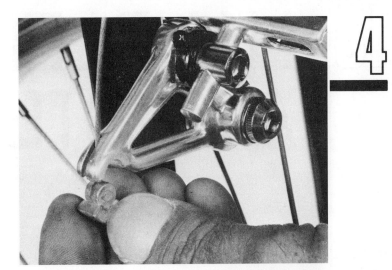

solidly contact the rim when the arm is pushed toward the wheel.

Cantilever brakes, like centerpull calipers, make use of a short cable—known as the transverse, stirrup, or straddle cable—to connect the two braking arms. This cable may have a permanent fitting on only one end. If so, the other end is anchored by bolt and the cable length is adjustable.

Hook the end with the fitting into the cantilever arm that has a slot made to receive it. (Photo 4) Thread the other end through the anchor bolt found on the other arm. Where you anchor it depends in part on the frame of your bike. As a general rule, set the stirrup cable length such that when you pull up on its center the angle formed there is less than 90 degrees.

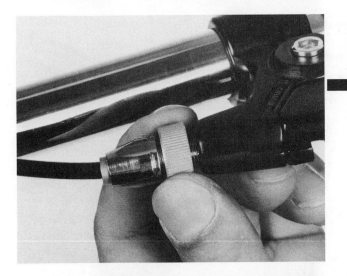

Give the main cable a light coating of grease, then push it through the housing and seat the fitting on its upper end into the groove provided for it on the lever. Hook the yoke around the center of the stirrup cable and run the loose end of the main cable through its anchor bolt.

Before anchoring the main cable to the yoke, thread the adjusting barrel at the lever end down almost against the lever to provide plenty of adjustment space as the cable stretches. (Photo 5)

Hold the cantilever arms against the wheel rim, pull the main cable taut, and tighten the bolt to anchor it. (Photo 6)

Release the braking arms and test the brake. Make further adjustments in shoe position and cable length if needed. If the brakes do not contact the rim at the same time, try shifting the position of the yoke along the stirrup cable toward the slower side. If that does not solve the problem, remove that cantilever arm and bend the spring to give it more tension. ▲

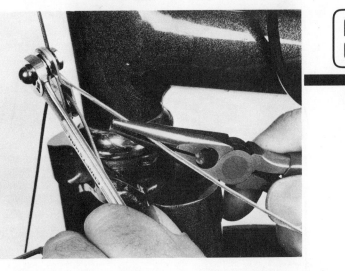

# 13 HANDLEBARS AND STEMS

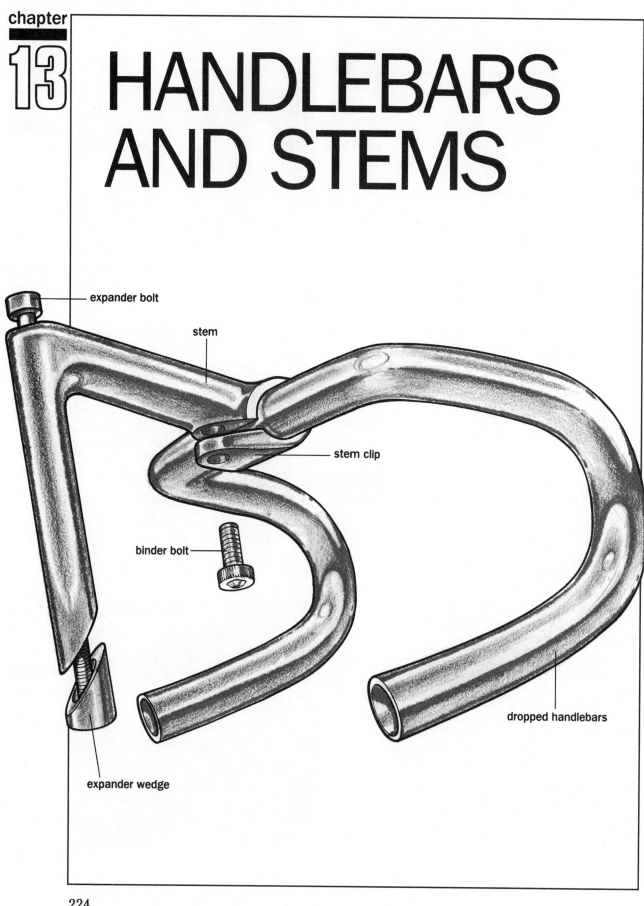

expander bolt

stem

stem clip

binder bolt

expander wedge

dropped handlebars

How much effort do you put into the selection of a saddle? If you are like us, a lot of time is expended to find a comfortable saddle and to get it set at the right height and angle on the bike. Yet, the saddle supports only part of a cyclist's weight. The remainder, ideally, rests on the handlebars.

When you are shopping for a new bike or new bike components, as much time and care should be taken in the selection of the right handlebars and stem as in the selection of the right saddle. The size and shape of the bars and stem determine the positioning of your upper torso on the bike and affect the position of the rest of your body. The bars and stem and the height at which they are set not only greatly influence your comfort, they also affect your pedaling effectiveness on the bike.

## Finding the Right Stem

Before purchasing a new stem, first determine whether you have a frame with a French-dimensioned 22.0mm or the more universal 22.2mm diameter steering tube. If you don't have an inside micrometer or inside calipers, simply borrow a stem of each diameter and try them out or take your bike along to the bike shop to get the proper fit.

One way to get a pretty good idea about your steering tube dimension is to look at the headset or bottom bracket. If the threading there is either English,

Italian, Swiss, or Far Eastern, chances are your steering tube will be 22.2mm in diameter. On the other hand, if the headset or bottom bracket has French threading, the steering tube will probably be 22.0mm. There is a third size, .833 inch, that is unique to the United States. But it is normally found only on American-made sportster and juvenile bikes. However, in the vast majority of cases, American-made lightweight bikes use 22.2mm steering tubes.

It is very important in selecting a stem to determine the length of extension that is correct for your body. Unfortunately, there is no simple or foolproof method for doing this. The correct stem length is predicated on several variables that do not always correlate in the same way. The variables include torso length, lower and upper arm length, saddle position, top tube length, and choice of handlebars.

Getting a good fit between rider and bike begins with the selection of a frame. (See page 25 for a discussion of matching a body to a frame.) Once that choice is made, fine-tuning is done with the setting of the seat height and its limited room for fore-and-aft movement. These adjustments relate to leg and pedal position.

Once the saddle position is set, the proper handlebar position can be determined in relationship to it. One traditional technique is to place the back of the elbow against the nose of the saddle and extend the forearm and hand toward the stem and handlebars. As a general rule, the top of the handlebar should lie about 1 inch beyond the tips of the fingers. This is a fairly good place to start.

Some people will want the bars a little closer than this to allow for easier breathing and a more upright riding position. This is particularly the case for cyclists undertaking loaded touring or simply riding for long periods of time. Racers and some sport riders like to have their bars a bit farther out because they prefer a more stretched-out riding position.

Some people recommend using an adjustable stem for awhile to determine what works best for them. We would agree with this method as long as the special stem is used on the same frame and in conjunction with the same components with which the new stem will be used, or at least with a frame of the same geometry and similar components. Also, when working with an adjustable stem, make changes in small increments so your body has a chance to get accustomed to each change in order to properly evaluate it.

Stems used on all-terrain bikes are somewhat different from those used on lightweight bikes in that they are designed to take the pounding of rough terrain. On some ATBs, the stem is integrated into the handlebar and cannot be separated from it. Others have stems that clamp onto the bars using a method similar to what is found on lightweights with dropped handlebars.

The single-piece flat bar and stem combination is probably the strongest pound for pound, both because of its triangular shape and the chrome-moly steel generally used in bars of this type. The drawback of the one-piece units is the impossibility of adjusting the angle of the bars or replacing the stem separate from the bars.

For top-of-the-line ATBs, alloy and alloy/steel combination stems are the order of the day. These combine the weight-saving advantage of aluminum with the strength of steel. The biggest advantage of these stems is that they do

*Photo 13-1: The Bullmoose type of handlebar found on many all-terrain bikes integrates the bar and stem into one inseparable unit.*

permit adjustment of the bars. But they are more complicated and thus more expensive to produce than stems on the single-piece units.

As with lightweight bikes, so with ATBs, the steering-tube size will be predicated on where the frame was manufactured. The exception to this rule is with custom-built frames. In some cases a .833-inch tube may be found on such a frame, especially if the builder is located in the United States and also makes the stem that fits into the frame. However, most custom-builders with whom we have talked realize the problems of nonstandardization and try to stay with 22.2mm tubing.

## Selecting Handlebars

The size of the handlebars, like the stem, should be based on the physical characteristics of the rider. The width of the bars should be as wide as the distance between the shoulders to provide a position on the levers that permits unrestricted breathing. The reach of the bars should allow the brake levers to be grasped without stretching, and the hooks should offer a position that maximizes the pulling power of the arms and back.

Most road racers favor the "square" or road bar shape because of the variety of hand positions it offers. The flat top part of the bar allows an "upright" position with the hands placed not quite shoulder-width apart, but far enough to allow relaxed breathing while motoring along or engaging in steady, moderate climbs. A more prone position of the upper body is achieved when the hands are placed on the brake hoods or just above the hoods on the upper curved portion of the bars. This position is good for a faster effort, one requiring that the body generate less wind resistance. At the same time it leaves the chest cavity open for easy breathing. This position puts the hands at quite a different angle than the bar top position. Switching between the two thus varies the pressure, putting it on different parts of the hands.

As the hands move to the "drops" or bottom of the bar, the upper torso is forced down into a prone or nearly prone position, depending on how the bike is set up. This position exposes the least amount of body area to the head wind and also maximizes the use of the back muscles for all-out efforts, such as sprints. The drawback in riding for too long in this position is that most of the upper body weight is supported by the palms. This puts pressure on the ulnar nerve and can lead to numb hands, which may not regain their sensitivity for hours.

The "Belge" bar, now more generally known as the criterium bar, is an adaptation of a track racing handlebar. It is similar to the square bar except the tops are more limited, beginning the curve to the dropped part of the bar more quickly. The curve to the drop is more gradual and the drop is deeper. This shape allows the maximum amount of pull for the rider who has developed a powerful sprint. Because of the early curve and the deep drop, the criterium bar provides plenty of clearance for the forearms, so the rider can pull straight back against his arms. And since the drop is deeper, the stem does not have to be set so low. The rider can enjoy a fairly upright position when climbing and still tuck down into an aerodynamic position on the drops for faster riding.

*Illustration 13-1:*
*Three basic types of*
*handlebars.*

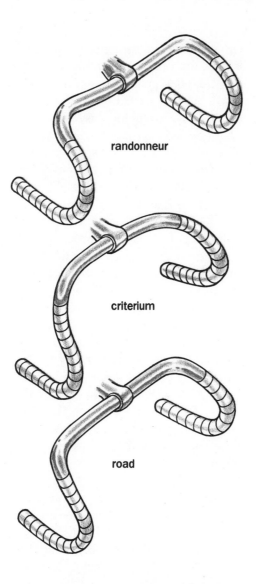

randonneur

criterium

road

A handlebar shape developed in France to answer the needs of the lightweight touring brigade was the randonneur bend. This shape has a flat top section that rises slightly and flares outward slightly as it reaches the hooks. The slight rise allows the head and torso to remain more upright since touring speeds are more sedate than those of riders hell-bent on being first across the finish line of a race. As it turns into the shallow drop section, some randonneur bars flare out a bit, providing extra wrist and forearm clearance. This is a very practical shape found on many loaded touring bikes. It probably would be seen more on high-quality bikes if most of them were not set up to please racers and faster sport riders.

The tourist bar is available for those riders who desire a permanent upright position. This bar is almost flat and is very similar to the handlebars used on the 3-speed English racers of years past. This bar essentially offers only one hand position, on the grips at the ends of the bar. Also, this bar must be equipped with straight brake levers similar to those used on ATBs.

Handlebars designed for all-terrain bikes are still in a state of flux, so there are a lot of different styles from which to choose. One distinctive style is the triangulated Bullmoose-type bar, in which the bar and stem form one inseparable unit. There are also numerous designs of a more conventional type that utilize separable bars and stems. Different models of bars vary in the amount of their rise from the stem area. Some bars are almost completely flat across the top. Others, such as those used on some of the hybrid "town and country" or "city" bikes, rise quite dramatically above the stem.

A new style of ATB handlebar is an adaptation of the criterium bar described earlier. This bar provides the alternative hand positions standard on lightweight bikes, but previously not available for ATB riders. The development of a dropped handlebar option for all-terrain bikes is a testimony to the versatility of this type of bike and an example of the continual evolution of its design.

# Installing Handlebars and Stems

The installation of a stem and a set of handlebars is a relatively simple operation if things are assembled in a logical order. It is often helpful to work the handlebars onto the stem before mounting the stem onto the bike. This way you can twist the handlebars in various directions without being in danger of hanging them up on the front fork of the bike.

The most frustrating part of handlebar mounting for beginners is getting the bar stuck inside the stem clip. There's a trick that will eliminate this problem. Look at the clip section of the stem and you'll notice that the width of the clip narrows at the bottom near the binder bolt. As you insert the bar, take your time and keep turning the bar so that the tighter inside radius of the bars is always next to the narrow part of the clip as you push the bar through the stem and center it. When you get the center of the bar inside the stem clip, snug up the binder bolt just enough to keep the bars from moving.

Once the bars and stem are together you will probably find it easier to mount them on the bike before attempting to install the brake levers or tape the bars. But before installing the bars and stem on the bike, determine the length of threading on the steering tube to see what the minimum insertion depth will be. The expander portion of the stem must extend beyond this depth or the chance of deforming or even splitting the steering tube will be greatly increased because of the thinner wall thickness at the threads. However, in no case should the insertion depth be less than 2 inches. Most stem makers are now marking the minimum insertion on their stems so you shouldn't have any problems.

Before inserting the stem into the steering tube, smear a generous coat of grease over the inserted portion to keep the dissimilar metals from corroding together and to provide a grease seal. Lower the stem to where you think you will want it and tighten the bolt.

If you perspire heavily while riding or frequently ride in the rain, moisture may work its way down inside your head tube. One way to cope with the problem is to replace the locknut on your headset with a locknut that has an o-ring seal built into it. This will minimize the possibility of corrosion developing, which, if left unchecked, will actually weld the stem to the steering tube. If you do decide to use such a locknut, such as the one by Specialized, be careful to maintain the same stack height of your headset for a proper fit.

## Padding the Bars

Many people find that after riding a bicycle for long periods of time, they begin to experience numbness in the hands. This is a problem that should not be ignored, because it can develop into a serious and chronic condition. One way to minimize the problem is to wear padded gloves. Another way is to place some kind of padding on the handlebars themselves. You should also check to see if the adjustment of your seat, stem and bars is contributing to the problem by throwing an excessive amount of weight onto the bars or placing your wrists in a strained position.

If you wish to pad the tops of your handlebars, do it before replacing the brake levers.

There are various commercial high-density handlebar padding materials that are available such as Grab-On and Cushion-Grip. They provide a lot of shock absorbency but they increase the diameter of the handlebar, so smaller hands may not feel secure gripping around them. A good compromise is just using the padding on the drops where the weight and pressure on the hands is the greatest.

An alternative to the factory-made bar padding is pipe insulation. It works almost as well as the padding but is not as dense, so it feels spongier and takes some getting used to. It comes in various sizes so you can find a fit either for bare or already-taped bars. The best source of this material is an air conditioning contractor or a heating/air conditioning supply house. Other padding alternatives to be used only under tape include foam-type carpet padding and old bicycle tubing. If you choose the tubing, we recommend two layers, one inside the other. Talcum powder or soap and water will aid in its installation.

Once you have padded the bar tops, if you choose to do it, you are ready to install the brake levers. Slip the levers onto the bars and partially tighten the clamp. Then position them. A good place to start is to install them with the tips of the levers even with the bottom section of the bars. Hold a straightedge along the underside of this part of the bars to help you align the levers. Snug up the levers a bit and try them out for fit. If you do not like the location, move them to the place that feels more comfortable. For more detailed instructions on installing brake levers, see page 210.

If you wish to use padding below your brake levers, add it now. Then proceed with the taping of your bars.

## Taping Handlebars

There are two ways that handlebar tape can be wrapped: from the top down or from the bottom up. Each method has its advantages and disadvantages. The advantage in wrapping from the top down is that the end where you begin can be neatly wrapped over, and the other end can be tucked into the end of the bar and sealed with a plug. Thus, there are no loose ends to unravel. The disadvantage with this manner of wrapping is that the overlaps face upward on the bends. With time and use, pressure from the hands has a tendency to peel or roll the tape back. This is especially true with cloth-type tapes. Plastic tapes are less of a problem.

This problem can be avoided by wrapping the tape from the bottom up. A little tape is left at the beginning to tuck into the bar end, so that end is secured with a plug. However, the finishing end at the stem sleeve has to be secured in some way to prevent unraveling. The accepted technique is to wrap a piece of electrician's tape or colored plastic stretch tape around that end. Electrician's tape has a good deal of elasticity in it, so as you wrap it around the bar, pull it taut. Then when you let go, it will shrink back into a tight bond around the handlebar tape.

Whichever taping method you choose, before beginning to actually wind tape around the bars, cut a short piece of tape from each roll, just long enough to cover one of the brake lever clamp bands on the side of the bars you are about to wrap. Don't cut off more

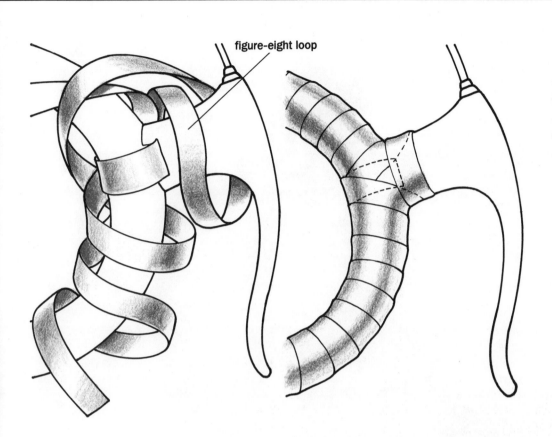

**figure-eight loop**

*Illustration 13-2: When taping around brake levers, hold a short strip of tape over the lever clamp, then cover it with a figure-eight loop of the main tape around the lever hood and handlebar.*

than you need or you may run short of tape.

As you wrap, try to overlap about one-half the width of the tape, if possible. When you reach curved sections of the bar, you will have to use more overlap on the inside curves and less on the outside. How much you can overlap depends on the length of tape provided. Unfortunately, you can only determine the proper overlap by trial and error. If you get to the end of the tape before you have wrapped the whole bar, just unwind the tape and try again. Also, don't forget to maintain some tension on the tape to stretch it a bit as you wrap. This will make for a smooth, snug fit and will help you get enough length out of the tape to cover the bar.

When you reach a lever, hold a cut-off piece of tape over the clamp band while you make a figure-eight loop around the lever hood and the bar along with an additional loop around the lever hood as shown in illustration 13-2. This will secure the short piece of tape and completely hide the clamp band. When the tape wrapping is complete, don't forget to plug the ends of the bars. Even if you did not need them to secure the tape, you need the plugs to protect your body from painful contact with the bar ends.

## Bar and Stem Adjustments

The height of your stem and handlebar cannot be properly set until the saddle has been adjusted to its appropriate height and angle. Once that is taken care of, check the height of the bar in

231

*Photo 13-2: Bar height and stem length can be checked by sitting on the bike with a straight back and arms, the hands resting on the brake lever hoods. In that position your back should be at a 45-degree angle.*

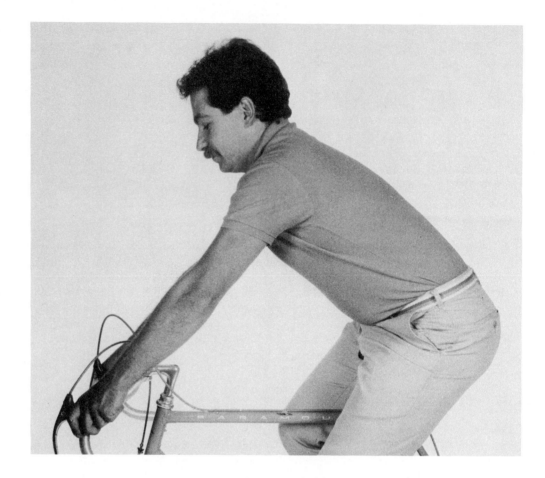

relation to it. For general-purpose riding, the bar should ideally be about 1 inch lower than the saddle. Another way of checking both the bar height and the stem length is to sit in the saddle and place your hands just behind the brake lever hoods. When you straighten both your arms and your back, your back should be at a 45-degree angle in relation to the ground.

Here again, the rule may vary somewhat for specialized riding needs. Cyclists who expect to ride primarily in an upright position may wish to set the bars at approximately the same height as the saddle, whereas those wishing to do a lot of fast riding in a low, aerodynamic position may wish to drop the bars

a couple of inches below the saddle. The 1-inch rule should be taken as a median, a starting place from which to find the height that suits your particular needs. If you wish to experiment with different bar and stem heights, try each one for a week or two and make changes in increments of no more than ¼ inch each time. This will make it easier for your body to adjust and thus give each setting a fair try.

After the stem height has been set, the last adjustment to be made is the handlebar position. Many riders seem to like having the flat portion of the hooks parallel to the top tube. Others like it with the hooks pushed forward a bit so the ends slope slightly downward. One suggested rule is to set the bars so that the slope of their ends follows an imaginary line that bisects the seatstays. The argument is that this position places the wrists in the most natural and comfortable position when the hands are on the drops.

Since the bar angle is easily adjustable, you can experiment with various settings if you'd like. Here again we would recommend that if you want to change your position, do it a little at a time and not all at once. Let your body get used to each increment of change before moving it again. Otherwise, your body may have difficulty adapting to the change.

Since your hands provide approximately one-third of the contact that occurs between your body and your bicycle and perform about 90 percent of the control work, it is worth expending some time and effort in finding the most comfortable and efficient handlebar position. An unsuitable riding position creates irritation of the nerves in the hands and arms and a strain on the back. That in turn leads to numb hands and sore neck, shoulder, and back muscles. Nothing is more likely to take the pleasure out of riding a bike. A little time spent in finding the right equipment and adjusting it to the optimum position will be more than repaid in riding enjoyment.

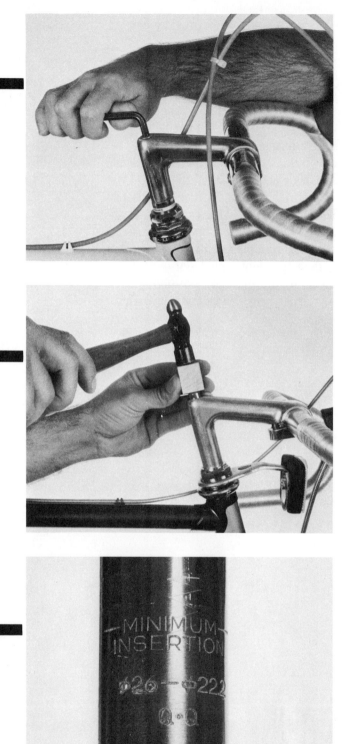

Often in a bike crash, the handlebars get twisted out of line. This may even occur as the result of a strong tug on the bars after hitting a pothole. Whatever the cause, a misalignment of the bars should be corrected as soon as possible. The stem should then be tightened sufficiently to minimize the possibility of it occurring again.

Before you can make a lateral adjustment in the handlebars, the stem must be loosened. Turn the stem expander bolt counterclockwise a turn or two, hold the front wheel of the bike between your knees, and twist the bar sideways until it is properly aligned with the wheel. Then retighten the bolt. (Photo 1)

When tightening a stem expander bolt with an Allen key fitting, make it as tight as you can get it with the leverage provided by the small wrench. If the bolt head can be turned by a large adjustable wrench, do not try to tighten it as far as possible because you might end up cracking the steerer tube.

One way to test the stem bolt for adequate tightness is to hold the front wheel between your knees and give the bar a vigorous twist. You should not be able to easily move it back out of line, since you want to eliminate the possibility of that happening while you are riding the bike.

For general riding purposes, the handlebars should be set about 1 inch below the level of the saddle. To adjust the height you must again loosen the stem expander bolt. If the stem has not been moved for some time, you may find the expander wedge does not drop down with the loosening of the bolt. In this case give the head of the bolt a sharp rap

with a padded hammer. Lacking that tool, hold a small block of wood on top of the bolt to cushion the shock and hit it with an ordinary hammer. (Photo 2)

When setting the handlebar height, make certain that at least 2 inches of stem extend down into the steerer tube. Many manufacturers mark their stems with a minimum insertion line. (Photo 3) Make sure the stem is in far enough to cover this line.

Some people like to set their handlebars with the lower part of the drops parallel to the top tube. Others prefer to set them along an imaginary line that runs from the bars back to the midpoint between the saddle and the rear axle. You should set them at least somewhere within this range. To adjust the angle of the bars, loosen the binder bolt on the stem clip. (Photo 4) Rotate the bars into the desired position and retighten the bolt.

Before you càn remove a set of handlebars from the stem, you must strip off the handlebar tape, unclamp and slide off the brake levers. Then loosen the binder bolt and work the bars out of the stem.

In installing or removing bars, when you reach a bend, the bar will become difficult to move. (Photo 5) To make it easier, rotate the bar so that its inside radius stays next to the narrowest part of the stem clip. You may find you have more room to maneuver if you mount the bars on the stem with the stem off the bike.

Before installing a new stem or reinstalling an old one, give the part of the stem that will be inserted into the steerer tube a good coating of grease. (Photo 6) ▲

**1**

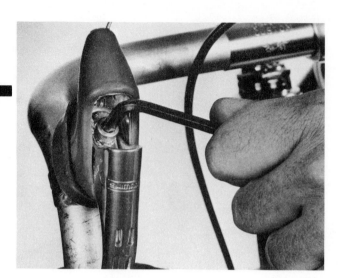

**2**

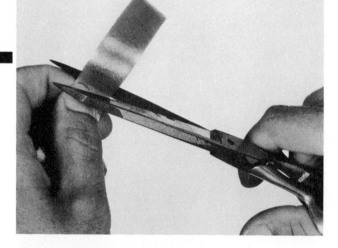

**3**

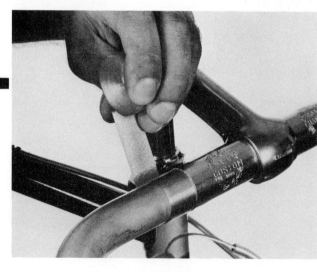

Tape on handlebars is both practical and decorative. It enables a set of bars to be gripped more firmly and more comfortably than if they remained bare metal. At the same time, brightly colored and nicely wrapped tape on handlebars adds a lot to the visual beauty of a bike.

No set of dropped handlebars looks complete without some sort of cover, be it bright or dull, spongy or firm, thick or thin. Thus, the final step in any handlebar installation is to cover the bars with padding or tape.

Even if the handlebars are never removed, from time to time they can use retaping. After a while any tape will become worn and dirty. New tape is inexpensive and is one nice way to recondition an old but still usable bike. Buy one roll for each side of the handlebars.

Before applying new tape, clean off any remaining residue from the old tape. Also, use this opportunity to check the location of the brake levers and the tightness of their clamps. The bolt for loosening and tightening these clamps is located inside the body of the lever. (Photo 1)

Cut a piece of tape off the end of each roll just long enough to fit over the visible part of the brake lever clamp. (Photo 2) Set it aside until your wrapping reaches that point.

The most common method of wrapping involves starting a couple of inches to the side of the stem. If the bar has a reinforcing sleeve in the stem area, start immediately next to that for a clean look. (Photo 3) You can also wrap handlebars starting at the end, working your way up to the stem area. To do that, reverse the sequence that follows.

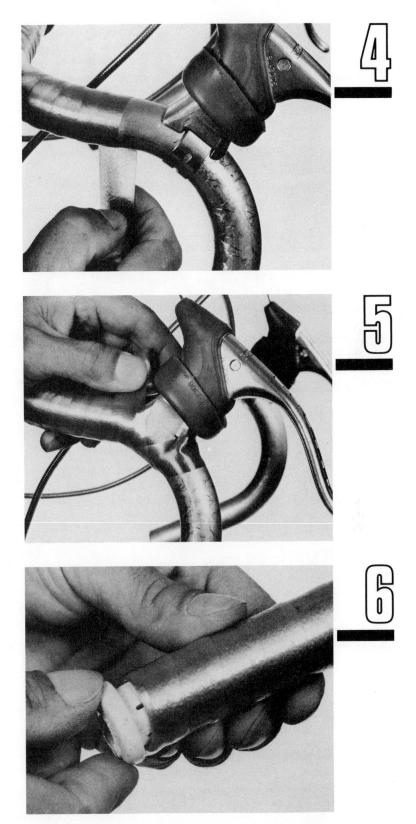

Overlap the beginning end completely, then continue along the straight section of the bar, overlapping between one-third and one-half the width of the tape. Keep tension on the tape as you wrap to make it stretch a little bit.

As you move into the curved part of the bar, use slightly more tape overlap on the inside of the curves and less on the outside. (Photo 4) When you reach the lever clamp, wrap the short piece of tape around it and hold it there while covering it with a figure-eight pattern of the rolled tape. (Photo 5)

At the ends of the figure eight, loop the roll of tape once around the brake lever hood to cover and fasten the ends of the short piece of tape, then continue the regular taping pattern along the bar.

When you reach the end of the bar, there should be enough tape left to go around the bar once, overlapping its end. After doing that, fold over the final loop of tape and push it into the end of the bar along with any tape remaining on the roll. Secure the tape by pressing a plug into the end of the bar. (Photo 6)

If you did not have enough tape to complete the job, you overlapped more than you should have. Unwrap most or all of the tape, winding it back into a roll as you go, and try again. Add a little more stretch to the tape this time so it will fit snugly and go farther.

If you reached the end of the bar with quite a bit of tape left, you could have overlapped more generously. You can simply stuff the leftover tape into the bar, if you choose, but you may wish instead to do the job over using more overlap. That will provide more value from the tape. ▲

# 14 SADDLES AND SEATPOSTS

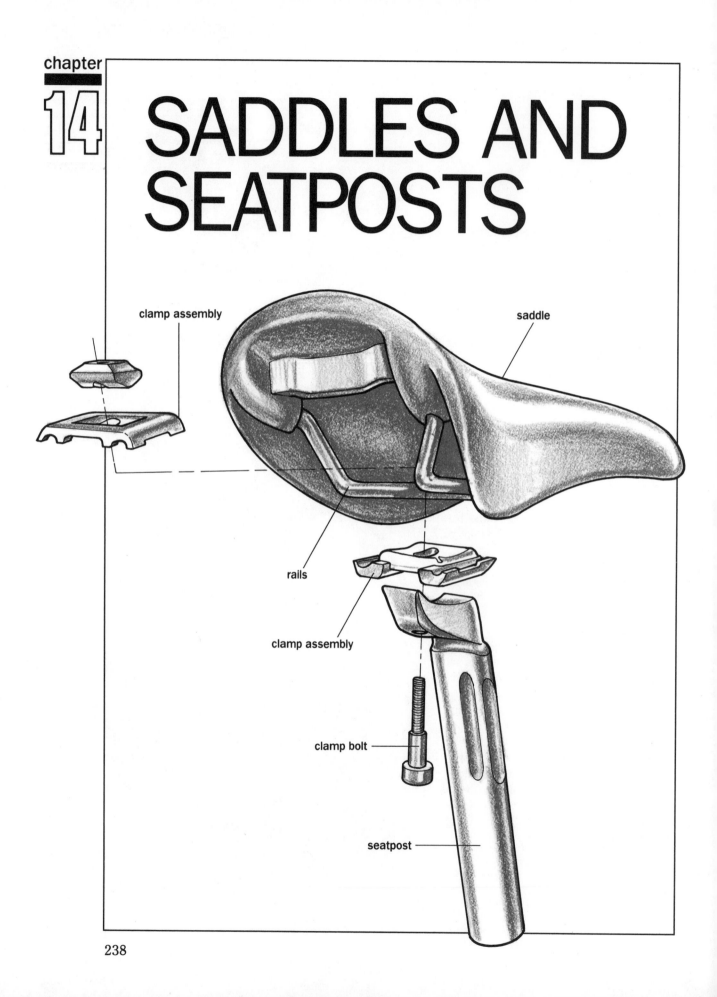

clamp assembly

saddle

rails

clamp assembly

clamp bolt

seatpost

When you think about it, there really aren't very many parts on a bicycle with which your body comes into contact as you ride. You rest your hands on the handlebars, your feet on the pedals, and your buttocks on the seat. Obviously, the seat (or saddle as it is often called) bears the burden of your weight, which is probably the principal reason why it is the prime source of complaints about discomfort on a bike. However, often the reason a saddle is uncomfortable is because it is improperly adjusted or simply not well matched to the cyclist's anatomy. Bicycle saddles are not all alike. There is an amazing diversity to be found both in design and construction materials. Somewhere in the midst of this diversity should be a saddle that is right for each cyclist.

The most important rule to remember about saddles is that everybody's posterior is different and what is comfortable to one person may be torture to another. Not only that, but a saddle well-suited to short, fast racing events may be ill-suited to long-distance touring. Proper saddle selection must take into account both bodily structure and riding needs. In short, saddles are a very personal thing, so no matter what anyone else says about a particular model, you have to make the final decision.

## Basic Construction of Saddles

The bicycle saddle consists of a shell, which is the part you sit on, and a carriage or frame, the part that supports the shell.

The shell can be made of steel, leather, or plastic. Steel shells are found on inexpensive adult and juvenile bicycles. The steel shell is covered with a piece of low-density foam topped with plastic. Though these saddles feel soft—cushy would be a better description—they aren't very comfortable. The foam compresses easily and you end up sitting on a plate of steel that doesn't conform to your body.

Saddles that feature leather shells mounted over metal frames are probably the oldest style still available. Given adequate time for proper break-in, the leather shell will become soft and resilient and will conform to the particular anatomy of the person using it. At one time leather saddles came in all price ranges, but these days are found only in the upper price ranges.

Leather saddles require special care. They should be protected from the rain and special covers are available for this purpose. Leather saddles also need some breaking-in before they are really comfortable and conform well to your hind side. You can help this process along by applying some type of saddle dressing. Some people use saddle soap, others use products like Lexal, Proofhide, or Hydropane, all of which are available from leather goods stores.

Plastic saddles are probably the most popular today. Some plastic saddles consist of nothing more than a bare plastic shell shaped much like a leather saddle. More exotic plastic saddles have shells that vary in thickness to allow for different levels of softness or hardness at different points. These saddles use special high-density foams for padding and feature "bumps" that put a little extra padding under the pelvic contact points. Saddles with these bumps are generally called anatomic saddles. Plastic saddles of this type usually have a cover made of vinyl or leather.

The carriage is the structure that supports the shell and connects it to the seatpost. Normally the carriage, sometimes called the frame, is made of steel, although aluminum and titanium models have been made. Generally steel is the best choice. The nose of the saddle is supported by one part of the carriage and the tail of the saddle is supported by the other. Connecting the two are the saddle rails. These rails also link the carriage to the seatpost.

# Kinds of Saddles

Generally there are two kinds of saddles, touring saddles and racing saddles. The touring saddles are designed with comfort in mind. While racing saddles consider comfort, efficiency of movement is the primary criterion that governs their design.

## Touring Saddles

Touring saddles have extra padding to help cushion the shock of spending long periods of time on the bike. The extra padding is usually placed under the ischials, the pelvic bones that press into the seat when you are sitting down. The ischials, sometimes called the sit bones, bear the weight of your upper body. You can see this extra padding on the saddle in the form of bumps. Some saddles don't appear to have bumps, but the extra padding is there; it's just that the bumps go down instead of up. The extra padding weighs a bit more so many racers forgo it.

## Racing Saddles

Racing saddles are built to allow full movement of the legs with a minimal amount of chafing. These design goals lead to some interesting and unusual-looking shapes. These special shapes not only allow the cyclist's legs to move very efficiently, they also tend to give the cyclist something to push against in order to get more power into every stroke.

## Women's Saddles

Because women have wider hips than men they also have wider ischial bones. This means that when they sit on a man's saddle the ischial bones are not supported by the saddle. This can be quite uncomfortable. Women's saddles are designed with an extrawide tail to ensure that the pelvic bones are properly supported by the saddle. The anatomic woman's saddle also has extra padding inserted just back of the nose for increased riding comfort.

## Alternative Saddles

For people that just can't seem to get comfortable, the inventors of the world have been busy. This is certainly true of bike saddles, which have been created in some amazing forms. For example, there is the Bummer, a sling saddle that consists of a transverse tubular steel frame from which is suspended two straps of auto safety webbing covered with foam-filled Naugahyde panels. This 19-inch-wide sling pivots forward and backward on its frame as the weight of the cyclist shifts. The sling offers couchlike comfort, but the ease with which it shifts position can be disconcerting to riders used to the stability of a conventional saddle.

Another nontraditional saddle is the Easyseat, a noseless two-part saddle. Each part moves independently as your hips move. The pads pivot forward and backward as the rider pedals and can be adjusted inward or outward to match the rider's pelvic width. Both these designs have to be tried to be understood. They are certainly quite different from the traditional stationary saddle and feel rather strange upon first trial.

If you are basically satisfied with the shape of your bicycle seat but would appreciate a little additional padding, you might wish to try a saddle cover such as the Spenco Saddle Pad or the cover made by Grab-On. Both of these products use special foam to make your ride more comfortable. There are also covers on the market that employ air or water to create a cushion between you and your saddle. Many people even use sheepskin saddle covers. These help prevent saddle chafing but they don't add much padding.

## Hints on How to Select a Saddle

Bicycle saddles, like most other products, are available in so many different models that it is helpful to solicit opinions from friends and acquaintances. Talk to other riders with a physical build and riding habits similar to your own. They can give you information on saddles they have tried, and that may help you narrow down your choices. Also, don't neglect to discuss the matter with your bicycle dealer. He will know what saddles are most popular with his customers and should know better than most people the quality and materials that go into each model.

One way to narrow down your choices is to decide first whether you prefer leather or plastic, and if the choice is leather then decide between tanned leather or suede. Thus you will have fewer saddles to compare closely. But in making this initial decision, remember a basic difference between materials. Leather saddles often feel very hard and uncomfortable at first. Sometimes they take a year or more to break in. But once broken in, a leather saddle may provide the kind of ride you want.

By contrast, don't buy a plastic saddle that feels uncomfortable, thinking that it will be OK once it is broken in, because they don't break in. Plastic saddles never feel better than when they are new.

If you like your saddle but want to try something new, never get rid of the old one until you are sure you like the new one. When you do decide to purchase a new saddle, be sure you are buying what works for you. Don't worry about what everybody else is riding. You have to find something that agrees with your anatomy and riding style. So, for example, if you are a male with wide hips, don't pick a skinny racing saddle just to be in style. If a wider saddle, such as one designed for a woman, fits your body, don't hesitate to give it a try.

## Seatposts

The seatpost attaches your saddle to the bicycle. It also allows you to adjust the height and the fore-and-aft position of the saddle on the bike.

A bicycle seatpost consists of both a pillar and a clamp. Sometimes these parts are integrated into one unit, in which case they are referred to as a one-piece seatpost. The two-part seatpost consists of a tube with a clamp attached around its upper end. The clamp simultaneously holds the rails of the seat in the chosen position and fastens the seat to the top of the seatpost. On this type of seatpost, the clamp is usually made of steel and has serrations that allow the saddle to be tilted up or down and set at various angles. These serrations are rather coarse in order to support a cyclist's weight and don't allow fine adjustment. The pillar part of the seatpost on which this clamp fastens may be made either of steel or aluminum.

A one-piece seatpost is more rigid than a two-piece model because of the way the clamp is integrated into the upper end of the post. This gives the rider a better base to push against and thus is more efficient. On the most basic level, the clamp assembly on this type of post is the same as that in a two-piece system, in that it controls tilt as well as fore-and-aft position of the saddle.

The cheapest one-piece seatposts are also similar to the two-piece models in that they employ a clamp with serrations, which allows only finite adjustments, and a bolt running through the side of the clamp. This type of one-bolt system is easy to use and quite reliable. Adjustment on these seatposts is finer than on old-fashioned models.

As you move up the scale of quality, you can find one-piece seatposts employing a single bolt that runs vertically through the clamp. Shimano manufactures several posts of this type, which make use of a set screw instead of serrations to set the tilt. These posts are thus infinitely or "micro" adjustable.

The double-bolt microadjusting seatpost has the best adjustment system available. The Campagnolo Record model is the standard by which all others are judged and is in many cases imitated. Two bolts pull in opposition to each other, which allows you to make very small changes in the angle of the seatpost. This system prevents the angle of the seat from changing unless a bolt breaks or the saddle rails bend.

## Adjusting the Tilt of a Seat

Often the discomfort people feel when riding is not the fault of the saddle design, but simply a matter of improper adjustment. If, for example, the nose of the saddle is tilted down, the cyclist's body weight is thrown forward, creating extra strain on the arms and shoulders. On the other hand, if the nose of the saddle is tilted up, the cyclist may feel discomfort in the genital area. This is particularly true for the male cyclist, and is especially likely to occur when he rides with his hands on the dropped part of the handlebars.

As a general rule, your bicycle seat should be set parallel to the top tube of your bicycle. This, of course, presupposes that you are riding a bike with a conventional frame shape and not one with a dramatically sloping top tube, such as you find on some all-terrain bikes. If you look at your saddle and find the top of it is sloped or curved, you may wonder how to determine what is parallel. Simply lay a straightedge (a ruler will work) along the top of your saddle, from the nose to the back, and use that as your line of reference.

If your seatpost has a standard clamp or is a single-bolt one-piece design, you should loosen the clamp, move the seat to the desired position, then retighten the clamp. Two-bolt designs require that you loosen the bolt on the end you want to go up and tighten the bolt on the end you want to go down. Two-bolt designs are more difficult to work with, but once your position is set on one of these seats, it won't slip.

## Seat Height

Proper height of the saddle is very important. If the saddle is too low, riding becomes very difficult. If it is too high, you cannot get the leverage you need on the cranks for efficient use of energy. Also, improper height in either direction can lead to bodily injuries. When the seat is too low, excessive stress is placed on the knees. When it is too high, your hip will tend to rock, causing you to rub an abnormal amount on the saddle, possibly creating saddle sores.

The correct seat height makes riding both comfortable and efficient. To find the correct seat height you must sit on the bicycle with both feet on the pedals. This will require you to be held up, either by a wall, a friend, or some other stable means of support. Pedal backward and stop when one pedal is in the 6 o'clock position and one pedal is in the 12 o'clock position.

Place your heel on the lower pedal. In this position your leg should be fully extended. If your knee is bent, raise the saddle. If your hips must rock to allow you to reach the pedal or your leg won't reach it, you should lower the saddle. When you spin the cranks and your foot is properly positioned on the pedal your leg will be almost, but not completely extended.

To adjust the height of the seat, loosen the seatpost binder bolt on the frame, move the seat up or down to the desired position, then retighten.

Most bicycles require an Allen key or some other type of wrench to loosen the seatpost binder bolt. However, some bicycles, primarily all-terrain bikes, use quick-release seatpost bolts. Such bolts allow you to adjust the seat height without tools, because different seat heights are needed at different times to ride efficiently off-road. For road use they aren't really that useful, since you should set your seat to the correct height before you set out on a ride. They also make your seat an easy target for thieves.

After using the recommended technique to set your saddle height, try it out. If your feet are long and you tend to point your toes down while pedaling, you may find that your seat now feels too low. But don't raise it right away. Your body may simply need to readjust to the correct pedaling position. So try it for a few rides and see if your riding comfort and efficiency improve.

Once you have your saddle at the proper height, you may want to reassess the saddle angle. Normally, parallel to the top tube is best. But ride your bike awhile to see how it feels. Then move the nose up or down a little, if necessary, to get it to the position most comfortable for you.

## Seat Position, Fore-and-Aft

The correct fore-and-aft seat position allows you to get the maximum leverage from your muscles. Too far forward and you sacrifice leverage; too far back and you experience back strain. As with height and tilt, this is an adjustment worth getting right.

To move the seat back and forth you will have to loosen the clamp. And to find the correct position you will once again have to sit on the bike with both feet on the pedals and have someone or something hold you up. This time back-pedal until the pedals are at the 3 and 9 o'clock positions.

Take a string with a weight on the end (a large nut or a small wrench will work fine) and hang it next to your knee on the leg that is forward. Hold the string so that it rides in the notch in the side of your knee cap. The string should pass through the center of the pedal axle. If the string is behind the pedal, move the saddle forward. If it is in front of the pedal axle, move the seat back. After completing this fore-and-aft adjustment, check again to make sure the saddle has the right tilt.

If you have put a lot of miles on your bike after making all the proper adjustments, but still find your saddle uncomfortable, then you simply ought to try a new one. Many people find that a change of saddles drastically changes their outlook on cycling. With such a wide range of saddles and saddle designs from which to choose, there is really no reason why any cyclist should experience persistent discomfort while riding a bike.

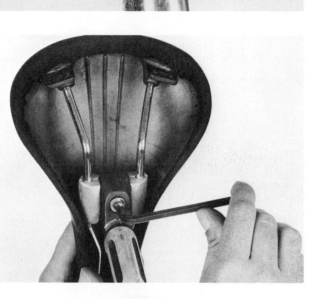

The seatpost on a bicycle is quite important because it supports most of a rider's weight, while allowing the height at which a rider sits to be adjusted for comfort and pedaling efficiency. The seatpost not only controls the saddle height, it also provides the means for adjusting the saddle from side to side, forward and backward, and up and down.

If a saddle feels uncomfortable, careful adjustment of its position may make a big difference. It certainly is critical to providing an overall proper fit between rider and bike. If adjusting the saddle does not help, there simply may be a poor match between the saddle and its rider's anatomy. The only remedy for that problem is to try a different saddle.

Saddle height is determined by how deep the seatpost is set within the seat tube of the bicycle frame. The tilt and fore-and-aft position of the saddle are controlled by the clamp that holds the saddle on the seatpost.

Old-fashioned seat clamps have a nut on either side that must be loosened before the seat can be removed or have its angle or horizontal position changed. (Photo 1) The serrations on this type of clamp are rather coarse and thus do not allow for very fine adjustments.

Among the newer types of seatposts is one fitted with a one-bolt clamping system, which does allow for very fine adjustments. When this single bolt is loosened the rails of the saddle can be slid forward or backward within the jaws of the clamp and the tilt of the clamp can be changed. The bolt is then retightened to hold the saddle in the new position. (Photo 2)

The best saddle adjustment system currently available is the micro-adjusting seat-

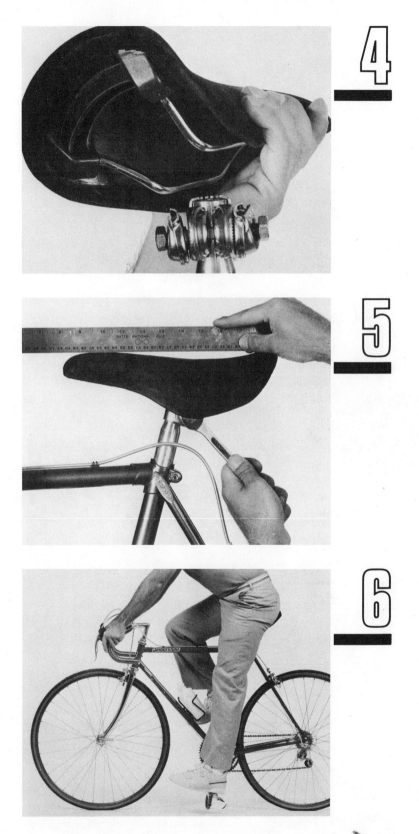

post, which employs two bolts working in opposition to one another. (Photo 3) Changing the tilt of the saddle involves loosening one bolt and tightening the other. This system not only allows very minute changes to be made in saddle tilt, it also holds the adjustment very securely.

To completely remove a saddle from a seatpost, you must loosen the clamp bolt or bolts enough for the saddle rails to slip out of the jaws of the clamp. (Photo 4) The clamp does not need to be this loose for adjusting saddle position.

To set the tilt of the seat, loosen the seatpost clamp just enough to allow the nose of the seat to be easily moved up or down. Place a straightedge along the top of the saddle and adjust the seat angle until the straightedge is parallel with the top tube of the bike. Then retighten the clamp bolt. (Photo 5)

The fore-and-aft position of the seat should be set according to how your knees relate to the pedals at a particular point in the revolution of the cranks. Since the saddle height will also influence this, it should be set first.

To determine the appropriate height at which your saddle should be set, you must sit on the bike in riding position. It is helpful to have a friend hold you and the bike upright while you do this. Otherwise, place your bike in a doorway, near a wall, or in some other place where you can hold yourself upright.

Rotate the cranks to the 12 o'clock and 6 o'clock positions. Then set your heel on the lower pedal and look at that leg. It should be fully extended in this position. (Photo 6)

You should be able to place your heel comfortably on the pedal in this position. If there is a noticeable bend in the knee, your

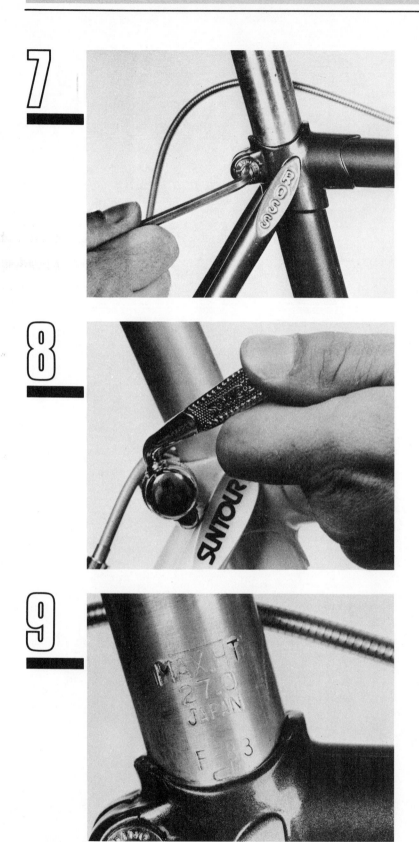

saddle is too low. If you have to rock your hips to reach the pedal, the saddle is too high. In either case, the height should be adjusted and retested.

To raise or lower the saddle, loosen the binder bolt located at the top of the seat tube. (Photo 7) Move the seatpost up or down as needed. Check to make sure the saddle is aligned with the top tube of the bike, then retighten the binder bolt.

Some city bikes and certain models of all-terrain bikes are equipped with quick-release binder bolts for rapid and frequent changes of seat height. (Photo 8) These work quite well and are certainly convenient if you need to adjust the seatpost. However, this system makes it easy for thieves to make off with your saddle and seatpost. For most types of riding, once you have determined the ideal height for your saddle, it should be set there and left alone.

One important thing to watch for when raising your saddle is the manufacturer's line indicating maximum recommended height. (Photo 9) Riding with the seatpost raised above that point is dangerous because there may not be enough post within the seat tube to support your weight. If you cannot set your saddle to the proper height without moving above that line, then you probably need a bike with a larger frame. A less expensive solution is to purchase a longer seatpost.

Anytime you pull the seatpost out of the frame, clean it off and apply a fresh coat of grease before sliding it back in. (Photo 10) This will help protect it from corrosion and make raising and lowering of the seat easier. This type of maintenance should be done periodically, in any case. You do not want

your seatpost permanently fixed in the frame thanks to rust.

After setting your saddle to the proper height, you can turn your attention to its fore-and-aft position. Sit on the bike as you did before, only this time rotate the cranks to the 3 o'clock and 9 o'clock positions.

Take a plumb line or a string with a weight tied on the end and hold it next to the knee of your forward leg. Place the top of the string in the groove next to your knee-cap and observe where the weight falls. It should touch your foot at a point in line with the pedal axle. (Photo 11)

If the weight falls in front of the pedal axle, the seat needs to be moved back a bit. If it falls behind the axle, the seat needs to go forward. Loosen the seatpost clamp and move the seat in the direction needed. But before retightening the clamp, check to make sure the tilt of the saddle is still right.

Once the seat height, tilt, and horizontal position have been properly set, the position of the handlebars and stem should be checked. For general riding purposes, the top of the bars should be set about 1 inch below the level of the top of the saddle.

Also, check the distance of the bars from the seat by placing your elbow against the nose of the seat and extending your fore-arm toward the handlebars. The tips of your fingers should fall about 1 inch short of touching the bars. (Photo 12)

Racers may want the bars a little lower and farther away from the seat. Tourists may want them a little higher and closer to the seat. But if the distance from the seat to the bars does not fall within a suitable range for your type of riding, you must replace the stem. ▲

# PEDALS

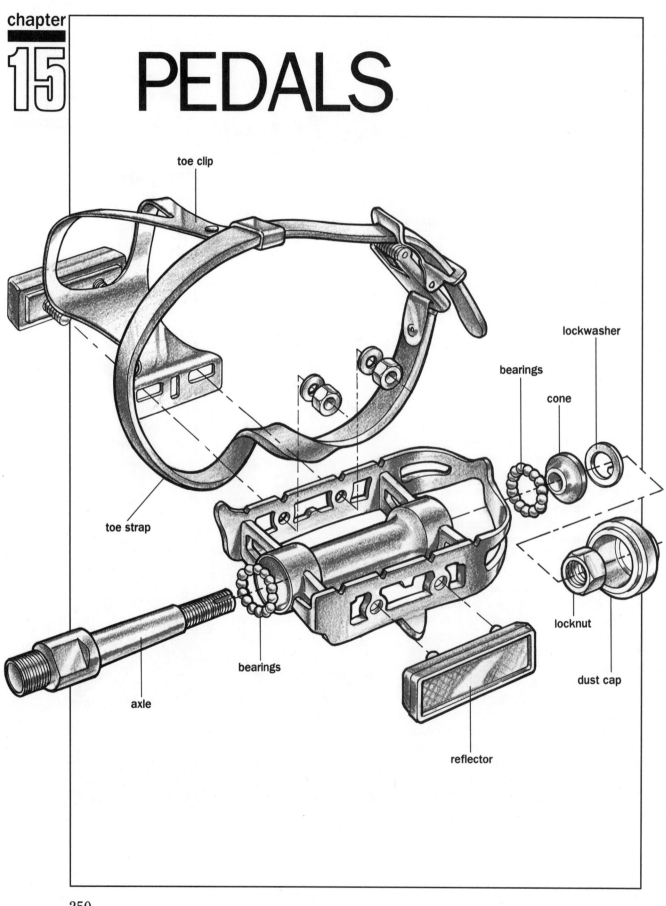

toe clip

lockwasher

bearings

cone

toe strap

bearings

axle

reflector

locknut

dust cap

Pedals are not complicated components, but they are one of the most important links between you and your bike. Not only do you transmit power that propels you through the pedals, you also use them as moving balance points that help you position yourself on your bike for hard cornering and stable descending. A mismatch between pedals and shoes can result in discomfort, and possibly even injury.

Bicycle pedals come in many different types and levels of quality. Some types can be used only with special cleated shoes. Others cannot be used with cleats. Certain types are designed for special uses, while many models have more general applications. Thus, it is important to become familiar with the different pedal types and to understand the applications for which they are best suited.

## Basic Pedal Design

Although pedals come in many different shapes, almost all pedals share several common characteristics. At the heart of a pedal is an axle that screws into the end of a crankarm. The inner races of two sets of bearings are located on this axle, one at the inside end of the axle next to the crankarm and the other at the axle's outer end. A separate body holds the outer races of the two bearing sets. Attached to this pedal body is a pair of rattraps, a quill cage, or some sort of platform, which acts as the pushing surface for your foot.

Most of the apparent differences between pedals are just that, cosmetic differences; their internal parts are usually strikingly similar. As we'll see later, that also means that servicing is usually the same procedure for different types and even different brands of pedals.

## Common Pedal Types

Most bicycles are equipped with pedals belonging to one of four basic types: rubber block, rattrap, quill, and platform. There are many variations within these basic types as well as some new pedals, which do not fit neatly into these categories.

### Rubber Block

If you see these on a bike, you know right away the machinery is not intended for serious use. These pedals shine in commuter situations where the cyclist will most likely be wearing dress shoes. If you've ever tried the slippery combination of leather soles on metal pedals, you can appreciate the sticky advantage of leather on rubber pedals. On the down side, rubber pedals are always heavy, nonserviceable, and don't provide any options for positive foot positioning.

### Rattrap

You'll find rattrap pedals on less-expensive 10-speed sport bikes. Their thin cage plates allow the use of cleated shoes and also provide location for bicycle touring shoes with transverse ridges in their soles. Unfortunately, the thin cage plates also mean that shoes without

*Photo 15-1: Pedals come in four basic styles (clockwise from upper left): rubber block, rattrap, quill, and platform.*

some sort of reinforcement in the soles, like your garden-variety sneakers, will transmit pressure unevenly to the soles of your feet. That's where you may develop tender spots on rides longer than 5 or 10 miles. If that happens and you do not wish to switch to a platform-type pedal, you should change to touring-style cycling shoes. They have stiffer soles than most athletic shoes, but are still flexible enough for moderate amounts of walking.

On many rattrap models the dust cap at the outer end of the pedal has no provision for a wrench or other tool to remove it. Normally this would mean that the pedal is unserviceable; that's often the case with inexpensive rattraps. However, don't despair too soon because you can sometimes pry the cap off with a small screwdriver and get to the bearings beneath it.

In case you think that the rattrap design is limited to cheap pedals, take a good look at what are often called "track" pedals. This specialized type of pedal uses the twin cage-plate rattrap design because of the extra ground, or banking, clearance it provides at the end of the pedal. For the same reason, some pedals intended for road use also utilize the same basic design.

## Quill

The only real difference between quill pedals and rattraps is that a quill pedal has a curved section of metal that connects the front and rear cage plates, making the two of them one part. This creates a stronger structure, as well as providing a little more shoe contact area. The latter point is especially important for people with large, wide feet.

For years, this was the only "acceptable" design for road racing pedals, and Campagnolo Record pedals were the model for a legion of imitators.

Quill pedals are almost always serviceable. However, you cannot disassemble a pedal without first removing its dust cap, and you may have to purchase a special dust cap wrench in order to remove that part.

## Platform

As you might guess from the name, platform pedals offer a flatter, larger area for foot contact than do other types of pedals. Generally speaking, these pedals are adaptable to different types of shoes, although many models were clearly designed to accommodate cleats. As cycling has steadily gained in popularity among people who are more interested in commuting, touring, or riding for fun and exercise than in participating in racing events, a rash of new platform-type pedals have been introduced to better fit the "touring" shoes these riders often prefer over competition shoes.

Platform pedals don't necessarily have a completely flat body, although some designs approach it. Even pedals that at first glance might appear to be rattrap or quill type can be classified as platform pedals if some parts of the pedal other than the cage plates are raised high enough to provide additional shoe contact. This is usually accomplished with the crossmembers that connect the barrel of the pedal body to the cage plates. Specialized Touring pedals manage to augment the same effect by flattening the top edge of the pedal quill as well.

Most modern platform pedals are variations on the single cage-plate design that consists of a single rear cage plate attached to the wide end of a V- or U-shaped body. This hybrid design works well with cleats, yet also provides a fair amount of contact surface for touring shoes. In addition, the internal parts are sometimes identical to those of rattrap or quill designs from the same manufacturer. The Ofmega Sintesi, Campagnolo Victory and Triomphe, Shimano 600 EX and Dura-Ace, and SunTour LePree models are good examples of this design.

Toe clips for these designs mount on the horizontal surface of the pedal body instead of the vertical surface of the missing front cage plate. Because in most cases this means the toe clip can move fore-and-aft as well as in the usual side-to-side direction, small adjustments can be made to accommodate shoes of different sizes. If a toe clip does not fit, this type of adjustment should be tried before a switch is made to clips of a different length.

## All-Terrain

Pedals for all-terrain bikes (ATBs) are usually either platform style or "bear trap" style. The former looks like a square doughnut with a spindle running through it, and the latter looks like a quill pedal with a round or rounded cage. The bear trap cage invariably has a notched or "tooth" profile for a secure grip on your shoes. Extra gripping power on the platform types is often provided by small, flat-top pins that are far less damaging to your shins than notches or teeth.

Happily, ATB pedal insides are virtually identical to those of their road cousins, with one difference: seals and sealed mechanisms are the rule here rather than the exception.

## Special Types

There's been a long-standing movement away from the traditional pedal, toe clip, and toe strap trio toward a system that invariably involves a pedal/cleat combination, which locks the rider's foot onto the pedal. This integrated locking feature makes clips and straps, and their adjustment, obsolete. The Look pedal, produced by the makers of Look ski bindings, has apparently perfected this new design. The maneuvers required to lock and unlock cleats into and out of these pedals are fast and easy operations, making them safer and more convenient than other contemporary pedals. The primary drawback with the Look system is that it requires permanent cleats on your shoes, and after you set up your shoes with the Look cleats to use with the Look pedals, you cannot wear those shoes to ride a bike equipped with any other type of pedals. Time will tell how well these new pedals catch the cycling public's fancy.

## Common Pedal Features

Pedals on higher-quality bikes are generally equipped with toe clips and toe straps. There is a misconception that the purpose of toe clips is to prevent your feet from slipping forward on the pedals; in reality their primary function is to hold up the toe strap loops so you can easily place your feet through them. The strap's function is to prevent your feet from slipping off the pedals, particularly if you wear cleated shoes that permit you to pull up slightly on the back side of your pedaling circle. Even under racing conditions, toe straps are not nor-

mally cinched down tightly. This is done only at the start of particularly steep hills and just before finish-line sprints.

Under normal riding conditions most people don't keep their straps tight, just without much slack. That way the straps provide a measure of security without preventing you from being able to quickly remove your feet from the pedals. With a little practice, the technique of lifting your foot up before you pull it back out of the strap becomes automatic.

If your bike is equipped with toe clips that seem too short to allow you to place your foot far enough forward to pedal on the ball of your foot, check with your dealer about getting larger toe clips. They come in a variety of sizes.

Many pedals feature replaceable cages. They permit you to maintain an otherwise serviceable pedal even when the rear cage plate becomes worn. That's important for your knees as well as your wallet, because a worn cage plate can allow your shoes, especially cleated ones, to cock themselves to one side or the other. That can result in knee damage such as tendinitis. Keep an eye on the top edge of the cage plates. If either appears to have a curve in it, check it by fitting the shoe onto the pedal by hand. Slide the shoe sideways and back and forth. See if it rocks from side to side. If it does, replace the cage plate, if possible, or else the entire pedal.

Pedals with replaceable cage plates use Phillips-head or flat-head Allen screws to hold the cage plate(s) on the pedal body. Pedals with irreplaceable cage plates use rivets. A small drop of low-strength Loctite on the screws is a worthwhile precaution when assembling new cages onto old pedals. This will discourage the screws from loosening and dropping out while the pedals are in use.

So-called sealed bearings are just as popular a feature in pedals as they are in other components. The term "sealed mechanism" is somewhat of a misnomer, although there are some pedals, such as the excellent SunTour Superbe Pro, that really use sealed cartridge-type bearings. This type of pedal requires special tools to remove the bearings for service and is best left to the attentions of a well-equipped shop.

In line with today's emphasis on serviceability, most recent "sealed" designs can be disassembled with regular tools. That's because the seals in question are actually shields incorporated around regular pedal bearing construction. These pedals can be serviced in the same manner as any "nonsealed" type.

## When to Service Pedals

There are usually only four conditions that indicate a need for pedals to be serviced. The first is simply the passage of time. In the absence of any other condition, once a year pedals ought to be serviced as a routine matter of preventive maintenance. Open up the pedal and make sure you don't have water or other contaminants trapped inside. (Those seals can work both ways!) These problems are difficult to detect from the outside.

The second condition is when you hear and/or feel a maddening *click* with every complete revolution of the pedal or crank. This could result from a loose bottom bracket cup, crankarm, or toe clip bolt, so check those easily rectified problems first. If those parts are all tight and the click continues, it is probably something within the pedal bearings. If

you've recently overhauled your pedals, try to isolate the offending side and service only that one. But if it's been a while since their last servicing, you might as well do both of your pedals now. Ironically, you'll most likely never find the small bit of dirt that causes the problem, which almost always goes away after cleaning and regreasing.

The last two conditions are easily detected with a simple inspection you should perform regularly, either before or after every few rides. Just hold each pedal body with your fingertips while you rotate it around the crankarm. A slight roughness to the touch suggests there may be dirt in the pedal bearings or they may be slightly out of adjustment. If the pedal binds, you have a very dirty or a badly adjusted set of bearings. If the pedal works OK to this point, try to rock it back and forth. An adjustment is called for if you discover any play in the bearings.

## Cleaning and Greasing

You can perform an adjustment on a pedal while it's still screwed onto its crankarm, but don't try to disassemble one without first removing it from the bike. You'll probably need a thin, 12mm wrench like that found at the small end of the fixed cup wrench in most bottom bracket tool sets. But remember! Pedals are threaded the same as the side of the bike they're on. That means that as you straddle the bike, the pedal on your right side unscrews counterclockwise, while the pedal on your left side unscrews clockwise.

To disassemble the pedal after taking it off the crank, hold its threaded end down in a vise with soft jaws or between two pieces of wood. Remove the dust cap with the appropriate tool. Underneath the dust cap you'll find the locknut and cone for the outboard bearings.

Hold the cone in place with one wrench while you loosen the locknut with another. In an emergency, if you don't have a wrench for the cone, you can sometimes hold it steady by wedging a screwdriver between it and the inside of the pedal body. Now unscrew the locknut and cone.

Either pick the ball bearings out of their race with a pair of tweezers or, holding the spindle (axle) firmly within the pedal body, turn the pedal upside down and dump the bearings into a container. Before you go any further, count the ball bearings—if you drop any during disassembly and the inside bearing has a different number of balls, you may not know if you found all of the ones you dropped. Don't lift the pedal body off the spindle or all the inboard bearings may drop on the floor. Next, turn the pedal upside down, if it isn't already, and lift the spindle out of the pedal body. If the pedal has a rubber seal you may have to gently pry it out of the body to make it easy to remove the inboard ball bearings. Count them before any get lost.

You should replace your ball bearings with new ones. The old ones are invariably slightly out of round, which will make adjusting them difficult when they're reassembled into the pedal. Most loose-ball pedals use ⅛-inch bearings, but take a sample to the bike shop to make sure you get a good match.

Clean everything well. Make sure you remove all the old grease from the inside of the pedal body. If there's a rubber seal at the inner end of the pedal body that you didn't remove and you can't get the area behind it clean, try gently prying it out of the body.

If any of the bearing races have pitted areas or more than a slight groove, check into replacement parts. Availability varies considerably between manufacturers.

Apply a layer of medium-weight grease to the races in the pedal body. Hold the inside end up and place the required number of ball bearings in the layer of grease. Carefully place the spindle halfway back into the body, then apply additional grease to the ball bearings either directly or by loading up the area next to the inside cone. Seat the spindle and turn it to make sure it isn't binding. Any grease that oozes out of the inboard bearings indicates that the bearings are fully packed and will resist contamination for the maximum amount of time.

Holding the spindle tightly in the pedal body, turn the assembly over and secure the spindle the same way you did to begin disassembly. Place the required number of ball bearings in the outboard race, then reinstall the cone finger tight, followed by the lockwasher and locknut.

## Pedal Adjustment

Loosen the locknut and back off the cone with a wrench and then tighten down the locknut. If you backed the cone off enough, there should be some play. Loosen the locknut, screw in the cone slightly, tighten the locknut, and check for play. Continue the process until the pedal turns smoothly on the spindle without any rough feel. It's better to work the play out of a loose bearing than to overtighten it to begin with and risk damaging the bearings or races.

Replace the dust cap and you're done. But take it easy when you tighten it; most dust caps are made of plastic.

Pedals may seem like an insignificant part of a bicycle, something you should be able to take for granted. While it is true that proper pedal adjustment is less critical to the safe operation of a bike than properly adjusting its brakes and headset, there is still no point in neglecting this process. Smooth-turning pedals add a lot to the joy and efficiency of cycling. All it takes is a little time and proper maintenance.

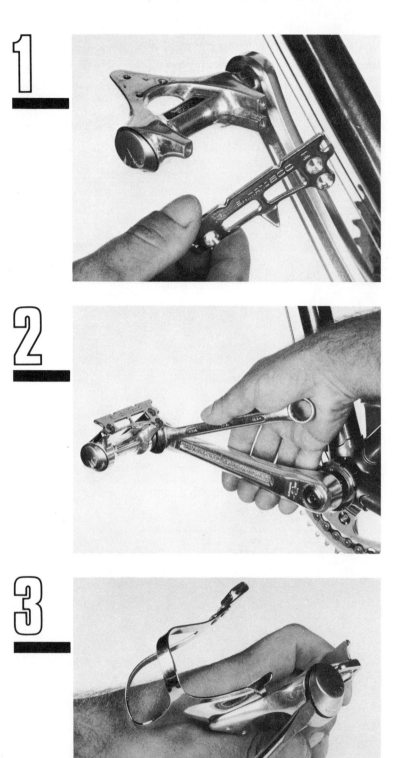

P edals are fairly simple, basic components. Thus, it is tempting to take them for granted and not give them the type of care given other parts of the bike. Some types of pedals are inexpensive enough not to be worth the time and trouble to service. When they cease to work well, they are not that difficult or costly to replace.

A good set of pedals, however, deserve the kind of respect given to hubs, headsets, and cranksets. All these components contain ball bearings, which need to be properly adjusted and lubricated and periodically replaced. This kind of treatment will ensure that the components work efficiently for a long time.

Pedals protrude from the sides of the bike and move near the ground. This makes them vulnerable to collisions with objects that do not treat them kindly. Often the damage done is only cosmetic—scratch marks on a previously shiny surface. But sometimes a critical part of a pedal may be bent or broken, making the pedal dangerous to use.

Some pedal parts are replaceable. If damage is done to such a part, it may be possible to take that part off and buy a replacement part instead of a completely new pedal. (Photo 1) That is especially desirable when replacing a complete pedal necessitates the replacement of the pair.

However, if you do need to replace a complete pedal, they are not difficult to remove. Just keep in mind that a left-hand pedal threads in the opposite direction from a right-hand pedal. The threads on pedals run in such a way that the top of the pedal turns toward the front of the bike when it is being tightened.

To loosen a pedal for removal, rotate its crank forward toward the front of the bike, fit on the wrench, then push the wrench

PEDALS

down toward the ground. (Photo 2) This procedure will work for each pedal in turn.

To disassemble a pedal, first remove the dust cap on the end of the axle opposite the threaded end. On many models you will simply have to pry off the dust cap with a flat-bladed screwdriver or similar tool. (Photo 3)

If you have a bench vise, use it to hold the pedal still in an upright position while you disassemble it. However, it is not that difficult to do the job without the aid of a vise.

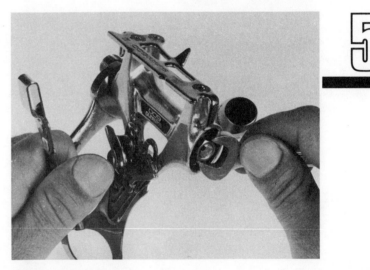

Once the dust cap is off, you will see a locknut on the end of the axle holding the axle and the bearings inside the body of the pedal. (Photo 4) Use a thin cone wrench to hold the cone still while loosening the locknut. If you do not have a suitable cone wrench, fit a wrench on the flats at the threaded end of the axle to prevent the axle from twisting while you loosen the locknut. (Photo 5)

Remove the locknut and the lockwasher behind it. Then thread off the cone. Be careful as you remove the cone, because there are bearings behind it that can easily spill out and become lost. (Photo 6)

The bearings can be removed in one of two ways. Either turn the pedal upside down and shake the bearings into a container or use a pair of tweezers to carefully pick them out one by one. (Photo 7) Make sure the axle remains inside the pedal body while the first set of bearings are being removed. Otherwise you may spill and lose some bearings from the inner set.

As soon as the outer bearings are all out, count them and record the number so you will know how many replacement bearings to put in when you reassemble the pedal.

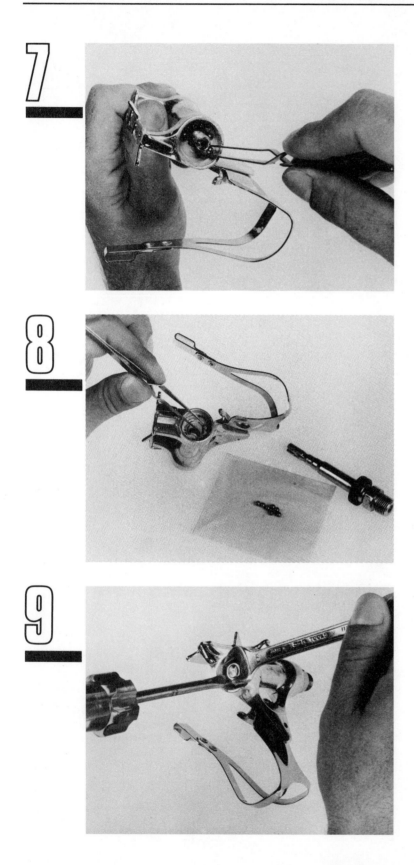

Turn the pedal over and pull the axle out. If the axle has a rubber seal, it may take some effort to pull it out. Once it is out, remove the second set of bearings, count and record their number. (Photo 8) Take a sample with you to buy replacements of the same size.

Clean all metal parts with solvent, but keep the solvent away from plastic parts and rubber seals. Use something mild like alcohol to clean those parts. Make sure you get all the old grease out of the inside of the pedal body. Inspect the bearing races. If they are pitted, check with the bike shop to see if replacement parts are available.

When you have a complete set of clean and usable parts, you are ready to reassemble the pedal. Pack medium-weight grease into the inner bearing race and install a new set of bearings. Coat the axle with grease and push it back through the pedal body until its cone seats against the bearings.

At this point, turn the pedal over, pack the outer race with grease, and install the other set of bearings. Put the cone on the end of the axle and thread it down with your fingers until you feel it make contact with the bearings. Put the lockwasher back in place and thread the locknut back on the end of the axle.

Make sure the locknut is loose enough to give you some working room, then back the cone off until you know it is too loose. Now slowly turn the cone down. Once you reach the point where most of the play is out of the adjustment, hold the cone still with a cone wrench and use a second wrench to tighten the locknut against it.

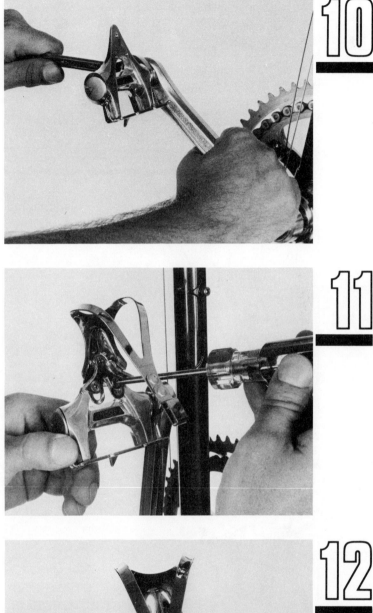

If you don't have a cone wrench to fit the pedal cone, use a screwdriver to prevent the cone from turning while you tighten the locknut. (Photo 9)

Now spin the pedal. If you feel any binding, your adjustment is too tight. If binding is no problem, but you feel play in the bearings when you wiggle the pedal up and down, loosen the locknut and turn the cone down a little more. Tighten the locknut and check the adjustment again.

Work in small increments in this way until you reach the point where there is neither binding nor looseness in the adjustment. Then make sure the locknut is firmly fastened and replace the dust cap.

Before threading the pedal back on its crankarm, coat its threads with a little grease. Carefully line up the two sets of threads, then thread on the pedal and use a wrench to snug it up. (Photo 10)

When adding or replacing toe clips, make sure you buy clips that are compatible with your particular type of pedals. Fasten the clips to the pedals with the screws provided by the manufacturer. (Photo 11)

When installing a leather toe strap, put a single twist in the strap as you run it between the two sides of the pedal. This will prevent the strap from shifting position.

Lace the strap through the upper end of the toe clip, then press the buckle open and run the end of the strap straight through both the inner and outer plates of the buckle. (Photo 12) When you release the buckle, the end of the strap should be caught between the cylinder of the inner plate and the teeth in the outer plate of the buckle. ▲

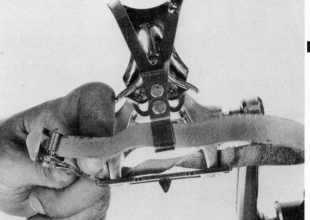

# 16 GEARS

The human body is in many ways a mechanical marvel. Nevertheless, as an energy-producing power plant the body has its limitations. Through training and proper conditioning, the maximum energy output of a body can be improved, but it always remains within a fairly restricted range of movement and speed. Like a diesel truck, the human body needs multiple gears in order to "keep on truckin" over widely varying road conditions.

This is why a bicycle is such an attractive vehicle. It is tailored to the human body and becomes an extension of it, providing it with the flexibility it lacks through natural endowment—low gears for climbing steep inclines and high gears for taking advantage of descents and flat terrain. Obviously, the availability of numerous gears on a bicycle plays a very important part in riding pleasure. Yet, gearing is also one of the most difficult areas of bicycling to master. Having 10, 12, 15, or even 18 speeds is just fine, but in between high and low on most people's gear charts lies an area marked "unexplored."

It's not just the numbers on the chart that many people find confusing. Jargon like crossovers, Alpine, and half-step with granny adds to the mystery. Unfortunately, you can't get away from the numbers, so we'll explain what they mean. As for jargon, just remember that most gearing setups have a rationale that addresses the pattern you use to get a set of usable gears. And that's what you need to know in order to ride without being constantly distracted by shifting decisions.

## Learning the Lingo

In America, the way we designate gear sizes is derived from the days of high-wheelers, the kind you see in Memorial Day parades. Since each complete revolution of the pedals of such a bike results in a single wheel revolution, people used to gauge how fast you could go on one by the diameter of the front wheel. A high-wheeler with a 45-inch front wheel is faster than one with a 36-inch-diameter wheel, but harder to ride up hills.

Nowadays we still refer to gears by the equivalent high-wheeler size that would give you the same distance traveled per pedal revolution as the distance you would cover with one pedal revolution on your 27-inch wheel bike. For example, when you ride on your 52-tooth chainring and a 14-tooth freewheel cog, your gear ratio is 52/14, or 3.714. If you multiply that ratio by the wheel diameter of a standard derailleur bike, 27 inches, you find that you're "in" a 100-inch gear. (See table 16-12 at the end of this chapter for the gear inch equivalents of all possible bicycle gear combinations.)

Notice in this example how the gear ratio is determined by dividing the number of teeth on the chainring by the number of teeth on the rear cog. A 52-tooth chainring and a 14-tooth freewheel cog are in a ratio of 3.714 to 1. If the chainring were reduced in size to 30 teeth and the size of the rear cog increased to 30 teeth they would be in a ratio of 1 to 1. Multiplying this ratio by the wheel diameter, we find that this combination of chainring and freewheel gives us a gear of only 27 inches. The difference in the size of these numbers reflects the different level of effort needed to propel a bicycle using the two gears. A 100-inch gear will move you 3.714 times as far down the road with each revolution of the pedals as will a 27-inch gear. However, the smaller gear will allow you to pedal up a steep grade with a heavy load while the larger gear is only useful on fast descents or, if you are quite strong, on flat terrain.

Later in this chapter we will provide numerous examples of different chainring and freewheel combinations and chart out the results of these combinations in terms of gear inches. For now, what we want to make clear is simply the logic of how these numbers are derived and what they mean in relationship to one another. The higher the number, the greater the size of the chainring in relation to the freewheel cog, and the greater the effort needed to use the gear; the lower the number, the smaller the size of the chainring in relation to the freewheel cog and the less effort needed to propel the bike.

From this you can see that there are two ways you can move to a gear that is larger or smaller than the one you are in. To move to a larger gear, you can either leave the chain on the same rear cog and shift it onto a larger chainring or you can leave it on the same chainring and shift it onto a smaller rear cog. Either move will increase the gear ratio and thus the size of the gear. Conversely, you can move to a smaller gear either by staying on the same chainring and shifting onto a larger rear cog or by staying on the same rear cog while shifting to a smaller chainring.

The manner in which gearing systems are set up on bicycles makes the distinction between larger and smaller gears easy to remember. The smaller the chainring or the larger the rear cog, the closer it is to the bicycle frame; the larger the chainring or the smaller the cog, the farther it is from the bicycle frame. Thus, the lowest gear is always formed with the chain all the way to the inside on both front and rear and the highest gear with the chain as far to the outside as it can be shifted front and rear.

To simplify references to different gear combinations in the discussion that follows, we will assign numbers to the freewheel cogs and letters to the chainrings. The cogs we will number consecutively from inside to outside in order to reflect their relative effects on gear size. Thus, the innermost cog will be referred to as "1" and the outermost as "5" or "6," depending on the total number. In a similar way we will use an "L" to refer to the inner chainring (the one that produces lower gears) and "H" to refer to the outer chainring (the one that produces higher gears). In the case of triple chainring cranksets we will add the letter "M" to designate the gears formed on the middle chainring.

By means of this code, we can refer to the gear formed on the inner chainring and the inside cog as L-1 and the gear formed on the outer chainring and outside cog as H-5 or H-6 (depending on whether there are 5 or 6 freewheel cogs). This works for either a double or triple chainring system, since the gears formed on the middle ring of a triple will be identified as M-1, M-2, and so on.

The most common method used for charting a gearing system is simply to write the chainring sizes across the top and the cog sizes down the left side of vertical columns, calculate all combinations of the two, and list the results in gear inches within the columns. This is the type of gearing information characteristically found in the bicycle road test articles that appear in *Bicycling* magazine. We have, in fact, created charts of this type for all the primary examples of gearing systems discussed in this chapter. (See, for example, table 16-1.)

The primary value of creating gear charts of this sort is that they allow a quick numerical comparison to be made of different gearing systems. By adding arrows, as we have done to the tables found in this chapter, the conventional gearing chart can be turned into a practical guide for learning how to properly shift through the available gears in a particular system. In addition to the arrows, we have added shading to the upper left and lower right corners of each of our gear charts to show that the L-5 and H-1 gears, while theoretically possible to create, should not be used. These gear combinations bend the chain to its maximum deflection, which can greatly accelerate chain, cog, and freewheel wear.

The difference in gear size created by moving the chain from any freewheel cog to an adjacent cog is referred to as a "step." In certain types of gearing systems, such as half-step and Alpine, the percentage of change for each step is kept relatively constant. For example, if you start with a 14-tooth outer freewheel cog and increase cog size by 15 percent each step, you'll end up with a 14-16-18-21-24T freewheel. No matter what size chainring you use with this freewheel, when you shift back and forth between adjacent freewheel cogs, the resulting gears will change by 15 percent. The important thing to note here is that, although the difference in teeth is not the same between each pair of these cogs, the *percentage* difference between

them is the same. This means that, to your legs, consecutive gears created by moving the chain from one cog to the next on this freewheel will feel about the same amount harder or easier to use.

Ideally, all gearing systems would have consecutive gears in a constant percentage relationship. However, as our subsequent discussion will show, it is quite difficult to create a system which has an optimum high and low gear, even spacing among all gears, and a shift pattern that is easy both to remember and to execute.

## Common Gearing Patterns

At this point we would like to begin a fairly detailed and systematic examination of the most common gearing patterns used on derailleur bicycles. We will pick a specific chainring/freewheel combination to illustrate the unique features of each, explaining how the pattern should be shifted, and underscoring both its advantages and disadvantages. We will also describe optional shift patterns, where they exist, and explain why they may sometimes be preferred over the recommended patterns. Finally, we will discuss ways in which various gearing systems may be altered in order to tailor them to your particular needs.

### Half-Step

Although it is unlikely you have half-step gearing on your bike, let's cover it first because it is straightforward and illustrates the general principles of gearing quite well. We will take as our example of this type of gearing a system comprised of a 14-17-21-26-34T freewheel and 47/52T chainrings. The gears produced by this combination of cogs and chainrings are charted in table 16-1.

A quick glance at table 16-1 reveals that this system offers eight usable gears, the lowest being 37 gear inches and the highest 100 gear inches. However, unless you are quite experienced in translating numbers on a chart into a feeling in the legs, you are not likely to know simply by looking at these numbers how close this system comes to fulfilling the ideal of even spacing among gears. The easiest way to gain this information is to begin with the lowest gear in the set and divide each gear into its neighbor, moving up the scale of size. Thus, we look at the table and see that

the L-1 gear is 37 inches and L-2 is 49 inches. Dividing 37 into 49 we get a result of 1.32, which tells us that shifting from L-1 to L-2 in this particular system involves a gear step of 32 percent.

Looking back at the table, we see that the next highest gear (L-3) that can be formed on the inner chainring in this system is 60 inches. So we divide 49 into 60 and discover that the L-2 to L-3 shift involves a step of 22 percent. Continuing in this manner we find that moving from L-3 to L-4 involves a step of 25 percent and L-4 to L-5 a step of 20 percent. Actually, L-5 is not recommended for use, but the same freewheel step can be made when your chain is on the outside chainring, so the information is useful. What we learn from this exercise is that this freewheel has a large inner cog that provides a relatively low first gear. Then, after a giant step from the first to the second cog, steps between the remaining cogs on this freewheel are fairly even.

Look once more at table 16-1. Focus your attention this time on the arrows that indicate the recommended shift pattern for the system. Each vertical arrow represents a shift involving only the rear derailleur, each horizontal arrow represents a shift involving only the front derailleur, while each diagonal arrow represents a double-shift involving both derailleurs. Right away you can see that except for the simple freewheel shifts at the lower and upper ends of the system, the recommended pattern involves constant shifts from one chainring to another and two double shifts involving both derailleurs. If the H-1 and L-5 gears were usable, the pattern would consist solely of chainring crossover and double shifts.

Since a change of chainrings is involved in most gear changes, the in-

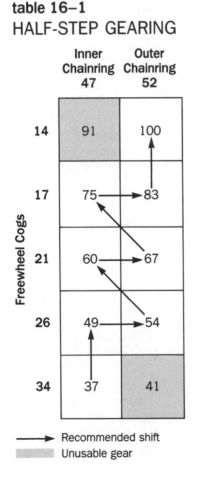

**table 16–1**

## HALF-STEP GEARING

| | Inner Chainring 47 | Outer Chainring 52 |
|---|---|---|
| 14 | 91 | 100 |
| 17 | 75 | 83 |
| 21 | 60 | 67 |
| 26 | 49 | 54 |
| 34 | 37 | 41 |

Freewheel Cogs

→ Recommended shift
▨ Unusable gear

formation we previously learned about the size of freewheel steps is not sufficient for us to judge the spacing of the eight usable gears in this system. What we need to see is the percentage relationship between all these gears as they occur in sequence. So let's rearrange the gears in sequential order. Beginning again with the lowest gear, let's divide each into the next one in line to determine the percentage difference involved in each change of gear position. The result is shown in table 16-2.

What we see from this table is that each shift that involves moving from one chainring to another reduces the percentage change in gear positions by about half of what occurs when the shift occurs only on the rear. Shifts of a full freewheel step occur only at the low and high ends of the system if the recommended pattern is followed. The rest of the shifts are only "half-steps."

This relationship between chainring shifts and freewheel shifts in a half-step system is no accident, but is the key to this particular system. It is the feature that gives the system its name and its uniqueness. The way it is achieved is by fitting the bike with a pair of chainrings that differ from one another in size only half as much as the freewheel cogs differ from one another. In our model half-step system, moving from one to the next among the four outside freewheel cogs results in a change of between 20 and 25 percent.

By contrast, moving from one chainring (47T) to the other (52T) results in a change of 11 percent, approximately half of one freewheel step.

Sure, there are large steps at the two ends of the sequence. However, at the low end, this is not especially critical, since the lowest gear will rarely be needed anyway. It is there only for those occasional steep hills. The gap at the top may be more of a problem; though, there again, the 100-inch gear will probably be used by most cyclists only on rare occasions. It is in the middle range, the area that will be used the most, that this system really shines, because the middle range of gears in this half-step system are comfortably close together and spaced beautifully even. As for the shifting pattern, it is simple for the mind, if not the hands.

If you plot this set of gears on a logarithmic graph, as we have done in table 16-3, the percentage relationship between adjacent gears becomes quickly evident, because a logarithmic arrangement makes all distances between gears of equal percentage the same no matter where they are on the scale. A log graph shows gear steps as they are actually experienced rather than simply in terms of numbers, which (as we have seen) can be misleading. That makes it easy to visually compare different gearing systems. A quick glance at the arrangement of dots in table 16-3 shows that a lot of variation exists in the size of gear steps,

## table 16–2
## PERCENTAGE DIFFERENCES BETWEEN GEARS IN A 14-34T, 47/52T HALF-STEP SYSTEM

```
              32%     10%     11%     12%     12%     11%     20%
             /   \   /   \   /   \   /   \   /   \   /   \   /   \
Gear inches: 37————49————54————60————67————75————83————100
```

the effect of chainring shifts, and the evenness with which gears are spaced within the five systems depicted.

On our log graph, the lower the gear, the closer it is to the left side of the graph. (The gear inches are noted at the bottom). Where there is a single horizontal line separating dots, dots above the line represent gears formed on the inner chainring and dots below the line represent gears formed on the outer chainring. The line itself thus represents the space between chainrings and movement across the line a shift across chainrings. The final example found in the graph is a triple-chainring system, which is the reason for the additional line and additional string of dots. In all five examples, dots with an "+" through them represent either extreme combinations or optional gears that may or may not be included in the shifting sequence. A graph of this type brings out beautifully the unique quality of the half-step system. The "half-step" effect of a chainring shift can be clearly seen by the manner in which the dots below the horizontal line in the half-step example relate to the dots above the line.

By contrast, look at the second system depicted on this graph, the Alpine pattern. Notice, in this case, that the first dot below the line falls approximately halfway between the second and third dots plotted above the line. This means that a chainwheel shift (from L-2 to H-2, L-3 to H-3, etc.) on an Alpine setup involves moving 1½ gear positions, instead of the ½ position of the half-step system. This is why the Alpine system is sometimes referred to as "one-and-a-half-step" gearing.

Shifting the middle range of a half-step pattern is not really that difficult once you get accustomed to doing it. If the shift can be made with the front de-

railleur in the direction you wish to go, then you only have to make a single shift. For example, if you're cruising on your large chainring and want to pedal in a slightly smaller gear, you can simply downshift ½ step onto your inner chainring. That is, you can shift from H-4 down to L-4, or from H-3 down to L-3.

However, if you are in the middle range and want to move into a slightly higher gear, you cannot shift up from your large chainring. In that case you must first shift down ½ step with your front derailleur and then back up a full step with your rear derailleur. The net result (for example, moving from H-3 over to L-3, then up to L-4) is a half-step upshift. The pattern is reversed if you start on the inner chainring.

In sum, the advantages of half-step gearing are its simple shifting sequence, the easy shifts across the small chainring spread, and its evenly spaced middle-range development.

Disadvantages with the half-step system include the need to double-shift many of the gears, gaps at the upper and lower ends of the range, and a limited low-gear potential. As we'll see later, adding an inner chainring can take care of the low-gear problem. Considering the even, close pattern of cogs in this system, using a 6-speed freewheel would not produce much of an improvement in gear choices for most cyclists.

## Alpine

Almost all bikes sold today are equipped with some form of Alpine gearing. In a way, that's unfortunate, because the shift sequence for Alpine is the most difficult to master. It persists today as a continuation of the traditional means for getting a full set of usable gears with the middle-range derailleurs

**table 16–3**

# COMPARISON OF STEPS IN DIFFERENT GEARING SYSTEMS

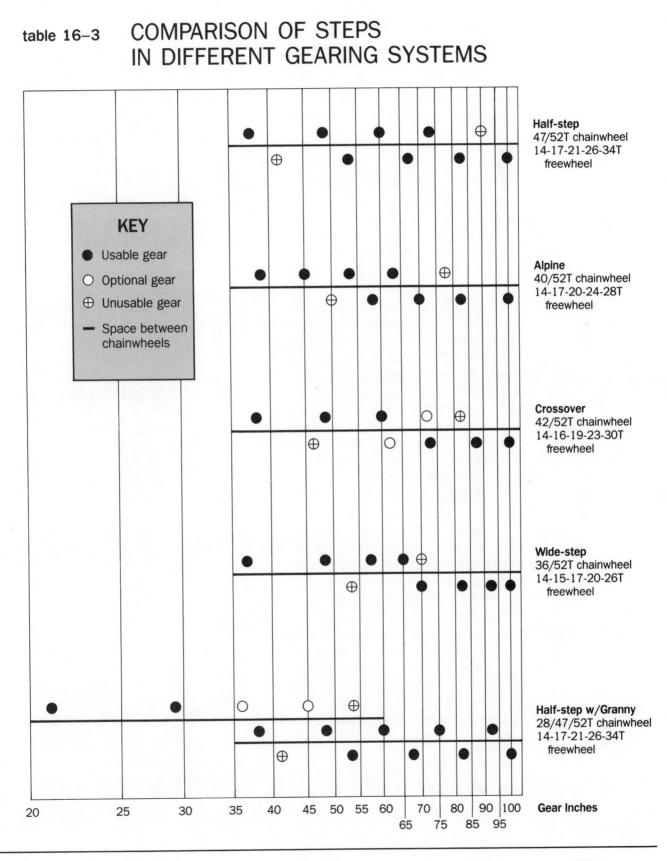

**KEY**

● Usable gear

○ Optional gear

⊕ Unusable gear

— Space between chainwheels

**Half-step**
47/52T chainwheel
14-17-21-26-34T
freewheel

**Alpine**
40/52T chainwheel
14-17-20-24-28T
freewheel

**Crossover**
42/52T chainwheel
14-16-19-23-30T
freewheel

**Wide-step**
36/52T chainwheel
14-15-17-20-26T
freewheel

**Half-step w/Granny**
28/47/52T chainwheel
14-17-21-26-34T
freewheel

**Gear Inches**

20   25   30   35   40   45   50   55   60   70   80   90   100
                                        65   75   85   95

COMPLETE GUIDE TO BICYCLE MAINTENANCE AND REPAIR

that were the best available before today's wide-range marvels appeared on the market.

Look at the horizontally charted gear development for the standard Alpine setup, a standard 14-17-20-24-28T freewheel coupled with a 40/52T set of chainwheels (table 16-3). As we noted earlier, shifts between chainrings in this system result in a shift along the horizontal line of 1½ gear steps. That is why some people refer to Alpine gearing as one-and-a-half-step gearing. Unlike the patterns we'll see later, which have a lot looser rules for their creation, Alpine gearing shares with half-step gearing the distinction of having a definite mathematical structure. Freewheel steps are of approximately equal percentage, while the step between chainrings is 1½ times that percentage.

Of the eight usable gears created by Alpine gearing, the lowest three and the highest three gears are shifted easily with just the rear derailleur. It's in the middle ground that difficulties arise. To take advantage of an Alpine's evenly spaced gears, the shift sequence must be L-1, L-2, L-3, H-2, L-4, H-3, H-4, H-5. (See the shift pattern in table 16-4.) The double shifts between several of the gears are not particularly difficult; it's the complicated Alpine shift (from H-2 to L-2 then up to L-4) that's difficult to remember. If you do remember, however, you'll be rewarded with shift gains of 18, 22, 5, 9, 13, 11, and 20 percent. If you don't, and skip the shift from H-2 to L-4 and go directly from H-2 to H-3, you'll exchange a 9 percent jump for a 22 percent one in an important part of your gear range. Your legs will notice the difference!

There is an interesting alternative, although it means giving up one gear.

Make your shift sequence L-1, L-2, L-3, L-4, H-3, H-4, H-5. This avoids one double-shift as well as the dreaded front shift/double rear shift and still gives you shift gains of 18, 22, 15, 13, 11, and 20 percent.

Here's another tip that may make living with an Alpine gear setup a lot easier. Make your own small gear chart like the one in table 16-4 on a piece of paper small enough to place on the top surface of your handlebar stem. Cover it with clear tape. There, at a glance, you can see your gears. You may want to just put a diagram of the shifting pattern

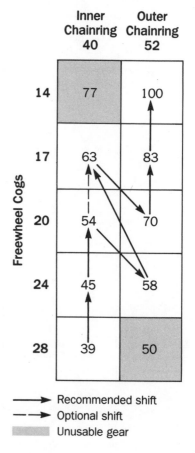

**table 16–4**
## ALPINE GEARING

|  | Inner Chainring 40 | Outer Chainring 52 |
|---|---|---|
| 14 | 77 | 100 |
| 17 | 63 | 83 |
| 20 | 54 | 70 |
| 24 | 45 | 58 |
| 28 | 39 | 50 |

(Freewheel Cogs)

→ Recommended shift
- - → Optional shift
▨ Unusable gear

there, instead of the gear-inch numbers. But whatever you do, don't study it too long while you're riding!

The advantages of Alpine gearing are its use of inexpensive, readily available middle-range cranksets, freewheels, and derailleurs; its eight usable gears (on a 10-speed); and the even half-steps in its middle range. Alpine disadvantages include the large jumps at either end of the gear range and its shift pattern, which is as difficult to perform as it is to remember.

## Crossover

If simplicity is what you value most in a shifting pattern, then a crossover pattern is what you want. It's the shifting sequence of racers by choice, and of most Alpine riders by ignorance. For a 10-speed bike, the shift sequence would be L-1, L-2, L-3, H-3, H-4, H-5. There are no double-shifts and a minimum of chain deflection. The down side to crossover gearing is that you get only six usable gears on a 10-speed or seven with a 12-speed.

If you plot the gears for a 14-16-19-23-30T freewheel and a 42/52T chainring set, you will see that in addition to the smaller number of gears provided by this system when compared to Alpine or half-step gearing, crossover has some large steps. They're 38, 16, 25, 19, and 14 percent. But look at the flexibility. You can make your crossover front shift while you're on the second, third, or fourth freewheel cogs and the gears you use are almost identical each way (table 16-5).

Here is a practical example of what we mean. If you are in your 59-inch gear (L-3) and need a slightly higher gear for just a short distance, you can make the

**table 16–5**
## CROSSOVER GEARING

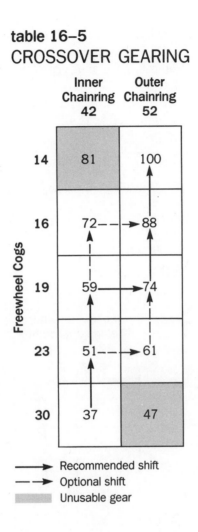

| | Inner Chainring 42 | Outer Chainring 52 |
|---|---|---|
| **14** | 81 | 100 |
| **16** | 72 - - → 88 | |
| **19** | 59 → 74 | |
| **23** | 51 - - → 61 | |
| **30** | 37 | 47 |

Freewheel Cogs

→ Recommended shift
- - → Optional shift
▨ Unusable gear

shift to L-4 and back to L-3 with your rear derailleur instead of the two front derailleur shifts required to go to H-3 and then back to L-3. You have the same sort of option when you want to shift to a slightly lower gear from H-3.

But don't be afraid to get creative with your gearing. Your needs are unique, and sometimes they can be addressed with a little ingenuity. For example, a marriage of crossover and half-step gearing can produce an even range of gears with flexible shifting. A 14-15-17-19-21-24T 6-speed freewheel combines with a 42/52T crankset to give you eight usable gears with shift gains of 15, 11, 12, 10, 12, 13, and 6 percent. In this case you can make your crossover/half-step shift from inner to outer chainring at either the third, fourth, or fifth freewheel cog (see table 16-6). In each case you will also have to shift one step with your rear derailleur. And, in riding situations where you can handle a slightly larger step, you can cross over at any of the four middle freewheel cogs. At least the sequence is easy to remember; most of the time you can stay on one chainring and ride your bike like a 5-speed with two ranges that overlap by two gears.

In sum, the advantages of crossover gearing are its simple shift pattern and lack of double-shifts, while its disadvantages include a small selection of gears with correspondingly large gaps between them.

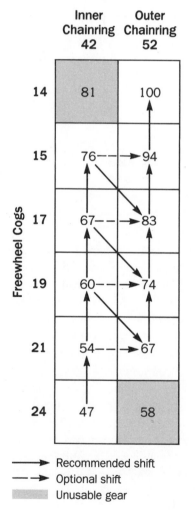

**table 16–6**
SIX-SPEED HYBRID GEARING

| Freewheel Cogs | Inner Chainring 42 | Outer Chainring 52 |
|---|---|---|
| 14 | 81 | 100 |
| 15 | 76 | 94 |
| 17 | 67 | 83 |
| 19 | 60 | 74 |
| 21 | 54 | 67 |
| 24 | 47 | 58 |

——▶ Recommended shift
– –▶ Optional shift
▒ Unusable gear

## Wide-Step

This gearing pattern will produce the lowest low gear generally possible with a double crankset. The theory is to couple two ranges of straight sequence gears with one "wide" jump between chainring sizes. If the freewheel is narrow enough in range, a pattern can result like the "crossover/half-step" discussed above. However, its low isn't low enough for most riders.

With a 36/52T crankset and a slightly wider 14-15-17-20-26T freewheel, we get to see the worst face a wide-step can wear (table 16-3). Although this arrangement has eight available gears out of ten, the shift gains, at 32, 16, 14, 8, 19, 13 and 6 percent, are uneven. (For the precise size of each of these combinations in terms of gear inches, see table 16-12.) In addition, there's a difficult Alpine shift (between L-4 and H-2) in a crucial part of your gear range that has no alternative shift (see table 16-7). Contrast this to the 14-28T, 42/52T Alpine, which has the same number of legitimate gears, the same range, and a similar shift pattern, but offers some shifting alternatives, particularly in the midrange.

If we were to change the freewheel to 14-16-19-25-34T (table 16-7), we

achieve more consistent shift gains of 34, 31, 20, 21, 19, and 13 percent with a shift pattern that stays on the inner chainring until L-4, then half-steps to H-3 to finish on the outer chainring. Switching the half-step by shifting from L-3 to H-2, or even making an Alpine middle, by shifting L-3, H-2, L-4, H-3, are legitimate alternatives. In addition, you get a 28 percent lower low gear! That's why wide-step gearing is your solution if you need a wide gear range and cannot convert your double crankset to a triple, can't afford a new one, or don't want to change cranksets.

## table 16–7
## WIDE-STEP GEARING

| Freewheel Cogs | Inner Chainring 36 | Outer Chainring 52 |
|---|---|---|
| 14 | 69 | 100 |
| 16 | 61 | 88 |
| 19 | 51 | 74 |
| 25 | 39 | 56 |
| 34 | 29 | 41 |

→ Recommended shift
- - → Optional shift
▨ Unusable gear

## Triple

As you might have noticed by now, it's not easy to get a set of easily shiftable, evenly spaced gears *and* a low, low gear. To achieve that goal is precisely the rationale for triple cranksets, that rather than the acquisition of a whole handful of closely spaced gears. In fact, many good triple gear patterns have only about ten usable gears. That's because the optimal triple arrangement uses the two outer chainrings to make up an easy-shifting set of mid- to upper-range gears, while the inner "granny" chainring is used only with the two, or at most, the three innermost freewheel cogs. The obvious companions for granny are half-step and crossover gearing.

If we return to our 14-34T, 47/52T half-step example, all we have to do is add another column for a 28-tooth, third chainring (table 16-8). That lowers the bottom end of our gear range by 60 percent, thanks to granny and the two inner freewheel cogs. It doesn't matter that in this setup L-3 overlaps M-1.

There's a bonus to adding that third chainring. Because the crankset has to be moved away from the frame (with a longer crank axle) to provide clearance for the inner chainring, the middle chainring should now be centered on the freewheel. That means you do not have to avoid using the outermost cog when you're on what is now the middle chainring. The extra combination in turn conveniently puts another half-step gear in the fair-size gap that existed between the 52×17T and 52×14T combinations, giving you a complete, even set of gears.

You can receive similar benefits when you add a third chainring to a 10-speed crossover pattern. If we use the 14-30T, 42/52T example from our

### table 16-8
## HALF-STEP WITH GRANNY

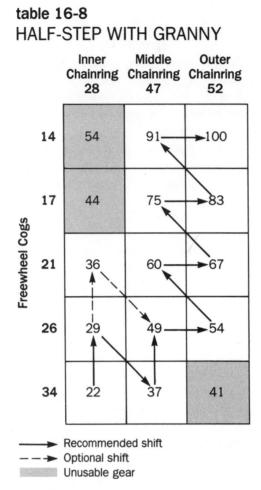

| Freewheel Cogs | Inner Chainring 28 | Middle Chainring 47 | Outer Chainring 52 |
|---|---|---|---|
| 14 | 54 | 91 | 100 |
| 17 | 44 | 75 | 83 |
| 21 | 36 | 60 | 67 |
| 26 | 29 | 49 | 54 |
| 34 | 22 | 37 | 41 |

→ Recommended shift
--→ Optional shift
▨ Unusable gear

crossover section, we can see that we need an inner ring that will combine with the 23T cog to make a gear that will "cross over" to the 51-inch gear (table 16-9). If we decide on a 35 percent jump to the 51-inch gear as a good starting point, we multiply 51 by .65 and get 33 gear inches. Using the gear chart at the end of the chapter, we see that we can make that 33-inch gear a reality by using the 23-tooth cog coupled to a 28-tooth chainring.

The resulting gear arrangement provides even more single-shift options than before, in addition to the same hole-filling half-step M-5 combination as the half-step with granny. And, because you

can achieve an 80-inch gear without shifting to the outer chainring, there will be even fewer occasions when you'll have to "cross over" to another chainring. If you want to keep things really simple, use only the 28T chainring with the 30T freewheel cog and cross over to the middle chainring there. Remember, in this triple setup you can go down to a 37-inch low on the middle ring.

As we mentioned before, the price you pay for this simple-shifting indolence is slightly higher gaps between gears than with a half-step outer section. You can make the gaps slightly smaller by using a 6-speed freewheel, such as

### table 16-9
## CROSSOVER WITH GRANNY

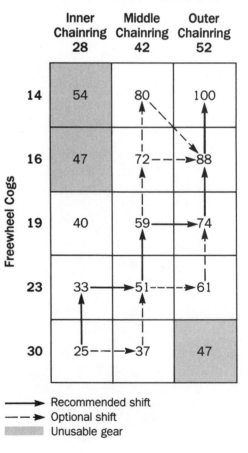

| Freewheel Cogs | Inner Chainring 28 | Middle Chainring 42 | Outer Chainring 52 |
|---|---|---|---|
| 14 | 54 | 80 | 100 |
| 16 | 47 | 72 | 88 |
| 19 | 40 | 59 | 74 |
| 23 | 33 | 51 | 61 |
| 30 | 25 | 37 | 47 |

→ Recommended shift
--→ Optional shift
▨ Unusable gear

14-15-17-20-25-32T with the same chainrings. (Use table 16-12 to calculate the set of gears produced by these components.)

The advantages of triples, then, include: one or two very low gears below 30 inches; a complete set of evenly spaced mid- to high-range gears with easy shift patterns; easy and relatively easy front shifting, respectively, for half-step and crossover configurations; and a set of five usable gears on the middle chainring.

Triple disadvantages include slight extra cost and the need to center the front derailleur on the middle chainring.

## Designing Your Gearing

In order to fit a gearing system to your particular needs, you need to determine five things: an optimum high gear; an optimum low gear; an appropriate shift pattern; chainring and freewheel cogs to combine those high-low limits with the chosen shift pattern; and the appropriate derailleurs and chain to make your design a reality.

If you just want to modify your current bike without a complete replacement of your drive train, you will still need to determine the optimum high and low gear, decide on a shift pattern, and pick replacement cogs and chainrings that are compatible with your derailleurs. Use table 16-12 to quickly determine which combinations will give you gears in the desired range.

### How High?

The 100-inch gear found on most bikes represents a kind of human limit. Even the strongest racers use only slightly larger gears, such as 104- or 108-inch gears. In fact, average riders can't maintain a brisk cadence in a 100-inch gear even on level road; it's there for downhills and tail winds.

If you're not concerned, as racers are, about the little bit of extra speed you can gain by pedaling downhill instead of coasting, you can use a slightly smaller high gear, something in the mid to upper 90s, and shift your whole gear pattern down to emphasize the middle and low ranges. It's a trade-off commonly made by heavily laden tourists and ATB riders. If there's a gap in your intended shift pattern in the 84- to 92-inch range, which is the size of a very handy cruising gear, you might consider filling it by using a 15-tooth outer cog instead of a 14. The 15 combines with a 52-tooth chainring for a 94-inch gear.

### How Low?

Deciding on the optimum lowest gear is a lot more difficult than choosing the highest. Some of the factors you have to consider are the following: your strength; the steepness and length of the worst hills you usually encounter; and the amount of extra weight you might carry, if any. Also, you should take into account the size of gaps between gears and the extra shifting difficulty you would be willing to put up with in order to get extra-low gears.

Obviously, a lot of personal factors will influence your decision of how low your lowest gear needs to be. Nonetheless, we can make some rough recommendations in table 16-10 for those of you who don't have a good idea, based on your own personal experience, of what your low should be. The recommended gears range from those suitable for an average to a strong rider *within each*

table 16-10

# RECOMMENDED LOW GEARS

| Type of Riding | Terrain | Gear Inches |
|---|---|---|
| Loaded touring | Steep hills | 20-27 |
| | Medium hills | 24-32 |
| Sport touring | Steep hills | 27-37 |
| | Medium hills | 32-42 |
| | Flatlands | 37-47 |
| Racing | Steep mountains | 47-60 |
| | Flatlands and rolling hills | 57-66 |

*category*. Thinking in terms of categories is important because an average racer planning some loaded touring can use a larger low gear than what's recommended for a strong loaded tourist.

## How Many Gears?

The number of gears in your drive train won't affect your choice of high or low gears, only how many steps you have for intermediate gears. Most riders' needs can be satisfied with the eight gears produced by a well-chosen 5-cog freewheel and a double crankset. The single exception arises in crossover gearing, which produces only six usable gears (or seven if you don't mind doing a half-step crossover) out of ten. So, for the racer's narrow crossover and the tourist's wide crossover, using the 12-speed format gives you one more usable gear.

You might be tempted to go for 12 speeds anyway for whatever marginal utility they might provide, but there is a penalty. Wheels built for standard-width, 6-speed freewheels are definitely more fragile than 5-speed wheels on two counts. First, the extra width of the 6-speed freewheel requires a longer unsupported right section of the hub axle, which makes the axle more susceptible to bending. And second, that same extra width requires more "dish," which means the right side spokes are angled more toward the vertical. This weakens the wheel, allowing it to go out of true and break spokes more easily.

Narrow-width, or "ultra," freewheels were introduced by SunTour to address these problems by fitting six closely spaced freewheel cogs in the same space as five regular ones. Dish and axle problems are not aggravated with this design (which almost everyone has copied), but the narrow spacing doesn't shift as well as standard-width systems. Usually it's not too noticeable with narrow-range racing gearing, but becomes more apparent with wide-range freewheels.

Shimano's Freehub system manages to fit 6 *standard*-width cogs in a 5-cog space without significantly increasing wheel dish. In addition, the right-side axle bearing is located almost at the end of the axle, which makes it so resistant to bending that these hubs are popular with serious ATB riders. The only drawback is the fact that the freewheeling mechanism is built into the hub (which only Shimano makes) and not a separate freewheel. The subsequent limitation on finding available replacement parts is more of a concern for the long-distance tourist than the local sport rider.

In general, we conclude that most riders should stick to standard-width 10-

speed configurations. The most appropriate use of a 12-speed gearing system is in a racing situation where a crossover pattern is desired for simplicity and speed of shifting.

What about those who need lows under 30 inches and don't want to sacrifice the spacing of their intermediate gears to get them? The answer, as you might have guessed from our earlier discussion, is to turn to a 15-speed gear system. This will provide you with an excellent set of easy-shifting medium-to-high range cruising gears as well as some stump-pulling lows. A move to an 18-speed may gratify your ego, but you risk encountering the same problems we mentioned with respect to 12-speeds.

## Picking a Pattern

We've reviewed the principal vices and virtues of the major gearing arrangements. Now let's summarize them.

Depending on whether you're more visually or mathematically oriented, lay out prospective gearing arrangements on logarithmically arranged "gear lines" (like table 16-3) or use gear tables (like tables 16-1, 16-4, etc.) and check for percentage jumps.

The big problem, of course, is not how to get your particular high and low, but how to evenly fill in the middle range of your gearing requirements. Take the size of your required gear range into consideration when you consider the different gear arrangements. For example, the many evenly spaced gears of the half-step system are better suited to a wide gear range, while the smaller number of crossover gears and their larger gaps are less noticeable on a narrow range of gears. Don't forget to use arrows to indicate your shifting path through the gears.

table 16-11

# BASIC CHARACTERISTICS OF MAJOR GEARING SYSTEMS

| Type | Shifting | Double Shifts | Low Range | Usable Gears* |
|------|----------|---------------|-----------|---------------|
| Half-step | Easy | Yes | 36-55 | 8 |
| Alpine | Difficult | Yes | 30-45 | 8 |
| Crossover | Easiest | No | 32-47 | 6 |
| Wide-step | Difficult | One | 24-33 | 7 or 8 |
| Triple | Easy | Yes | 20-30 | 9-12† |

*With 5-speed freewheel and two († three) chainrings.

Whatever you do, don't underestimate the importance of that shifting pattern. After all, *you* are the person who's going to have to shift your bike. It's worth giving up a special gear development that's difficult for you to shift so you can enjoy the peace of mind and pleasure that are supposed to be part of riding a bike.

Of course, if memorizing the shift pattern you want isn't too difficult and you've acquired the skills needed to execute it, by all means don't be afraid to give yourself the advantage of a well-thought-out set of gears.

## Putting It Together

Let's start by saying that if you need to change most of the drive train components on your bike to get the kind of gearing you want, it might be more economical to sell your present bike and buy one that's already a lot closer to what you desire. On the other hand, if

## table 16-12  GEAR INCH CHART

Formula:  $\dfrac{\text{Wheel diameter X number of teeth on chainwheel}}{\text{Number of teeth on freewheel cog}}$ = Gear Inches

CHAINWHEEL COG TEETH

| | 34 | 33 | 32 | 31 | 30 | 29 | 28 | 27 | 26 | 25 | 24 | 23 | 22 | 21 | 20 | 19 | 18 | 17 | 16 | 15 | 14 | 13 | 12 |
|---|---|---|---|---|---|---|---|---|---|---|---|---|---|---|---|---|---|---|---|---|---|---|---|
| 56 | 44.5 | 45.8 | 47.3 | 48.8 | 50.4 | 52.1 | 54.0 | 56.0 | 58.1 | 60.4 | 63.0 | 65.7 | 68.7 | 72.0 | 75.6 | 79.6 | 84.0 | 88.9 | 94.5 | 100.8 | 108.0 | 116.3 | 126.0 |
| 55 | 43.7 | 45.0 | 46.4 | 47.9 | 49.5 | 51.2 | 53.0 | 55.0 | 57.1 | 59.4 | 61.8 | 64.5 | 67.5 | 70.7 | 74.2 | 78.1 | 82.5 | 87.3 | 92.8 | 99.0 | 106.0 | 114.2 | 123.8 |
| 54 | 42.9 | 44.2 | 45.6 | 47.0 | 48.6 | 50.2 | 52.0 | 54.0 | 56.0 | 58.3 | 60.7 | 63.3 | 66.2 | 69.4 | 72.9 | 76.7 | 81.0 | 85.8 | 91.1 | 97.2 | 104.1 | 112.1 | 121.5 |
| 53 | 42.1 | 43.4 | 44.7 | 46.2 | 47.7 | 49.3 | 51.1 | 53.0 | 55.0 | 57.2 | 59.6 | 62.2 | 65.0 | 68.1 | 71.5 | 75.3 | 79.5 | 84.1 | 89.4 | 95.4 | 102.2 | 110.0 | 119.3 |
| 52 | 41.3 | 42.5 | 43.9 | 45.3 | 46.8 | 48.4 | 50.1 | 52.0 | 54.0 | 56.2 | 58.5 | 61.0 | 63.8 | 66.9 | 70.2 | 73.9 | 78.0 | 82.6 | 87.8 | 93.6 | 100.3 | 108.0 | 117.0 |
| 51 | 40.5 | 41.7 | 43.0 | 44.4 | 45.9 | 47.4 | 49.2 | 51.0 | 53.0 | 55.1 | 57.4 | 59.9 | 62.6 | 65.6 | 68.8 | 72.5 | 76.5 | 81.0 | 86.1 | 91.8 | 98.4 | 105.3 | 114.8 |
| 50 | 39.7 | 40.9 | 42.2 | 43.5 | 45.0 | 46.5 | 48.2 | 50.0 | 51.9 | 54.0 | 56.3 | 58.7 | 61.4 | 64.3 | 67.5 | 71.0 | 75.0 | 79.4 | 84.4 | 90.0 | 96.4 | 103.8 | 112.5 |
| 49 | 38.9 | 40.1 | 41.3 | 42.7 | 44.1 | 45.6 | 47.2 | 49.0 | 50.9 | 52.9 | 55.1 | 57.5 | 60.1 | 63.0 | 66.2 | 69.6 | 73.5 | 77.8 | 82.7 | 88.2 | 94.5 | 101.7 | 110.3 |
| 48 | 38.1 | 39.3 | 40.5 | 41.8 | 43.2 | 44.6 | 46.3 | 48.0 | 49.9 | 51.8 | 54.0 | 56.3 | 58.9 | 61.7 | 64.8 | 68.2 | 72.0 | 76.2 | 81.0 | 86.4 | 92.6 | 99.6 | 108.0 |
| 47 | 37.3 | 38.5 | 39.7 | 40.9 | 42.3 | 43.7 | 45.3 | 47.0 | 48.8 | 50.8 | 52.9 | 55.2 | 57.6 | 60.4 | 63.4 | 66.8 | 70.5 | 74.6 | 79.3 | 84.6 | 90.6 | 97.6 | 105.8 |
| 46 | 36.5 | 37.6 | 38.8 | 40.1 | 41.4 | 42.8 | 44.4 | 46.0 | 47.8 | 49.7 | 51.8 | 54.0 | 56.5 | 59.1 | 62.1 | 65.4 | 69.0 | 73.1 | 77.6 | 82.8 | 88.7 | 95.5 | 103.5 |
| 45 | 35.7 | 36.8 | 38.0 | 39.2 | 40.5 | 41.8 | 43.4 | 45.0 | 46.7 | 48.6 | 50.7 | 52.8 | 55.2 | 57.9 | 60.8 | 64.0 | 67.5 | 71.5 | 76.0 | 81.0 | 86.7 | 93.4 | 101.3 |
| 44 | 34.9 | 36.0 | 37.1 | 38.3 | 39.6 | 40.9 | 42.4 | 44.0 | 45.7 | 47.5 | 49.5 | 51.6 | 54.0 | 56.6 | 59.4 | 62.5 | 66.0 | 69.9 | 74.3 | 79.2 | 84.9 | 91.3 | 99.0 |
| 43 | 34.1 | 35.2 | 36.3 | 37.5 | 38.7 | 40.0 | 41.4 | 43.0 | 44.6 | 46.4 | 48.3 | 50.4 | 52.8 | 55.2 | 58.1 | 61.1 | 64.4 | 68.2 | 72.5 | 77.4 | 82.9 | 89.3 | 96.8 |
| 42 | 33.4 | 34.4 | 35.4 | 36.6 | 37.8 | 39.1 | 40.5 | 42.0 | 43.6 | 45.3 | 47.2 | 49.3 | 51.5 | 54.0 | 56.7 | 59.6 | 63.0 | 66.7 | 70.8 | 75.6 | 81.0 | 87.2 | 94.5 |
| 41 | 32.6 | 33.5 | 34.6 | 35.7 | 36.9 | 38.1 | 39.5 | 41.0 | 42.4 | 44.2 | 46.1 | 48.1 | 50.3 | 52.7 | 55.3 | 58.2 | 61.5 | 65.1 | 69.1 | 73.8 | 79.0 | 85.1 | 92.3 |
| 40 | 31.8 | 32.7 | 33.8 | 34.8 | 36.0 | 37.2 | 38.6 | 40.0 | 41.5 | 43.2 | 45.0 | 47.0 | 49.1 | 51.4 | 54.0 | 56.8 | 60.0 | 63.5 | 67.5 | 72.0 | 77.1 | 83.0 | 90.0 |
| 39 | 31.0 | 31.9 | 32.9 | 34.0 | 35.1 | 36.3 | 37.6 | 39.0 | 40.5 | 42.1 | 43.9 | 45.8 | 47.9 | 50.1 | 52.6 | 55.4 | 58.5 | 61.9 | 65.8 | 70.2 | 75.2 | 81.0 | 87.8 |
| 38 | 30.2 | 31.1 | 32.1 | 33.1 | 34.2 | 35.3 | 36.6 | 38.0 | 39.4 | 41.0 | 42.7 | 44.6 | 46.6 | 48.8 | 51.3 | 54.0 | 57.0 | 60.3 | 64.1 | 68.4 | 73.2 | 78.9 | 85.5 |
| 37 | 29.4 | 30.3 | 31.2 | 32.2 | 33.3 | 34.4 | 35.6 | 37.0 | 38.4 | 40.0 | 41.6 | 43.4 | 45.4 | 47.5 | 50.0 | 52.5 | 55.5 | 58.7 | 62.4 | 66.6 | 71.3 | 76.8 | 83.3 |
| 36 | 28.6 | 29.5 | 30.4 | 31.4 | 32.4 | 33.5 | 34.7 | 36.0 | 37.3 | 38.8 | 40.5 | 42.2 | 44.1 | 46.2 | 48.6 | 51.1 | 54.0 | 57.1 | 60.7 | 64.8 | 69.4 | 74.7 | 81.0 |
| 35 | 27.8 | 28.6 | 29.5 | 30.5 | 31.5 | 32.5 | 33.7 | 35.0 | 36.3 | 37.8 | 39.3 | 41.0 | 42.9 | 45.0 | 47.2 | 49.7 | 52.5 | 55.5 | 59.0 | 63.0 | 67.5 | 71.9 | 78.8 |
| 34 | 27.0 | 27.8 | 28.7 | 29.6 | 30.6 | 31.6 | 32.7 | 34.0 | 35.3 | 36.7 | 38.2 | 39.9 | 41.7 | 43.7 | 45.9 | 48.3 | 51.0 | 54.0 | 57.3 | 61.2 | 65.5 | 70.6 | 76.5 |
| 33 | 26.2 | 27.0 | 27.8 | 28.7 | 29.7 | 30.7 | 31.8 | 33.0 | 34.2 | 35.6 | 37.1 | 38.7 | 40.5 | 42.4 | 44.5 | 46.8 | 49.5 | 52.4 | 55.6 | 59.4 | 63.6 | 68.5 | 74.3 |
| 32 | 25.4 | 26.2 | 27.0 | 27.8 | 28.8 | 29.7 | 30.8 | 32.0 | 33.2 | 34.5 | 36.0 | 37.5 | 39.2 | 41.1 | 43.2 | 45.4 | 48.0 | 50.8 | 54.0 | 57.6 | 61.7 | 66.4 | 72.0 |
| 31 | 24.6 | 25.4 | 26.2 | 27.0 | 27.9 | 28.8 | 29.8 | 31.0 | 32.1 | 33.4 | 34.8 | 36.4 | 38.0 | 39.8 | 41.8 | 44.0 | 46.5 | 49.2 | 52.3 | 55.8 | 59.7 | 64.3 | 69.8 |
| 30 | 23.8 | 24.5 | 25.3 | 26.1 | 27.0 | 27.9 | 28.9 | 30.0 | 31.1 | 32.4 | 33.7 | 35.2 | 36.8 | 38.5 | 40.5 | 42.6 | 45.0 | 47.6 | 50.6 | 54.0 | 57.7 | 62.3 | 67.5 |
| 29 | 23.0 | 23.7 | 24.5 | 25.3 | 26.1 | 27.0 | 28.0 | 29.0 | 30.1 | 31.3 | 32.6 | 34.0 | 35.5 | 37.2 | 39.1 | 41.2 | 43.5 | 46.0 | 48.9 | 52.2 | 55.9 | 60.2 | 65.3 |
| 28 | 22.0 | 22.9 | 23.6 | 24.4 | 25.2 | 26.0 | 27.0 | 28.0 | 29.0 | 30.2 | 31.5 | 32.8 | 34.3 | 36.0 | 37.8 | 39.7 | 42.0 | 44.4 | 47.2 | 50.4 | 54.0 | 58.1 | 63.0 |
| 27 | 21.4 | 22.1 | 22.8 | 23.5 | 24.3 | 25.1 | 26.0 | 27.0 | 28.0 | 29.2 | 30.4 | 31.7 | 33.1 | 34.7 | 36.5 | 38.4 | 40.5 | 42.9 | 45.6 | 48.6 | 52.1 | 56.0 | 60.8 |
| 26 | 20.6 | 21.3 | 21.9 | 22.6 | 23.4 | 24.2 | 25.1 | 26.0 | 27.0 | 28.0 | 29.3 | 30.5 | 31.9 | 33.4 | 35.1 | 36.9 | 39.0 | 41.3 | 43.9 | 46.8 | 50.1 | 54.0 | 58.5 |
| 25 | 19.9 | 20.5 | 21.1 | 21.8 | 22.5 | 23.3 | 24.1 | 25.0 | 26.0 | 27.0 | 28.1 | 29.3 | 30.7 | 32.1 | 33.8 | 35.5 | 37.5 | 39.7 | 42.2 | 45.0 | 48.2 | 51.9 | 56.3 |
| 24 | 19.1 | 19.6 | 20.3 | 20.9 | 21.6 | 22.3 | 23.1 | 24.0 | 24.9 | 25.9 | 27.0 | 28.2 | 29.5 | 30.9 | 32.4 | 34.1 | 36.0 | 38.1 | 40.5 | 43.2 | 46.3 | 49.8 | 54.0 |

FREEWHEEL COG TEETH

you're considering starting with a bare frame and custom equipping it, the sky's the limit as to what you can do with the gearing.

Most people's needs can be satisfied with some freewheel cog changes and maybe a new chainring. Those are the cheapest options. When you start changing cranksets, or even adding a third chainring and making the required axle change, the cost mounts up rapidly. Substantial changes in the range of your bike's gearing may also require new derailleurs. Be sure to check their gearing capacities before you start.

In general, if you have to buy a new inner chainring or a new crankset, it is wise to get a smaller chainring than you think you'll need. You can always match it with smaller freewheel cogs to get big enough gears. And, if you need smaller gears, it's a lot easier and cheaper to make further modifications at the freewheel end of your drive train than it is to go back and order smaller chainrings.

Your source for new cogs, whether it's a local shop or a catalog house, should be able to tell you what size cogs are available to match your equipment. Make sure you order the right type of cog for its particular position on the freewheel. And remember, it may be less expensive to buy a new freewheel with the cogs you want already on it than to replace more than two cogs on the freewheel you already own.

The gearing system on a bicycle makes it possible for the low-output, almost fixed speed engine we call a human being to transcend its boundaries of speed and distance by several quantum leaps. To not utilize the full potential of today's easy-shifting, wide-range gearing systems is to ignore the most significant advance that has been made in the designing and equipping of the modern bicycle. So even if you're not planning to revamp your drive train, take the time to get to know its strengths and weaknesses. The bottom line, whether you're creating a gearing masterpiece or just learning to properly use the gears the factory sent you, is to have a friendly relationship with your bike.

# GLOSSARY

**adjustable cup**—the left-hand cup in a bottom bracket, used in adjusting the bottom bracket bearings and removed during bottom bracket overhaul

**Allen key (Allen wrench)**—a small L-shaped hexagonal wrench that fits inside the head of a bolt or screw

**Allen wrench**—see Allen key

**all-terrain bike (ATB)**—a bicycle with straight handlebars, sturdy fat tires, and wide-range gearing designed for off-road use

**Alpine gearing**—a gearing system in which a shift between chainwheels is equivalent to one-and-a-half shifts on the freewheel

**binder bolt**—the bolt used to fasten a stem inside a steerer tube or a seatpost inside a seat tube

**bottom bracket**—the cylindrical part of a bicycle frame that holds the crank axle, two sets of ball bearings, a fixed cup, and an adjustable cup

**brake block**—see brake pad

**brake pad (brake block)**—a block of rubberlike material fastened to the end of a brake caliper; it presses against the wheel rim when the brakes are applied

**brake shoe**—the metal part that holds a brake pad and is bolted to the end of a brake caliper

**braze-ons**—parts for mounting shift levers, derailleurs, water bottle cages, and racks, which are fastened to a bicycle frame through a type of soldering process known as brazing

**butted tubing**—tubing whose outside diameter remains constant but whose thickness is reduced in midsection where less strength is needed

**cage**—on a front derailleur, a pair of parallel plates that push the chain from side to side; on a rear derailleur, a set of plates in which pulleys are mounted to hold and guide the chain from cog to cog

**calipers**—brake arms that reach around the sides of a wheel to press brake pads against the wheel rim

**cantilever brakes**—rim brakes with pivoting arms mounted on fork blades or seatstays at or below rim level

**chain**—linked metal rope that connects the chainwheel to the back wheel, sized differently for different types of bikes (see derailleur chains)

**chainring (chainwheel)**—a sprocket attached to the right crankarm to drive the chain

**chainring nut spanner**—a special tool used to loosen the slotted nuts that fasten a chainring to a crankarm

**chainstays**—the two tubes of a bicycle frame that run from the bottom bracket back to the rear dropouts

**chainwheel**—see chainring

**chain whip (chain wrench)**—a tool consisting of a metal bar and two sections of chain, used in changing cogs on a freewheel

**chain wrench**—see chain whip

**clincher tire**—a tire whose edges hook under the curved-in hooked edge of a special rim, not commonly found anymore and often confused with the common wired-on tire (see wired-on tire)

**cog**—a sprocket attached directly to the rear hub on a single-speed bike and mounted on a freewheel on a multi-speed bike

**cone**—a bearing race that curves to the inside of a circle of ball bearings and works in conjunction with a cup

**corncob**—a term used to describe a cluster of cogs on a racing freewheel because of the small variation in number of teeth on adjacent cogs

**cottered crank**—a crankset in which the crankarms are fastened to the axle by means of threaded cotter pins and nuts

**cotterless crank**—a crankset in which the crankarms are fastened to the axle by means of nuts or bolts instead of cotter pins

**crankarm**—a part, one end of which is attached to the bottom bracket axle and the other holds a pedal, whose forward rotation provides the leverage needed to power the bicycle

**crankarm fixing bolt**—the bolt that holds a crankarm on the end of the axle in a cotterless crankset

**crankset**—a group of components that includes the bottom bracket removable parts, two crankarms, and one or more chainrings

**crossover gearing**—a gearing system whose shift sequence involves moving from the lowest to the midrange of gears on the smaller chainring, then crossing over to the larger chainring for the remainder of the gears

**cross three**—a spoking pattern in which a spoke passes over two and under a third spoke before being attached to the rim

**C-spanner**—a wrench whose end is shaped like a C, used to loosen the lockring on a bottom bracket

**cup**—the bearing race that curves around the outside of a ring of ball bearings and works in conjunction with a cone

**derailleur**—a lever-activated mechanism that pushes the chain off of one sprocket and onto another, thus changing the gear ratio

**derailleur chain, narrow width**—chain made especially for use on an "ultra" or narrow freewheel, often recognizable by bulging inner link plates and flush chain pins

**derailleur chain, standard width**—chain designed to fit a freewheel of standard width, usually characterized by straight-edged plates and chain pins that protrude slightly beyond the outer link plates

**diamond frame**—the traditional men's bicycle frame, the principal parts of which form a diamond shape

**dish**—offsetting of the hub in a rear wheel on a derailleur bike to make room for the freewheel and still allow the wheel to be centered within the frame

**down tube**—the tube running from the headset to the bottom bracket, one part of the main triangle on a bicycle frame

**D-ring**—a D-shaped ring found on many models of shift levers, used to adjust the level of tension on the inner parts of the lever

**drop**—the vertical distance from the horizontal line connecting the two wheel axles and the bottom bracket, one way of determining the location of the bottom bracket in relation to the rest of the bicycle frame

**dropout**—a slot in the frame into which the rear wheel axle fits (see fork tips)

**dropout hanger**—a threaded metal piece that extends below the right rear dropout, used as a mount for the rear derailleur

**drops**—the lower, straight portion of a turned-down-type handlebar set

**dust cap**—a metal cap that fits into a hub shell to keep contaminants out of hub bearings; a metal or plastic end cover for a spindle in a pedal or a cotterless crankset

**face**—to shave the outer edges of a bottom bracket shell or the upper and lower ends of a head tube to make them parallel with one another and square to the tube's centerline

**fixed cup**—the right-hand cup in a bottom bracket, ordinarily not loosened or removed during bottom bracket disassembly (see adjustable cup)

**fixed gear**—a cog attached to a hub without a freewheel; it always turns as fast as the wheel

**fixed wheel**—same as fixed gear, the kind of rear wheel found on track bikes

**fixing bolt**—a bolt used to hold a crankarm on an axle in a cotterless crankset

**flange**—the parts of a hub shell to which spokes are attached; also sometimes used to designate the circle of metal inside the teeth on a chainring

**fork (front fork)**—the part of the frame that fits inside the head tube and holds the front wheel; a term also sometimes applied to the part of the frame where chainstays and seatstays join to hold the rear axle

**fork blades**—the parallel curved tubes that hold the front wheel

**fork crown**—the horizontal piece on the upper part of the front fork to which the fork blades attach

**fork rake (rake)**—the shortest distance between the front axle and an imaginary line extending through the head tube downward toward the ground

**fork tips**—the slotted tips of the fork blades into which the front wheel axle fits

**freewheel**—a removable component attached to the rear hub on most types of bikes; it carries gear cogs on the outside and contains a ratcheting mechanism inside that allows the wheel to rotate forward while the pedals, chain, and gear sprockets remain still or move in reverse

**front fork**—see fork

**front triangle (main triangle)**—actually a quadrilateral with one short side, it is the section of a bicycle frame that consists of the head tube, the top tube, the seat tube, and the down tube

**granny**—colloquial term for the tiny inner chainring on a triple chainring crankset

**half-step gearing**—a gearing system in which a shift between chainrings in a double chainring set is equivalent to half a gear step on the freewheel

**headset**—the combination of cups, cones, and ball bearings that creates the bearing mechanism that allows the fork column to rotate inside the head tube

**head tube**—the shortest tube in the main triangle, the one inside of which the fork column rotates

**hooks**—the curved, dropped sections of a set of turned-down handlebars

**hub**—the center of a wheel consisting of a shell to which spokes attach and contains an axle along with two sets of bearings, bearing cones, lockwashers, locknuts, and parts for attaching the wheel to the frame

**hub brake**—any type of brake (disc, drum, or coaster) that operates through the wheel hub rather than the rim

**idler pulley**—the pulley in a rear derailleur that stays farthest from the freewheel cogs and functions to keep tension on the chain

**jockey pulley**—the pulley in a rear derailleur that stays closest to the freewheel cogs and guides the chain from cog to cog during a gear shift

**knobby tires**—heavy-duty tires with large rubber knobs spaced relatively far apart to provide traction in wet, muddy terrain

**ladies' frame**—the type of frame in which the top tube is replaced by a second down tube to make mounting and dismounting the bike easier

**loaded tourer**—a bicycle whose structure, geometry, and equipment is designed to allow a cyclist to travel with 40 or 50 pounds of gear

**locknut**—a nut used in conjunction with a washer or a second nut to lock a mechanism in place, such as the nut found at the upper end of a headset and in front of the calipers on many caliper brakes

**lockring**—the notched ring that fits on the left side of a bottom bracket and prevents the adjustable cup from turning

**lockwasher**—a washer with a small metal tang to prevent it from turning, such as the washer beneath the locknut on a headset or between the locknut and cone on a hub

**lug**—an external metal sleeve that holds two or more tubes together at the joints of a frame

**main triangle**—see front triangle

**master link**—a special link on a bicycle chain that can be opened by flexing a plate, removing a screw, or some other means besides driving out a rivet

**mixte frame**—a frame that replaces the top tube with twin lateral tubes that run all the way from the head tube back to the rear dropouts

**mounting bolt**—see pivot bolt

**nipple**—a small metal piece that fits through a wheel rim and is threaded inside to receive the end of a spoke

**panniers**—luggage bags used in pairs and fastened alongside one or both wheels of a bike

**pick-up**—see yoke

**pin spanner**—a wrench with pins on forked ends, used to turn an adjustable cup on a bottom bracket

**pivot bolt (mounting bolt)**—a bolt on which the arms of caliper brakes pivot and which also serves as the means for mounting the brakes on the bike frame

**plain gauge tubing**—tubing whose thickness remains constant over its entire length

**Presta valve**—a bicycle tube valve whose stem has a small nut on top, which must be loosened during inflation, instead of a spring such as is found on the Schrader valve

**quick-release**—a cam-lever mechanism used to rapidly tighten or loosen a wheel on a bike frame, a seatpost in a seat tube, or a brake cable within cable housing

**quick-release skewer**—a thin rod that runs through the center of a wheel axle; a cam-lever is attached to one end and the other end is threaded to receive a nut

**quill**—similar to the rattrap type of pedal except that the two sides of the pedal frame are joined by a piece of metal that loops around the dust cap

**races**—curved metal surfaces of cups and cones that ball bearings contact as they roll

**rake**—see fork rake

**rattrap**—the type of pedals that have thin metal plates with jagged edges running parallel on each side of the pedal spindle

**rear triangle**—a frame triangle formed by the chainstays, seatstays, and the seat tube

**rim**—the metal or wooden hoop of a wheel that holds the tire and tube and the outer ends of the spokes

**rim brake**—any type of brake that slows or stops a wheel by pressing its pads against the sides of the wheel rim

**rollers**—a stationary training device that consists of a boxlike frame and three rotating cylinders (one for a bike's front wheel and two for its rear wheel) on which the bicycle is balanced and ridden

**saddle**—seat on a bicycle; metal piece on a centerpull brake (see yoke)

**Schrader valve**—a tire valve similar to the type found on automobile tires

**sealed bearings**—bearings fastened in sealed containers to keep out contaminants

**seamed tubing**—tubing made from steel strip stock that is curved until its edges meet, then welded together

**seamless tubing**—tubing made from solid blocks of steel that are pierced and drawn into tube shape

**seat cluster**—the conjunction of top tube, seat tube, and seatstays near the top of the seat tube

**seatpost**—part to which the saddle clamps and which runs down inside the seat tube

**seatstays**—parallel tubes that run from the top of the seat tube back to the rear axle

**seat tube**—the tube that runs from just below the saddle down to the bottom bracket

**sew-up tire**—a tire with an inner tube stitched inside the casing; also known as a tubular

**shallow angles**—angles that position frame tubes relatively farther from vertical and closer to horizontal than do steep angles

**spanner**—another name for a wrench, applied to many bicycle tools

**spider**—the multiarmed piece to which the chainwheels are bolted, usually welded to or part of the right crankarm

**spindle**—another term for an axle (such as a pedal axle or a bottom bracket axle)

**spoke**—one of several wires used to hold hub in the center of a wheel rim and to transfer the load from the perimeter of the wheel to the hub and on to the frame

**sports tourer**—a bicycle whose structure, geometry, and components are designed to make it a compromise between one suitable for racing and one suitable for loaded touring—good for general pleasure riding

**sprocket**—a disc bearing teeth for driving a chain, a general term that applies both to chainrings and to freewheel cogs

**steep angles**—angles that position frame tubes relatively closer to vertical than do shallow angles

**steerer tube**—the tube that forms the top of the fork and rotates inside the head tube

**stirrup cable (straddle cable, transverse cable)**—on centerpull brakes, a short cable, each end of which attaches to a brake arm and which is pulled up at the center to activate the brakes

**straddle cable**—see stirrup cable

**tandem**—a bicycle that provides seats, bars, and pedals for two or more riders, one behind the other

**tap**—to cut female threads inside a tube or opening; also the name of the tool that does the cutting

**top tube**—the horizontal tube that connects the seat tube with the head tube

**touring triple**—a triple chainring crankset designed to provide the wide range of gears needed for loaded bicycle touring

**tourist**—a cyclist who takes short or long excursions by bicycle, often carrying several panniers containing clothing and camping equipment

**transverse cable**—see stirrup cable

**trials**—a type of ATB cycling competition that tests riders not on speed but on ability to maintain balance while navigating a bicycle around and over numerous obstacles such as rocks, trees, and steep, slippery terrain

**tubular tire**—a type of tire that has a tube sewn up inside the casing, also known as a sew-up

**ultra 7**—a freewheel designed to allow seven cogs to fit into the space normally taken up by six

**ultra 6**—a freewheel designed to allow six cogs to fit into the space normally taken up by five

**wheelbase**—the distance between the front and the rear axles on a bicycle

**wide-step gearing**—a gearing system in which the step between the two chainrings is considerably greater than that found in most other systems

**wind trainer**—a training device consisting of a frame in which a bicycle is fastened for stationary riding and a fan that creates wind resistance to simulate actual road riding

**wired-on tire**—a tire with a wire bead edge that fits inside a trough-shaped rim; the type of tire often inaccurately referred to as a "clincher"

**yoke (pick-up)**—a triangular metal piece used to connect the main brake cable with the stirrup cable in a centerpull brake system (also known as a saddle)

# INDEX

Page entries in italics indicate illustrations and photographs; boldface entries indicate charts and tables.